The Hoosiers of Summer

By
W.C. Madden

GUILD PRESS OF INDIANA
6000 Sunset Lane
Indianapolis, Indiana 46208

TM

Guild Press of Indiana, Inc.
6000 Sunset Lane
Indianapolis, IN 46208

Printed in the United States of America

Library of Congress
Catalogue Card Number

ISBN 1-878208-44-6

Introduction

When I started writing this book, I decided I would interview every living Major League player who was born in Indiana. Little did I realize the enormity of that decision. I soon found out that would be impossible with some players, such as Kenny Lofton, who was the first to turn me down for an interview when he appeared at a card show in Indianapolis. Apparently, I didn't buy enough autographs.

That incident never stopped me from trying to interview players. I once traveled to Evansville and visited Don Mattingly's restaurant trying to interview the star. He decided not to frequent his place that night so I was out of luck. Only a few retired players turned me down for an interview. On the other hand, the active players became almost out of reach because the teams wouldn't issue me press credentials. The Pittsburgh Pirates was the only team that allowed me in their spring training camp.

Some active players and coaches did grant me an interview. Andy Benes called me from his home in San Diego one night as did Paul Splittorff, after I had written them requesting an interview.

I treated all biographies the same whether the players played one game or twenty-six years in the major leagues, like Tommy John. I tried to trace their baseball careers from the time they picked up a baseball until they retired. In the case of a living player, the biography includes what he or she is doing now.

I was unaware of how difficult it was for a player to get to the majors until I wrote this book. One player told me, "Nobody gives you a job. You have to take a job away from someone." Trying to make it to the majors is like going from a dishwasher to the owner of a restaurant. Some players I interviewed never thought they would ever get to the majors, but they didn't give up. Chuck Harmon didn't think he had a chance because of his color. But that barrier came down and he became the first African-American on the Cincinnati Reds.

I had thoughts of including up-and-coming minor league players, but gave up on that after failing to compile enough research. Information is tough to gather on minor leaguers from Indiana, because nobody publishes information that specifically identifies the players' birthplaces. The Fleer people put out a set of baseball cards on the bush ballplayers, but they only identify the player's place of residence, not birthplace. Bill James puts out a book on minor league players' statistics, but not where the players were born. And there were just too many teams to contact in this regard, so you will find nothing in this book about minor league players from Indiana.

This book wouldn't have been possible without some help and encouragement from my wife and friends. Dave Swavel in Ohio made photo reproductions from some old photos I had acquired and he took a photo of Mattingly in Cleveland. Randy Puterbaugh helped edit the book. Some people helped spread the word about the book, which led to getting some rare interviews. I received some help from

Introduction

the Indiana Baseball Hall of Fame. Others, such as Michael Byrum, have helped set up publicity for the book. Curator Dale Ogden of Indiana State Museum gave me a couple of rare photos to use, and his publisher, Guild Press of Indiana, Inc., allowed me to use some material from his book, *Hoosier Sports Heroes*. Paul S. Eriksson Publisher allowed me to use material from *Gil Hodges; The Quiet Man*. William G. Eidson from Ball State University permitted me to use material from his book, *State Champs; The Final Four in Indiana Baseball*. The Northern Indiana Historical Society allowed me to comb their files on the women's league and provided a photo for the cover. The Delaware County Historical Society also provided the back cover print of Babe Ruth with a Hoosier player. The National Baseball Hall of Fame helped greatly in providing information from their files on players in the book. And I owe gratitude to Kerry Smith for providing photos from his personal collection for the book. I owe the most to my wife who convinced me to continue with this book when I was about to throw in the towel and quit writing it because no national publisher was interested. And, too, my father, who passed away during the writing of this book, for passing his love for the game on to me. My father and his brothers once comprised the outfield for a semipro team in Chicago.

In compiling information and statistics of players for this book, I used a variety of source books, listings from team media guides, information from the files of National Baseball Hall of Fame and Northern Indiana Historical Society, and from "Baseball Weekly" newspaper. This was done to provide what I thought was the most accurate and fully documented information from a variety of the several sources.

Hoosiers have been involved in the game of "base ball," since Abner Doubleday invented the sport. Town ball was played in Indiana communities in the 1850s. When the game finally turned professional in 1876 with the coming of the National League, Hoosiers joined in and have been playing professionally ever since.

Players from Indiana have had quite an influence on the game. Amos Rusie, "The Hoosier Thunderbolt," is credited with the move of the pitching mound back fifteen feet because of his blazing fastballs. "Three Finger" Brown turned a handicap into an asset. Chuck Harmon broke the color barrier of the Cincinnati Reds. Tommy John overcame a career-ending injury to pitch again. Don Mattingly seems destined for immortality. In all, nine Hoosier players have been inducted into the National Baseball Hall of Fame in Cooperstown for their accomplishments and contributions to the game.

After basketball, baseball is the second most popular sport in Indiana. When the winter snows melt, Hoosiers turn their attention from the hardcourts to the grassy diamonds. The state simmers with hundreds of baseball teams in the summer, from Pee Wee leagues to minor leagues. Thousands of fans turn out to view the games.

The 329 baseball professionals have come from all corners of the state. Some enjoyed just a cup of coffee in the majors, while others spent decades. Most had one thing in common: they had a dream of making it to the majors one day and were able to live out that fantasy. They made it to the top despite the tremendous odds against them.

While the state may not be the hotbed for professionals, Indiana has had its fair share of professional baseball players. This book contains all of their names. Read it and you will learn something about how and why Hoosiers have played the game.

Autographs

Best Wishes!

Bill Madden

Charles "Babe" Adams
(Charles Benjamin)
Born: May, 18, 1882, Tipton
Died: July 27, 1968, Silver
Springs, Md.
5'11", 185, Pitcher
St. Louis, NL, 1906
Pittsburgh, NL, 1907, 09-16,
18-26
TR, 194-140, 15 SV, 2.76
ERA, 482 G
BL, .212, 1019 AB

Adams is the second best control pitcher in the history of the game. He is the only rookie pitcher to win three World Series games and was the first pitcher to win three series games.

The Hoosier moved to Missouri early in life and began playing baseball at age eighteen. The following year he signed on with the semipro Parsons.

St. Louis spotted the young pitcher and drafted him in 1906. The Cardinals tried the youngster in a game against Chicago. The Cubs clobbered him for nine hits and eight runs in four innings. The young player was too green for the majors and was sent to Denver for seasoning.

"Babe," as he was called, learned new pitches and matured the next two seasons in Denver. Adams was sold to Pittsburgh for $5,000 in 1907. He pitched in four games and was again bombed. Adams was shipped to Louisville for the 1908 season, where he was 22-12.

1909 became his rookie season in the majors. The control pitcher compiled an amazing 12-3 record with a 1.11 ERA. His claim to fame came in the World Series that year. The rookie was picked to start Game 1. He gave up a run in the first to Detroit then held the Tigers to six hits as his team won 4-1. In Game Five he was knocked around for four runs, but his teammates supported him eight runs.Then in the final game he threw a six-hit shutout to win the series for the Pirates. He gave up only one hit to the famed Ty Cobb.

Adams' career was going along fine until 1916. He lost control of his pitches and his record nosedived to 2-9 with a 5.75 ERA. The thirty-four-year-old Hoosier was shipped back to the bush leagues — his major league career seemingly over.

Adams worked on his control in 1917 with St. Joseph and Hutchinson. After going 14-3 with a 1.67 ERA at Kansas City in 1918, Pittsburgh called him back to the club. He made the comeback even more remarkable by pitching eight more seasons for the Pirates.

In 1926 the Tipton native made the mistake of backing Max Carey in a dispute with the manager over playing time. The Pirates released Adams, who played one more season in the minors at Johnstown, Pa., and Springfield, Mass.

During his career he walked only 430 batters in almost 3,000 innings. He averaged less than a walk a game during four of his nineteen seasons in the majors. He gave up only eighteen walks in thirty-five games in 1920! He still holds the Major League record for the longest game pitched without giving up a walk — twenty-one innings against the New York Giants on July 17, 1914. Adams led the league in

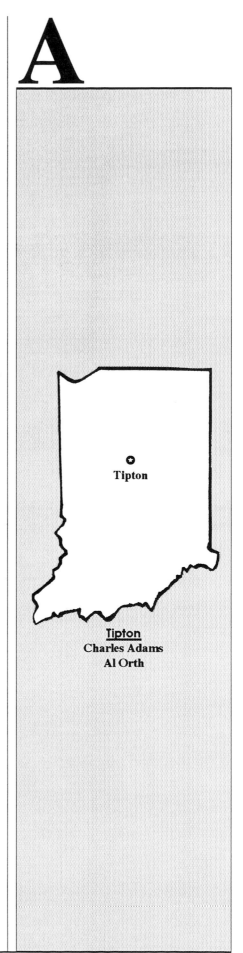

A

Tipton

Tipton
Charles Adams
Al Orth

A

shutouts in 1911 (7) and 1920 (8).

Jerry Akers (Albert Earl)
Born: Nov. 1, 1887, Shelby-ville
Died: May 15, 1979, Bay Pines, Fla.
5'11", 175, Relief Pitcher
Washington, AL, 1912
TR, 1-1, 1 SV, 4.95 ERA, 5 G
BR, .333, 6 AB

Akers was called up on May 4 and started one game in the majors.

Vic Aldridge (Victor Ed-dington)
Born: Oct. 25, 1893, Indian Springs
Died: April 17, 1973, Terre Haute
5'10", 175, Pitcher
Chicago, NL, 1917-18, 22-24
Pittsburgh, NL, 1925-27
New York, NL, 1928
TR, 97-80, 6 SV, 3.76 ERA, 248 G
BR, .229, 581 AB, 2 HR
2 WS, 2-1, 4.91 ERA, 26 IP

Aldridge was a consistent performer who did his best during the stretch drive and in the World Series. After baseball he became an Indiana state senator.

When Aldridge first entered professional baseball in 1915 with Indianapolis, he was known as the Hoosier Schoolmaster, because he was a teacher. He hurled a no-hitter with the Indians in 1916. In one stretch he allowed only twelve hits in six games.

Aldridge also pitched for Erie and Denver before joining the Chicago Cubs for the 1917 season. He made his debut on April 15 and was 6-6 in his rookie season.

After a brief stint with the Cubs in 1918, he joined the U.S. Navy. When the war ended, he played for three seasons with Los Angeles in the Pacific Coast League before rejoining the Cubs in 1922.

Aldridge was 47-36 for the Cubs over the next three seasons before being sent to Pittsburgh in 1925. During the drive for the pennant, he captured eight straight victories to help carry the Pirates to the World Series. In the series, he had the first two Pirate victories to help the team come back from a 3-1 deficit to win the series.

He again helped the Pirates to a pennant in 1927, but wasn't so successful in the series and lost the only game he started.

The former "Hoosier School-master became disgruntled with the Pirates and was traded to the New York Giants for Burleigh Grimes. He held out with the Giants before joining them late. Then he had only a 4-7 record to end his career in the majors.

After the 1928 season, Aldridge pitched in the minors for Newark and his hometown of Terre Haute.

When he was finished with baseball, he went to law school and became a state senator.

Bob Anderson (Robert Carl)
Born: Sept. 29, 1935, East Chicago
6'4", 210, Pitcher
Chicago, NL, 1957-62
Detroit, AL, 1963

TR, 36-46, 13 SV, 4.26 ERA, 246 G
BR, .134, 246 AB, 33 H

Anderson managed only one winning season during his seven years in the majors.

Even with losing records in 1959 (12-13) and 1960 (9-11), he was the second best pitcher for the second-division Chicago Cubs. The starter was sent to the bullpen in 1961 and his performance dropped off.

Anderson was traded to Detroit in late 1962 for Steve Boros. He was 3-1 in 1963 for the Tigers.

The Tigers dealt him to Kansas City in a multi-player trade involving Rocky Colavito. However, he never made it back to the majors.

Ernie "Junie" Andres (Ernest Henry)
Born: Jan. 11, 1918, Jeffersonville
6'1", 200, Third baseman
Boston, AL, 1946
BR, TR, 15 G, .098, 41 AB

Andres didn't have much success in baseball, but he was a professional basketball player for six years. After his professional playing days, he coached baseball at Indiana University for twenty-five years. He coached several college players who eventually made it to the major leagues themselves.

The farm boy from Midway didn't play organized baseball until he was fifteen, when he joined up with the semi-pro Midway Merchants. He was the youngest player on the team.

Basketball was the only sport at Jeffersonville High School his first two years. When baseball was added Andres was a junior and he played second and third base. During the summers he played for the local American Legion Post and began to pitch.

After graduating in 1935, he went to Indiana University to play baseball and basketball. In his junior year Branch McCracken became the head basketball coach and made Andres the team captain. "I was a big guard back then," Andres said. He lived up to his leadership abilities and was named to the All Big 10 team his last two years and All-American honors in his senior year. IU had a good team and was edged out for the Big 10 title in the last game of the season in his senior year.

Andres also excelled at college baseball and hit around .400 his junior year, which raised a few eyebrows of scouts. In the summers Andres played with semipro baseball teams, such as the Kentucky Dairy, Morgan Packing Company, and the Seymour Reds. After his senior year he tried out for the Louisville Colonels, a Class AA club. "I borrowed $100 from the bank and that's what they gave me," he explained about his signing bonus.

Louisville was an independent team at the time. "I hit a home run the first time I swung a bat at Louisville," he remembered. He also recalled a game in which the team was behind 4-0 and he hit a grand slam to send the game to extra innings.

He played thirty games for the Colonels, who finished fourth for the season, but the

Ernie Andres played for the Great Lakes Naval Air Station team when he was in the Navy.

Ernie Andres

A team still made the playoffs and ended up winning the league. "That's how ridiculous it was," Andres said about the playoff format.

At the end of the season he hung up his baseball jersey and quickly changed into a basketball uniform. He had signed on with the Indianapolis Kautskys of the National Basketball League, the predecessor to the NBA. He was paid twice as much to play professional basketball as he made in baseball.

In 1940 Louisville became a farm club of the Brooklyn Dodgers and he was paid a $2,500 bonus. Andres hit around .290 for the season. He also played for Indianapolis again in the off-season. In 1941 he again played baseball for Louisville, leading third basemen in fielding and hitting fifteen homers. At the end of the season, he played three pro basketball games before joining the Navy.

When Andres wasn't learning about submarine chasing, he played baseball for the Navy and was part of the Service All-Stars, which included such greats as Bob Feller and Mickey Cochrane. The team was afforded the opportunity to play the American League All-Star team in Cleveland. In 1943 it was off to war for the Hoosier. He was assigned to a sub chaser that went to Alaska.

The Armed Forces All-Star team was made up of mostly major league players, including Ernie Andres.

After the war ended, Andres was sold to the Boston Red Sox and he reported to spring training. He opened the 1946 season as the starting third baseman for Boston. Near the end of his first month he pulled a hamstring and was optioned to Buffalo, a Detroit farm club. After the season ended, Andres picked up playing basketball again with Indianapolis. Because he played basketball in the capital city, he asked Boston to sell him to the Indianapolis Indians. They obliged and he played both sports in Indianapolis through the 1948 season.

After his playing days were over in both sports, Andres was hired on as the head baseball coach at Indiana University. He coached some successful baseball players in his career at IU, such as Sammy Esposito, Bruce Miller, Ron Keller, and Bob Lawrence. He retired in 1973 and moved to Bradenton, Fla., in 1986, where he had once attended spring training. He lives there with his wife, Doris Mann of Delta, Ohio, whom he married in 1942.

" I may be the only basketball player who played before and after the war and is not getting a pension," he said. Had Andres played the year before and after his service obligations, he would now be getting a pension from the NBA.

Harry Arndt (Harry J.)
Born: Feb. 12, 1879, South Bend
Died: March 24, 1921, South Bend
Outfielder, infielder

Detroit, AL, 1902
Baltimore, AL, 1902
St. Louis, NL, 1905-7
TR, .248, 271 G, 985 AB

Arndt played professional ball for a decade before becoming a player/manager for South Bend of the Central League.

He began his professional career as an infielder for Battle Creek and Flint in 1901. He first made it to the majors in 1902 with Detroit and was traded to Baltimore in his first season. Then he played in the minors for two years with Columbus, Louisville, and Cincinnati before joining the St. Louis Cardinals in 1905.

After the 1907 season, Arndt played at Wilkes-Barre before returning to his birthplace to play and manage until 1912. He finally retired from baseball in 1915.

Lenna Arnold
Born: Fort Wayne
Pitcher
Fort Wayne, AAGPBL, 1946
2-4, 6 G, 40 IP
.214, 14 AB, 3 H

Jake Aydelott (Jacob Stuart)
Born: July 6, 1861, North Manchester
Died: Oct. 22, 1926, Detroit, Mich.
6', 180, Pitcher
Indianapolis, AA, 1884
Philadelphia, AA, 1886
5-9, 4.79 ERA, 14 G

Aydelott pitched for two professional teams in the early days of baseball. When pitching for New Orleans, he was struck in the left cheek by a line drive.

Ernie Andres relaxes in his Florida home, but he wishes he had a pension from the NBA.

A

Abbreviations

AA — American Association
AAGPBL — All-American Girls Professional Baseball League
AB — at-bats
BB — bats both
BL — bats left
BR — bats right
ERA — earned-run average
FL — Federal League
G — games
IP — innings pitched
K — strikeout
LCS — League Championship Series
NA — National Association
NL — National League
NNL — Negro National League
PL — Player's League
SHO — shutouts
TL — throws left
TR — throws right
UA — Union Association
WS — World Series

The impact crushed his cheek bones and left him scarred for life.

Kirtley "Whitney" Baker (Kirtley)
Born: June 24, 1869, Aurora
Died: April 15, 1927, Covington, Ky.
5'9", 160, Pitcher
Pittsburgh, NL, 1890
Baltimore, NL, 1893-4
Washington, NL, 1898-9
TR, BR, 9-38, 6.28 ERA, 58 G

Baker suffered from some arm troubles after the 1890 season and sat out a couple of years rather than participate in the Players League. He never posted a winning season in his five short stints in the majors before the turn of the century.

Bruce "Squeaky" Barmes (Bruce Raymond)
Born: Oct. 23, 1929, Vincennes
5'8", 165, Outfielder
Washington, AL, 1953
BL, TR, .200, 5 G, 5 AB

Bill Barnes
Born: Unknown, Indianapolis
Died: Unknown
Outfielder
St. Paul, UA, 1884
.200, 8 G, 30 AB

Tim Barrett (Timothy Wayne)
Born: Jan. 24, 1961, Huntingburg
6'1", 185, Pitcher
Montreal, NL, 1988
TR, 0-0, 5.79 ERA, 4 G

All of Barrett's appearances in the majors were in relief. He gave up two home runs in nine innings during his short stay with the Expos.

Paddy Baumann (Charles John)
Born: Dec. 20, 1885, Indianapolis
Died: Nov. 20, 1969, Indianapolis
5'9", 160, Outfielder, infielder
Detroit, AL, 1911-13
New York, AL, 1915-17
TR, BR, .274, 299 G, 904 AB, 4 HR

Baumann was a good base stealer and utility player during his lengthy professional career. He also managed and umpired.

His first professional season was 1908 with Cedar Rapids and Jacksonville. He went to New Bedford in 1909 and played there until a callup to Detroit and the end of 1911. He was called up again in 1914, but he went 0-for-11, which ended his stay at Detroit. He was sold to New York for $1,500.

The Yankees used Baumann quite a bit at second and third, and he came through by hitting .292 in seventy-six games. One of his best games ever came against the Washington Senators in his first year with the Yankees. He went 3-for-4, drove in two runs, and scored two.

The Hoosier continued to fill in where he was needed the next two seasons with New York. After hitting just .218 in 1917, he was sent back to the bush leagues. His stops included Toledo, Jersey City, Galveston, and Tulsa. He managed Dallas for several years then he became an umpire in the Three-I League.

Mary "Whimp" Baumgartner (Mary Louise)

B

**Born: Sept. 13, 1930, Fort
Wayne
Catcher
Peoria, AAGPBL, 1949
Kalamazoo, AAGPBL, 1950
South Bend, AAGPBL, 1950-
54
BR, TR, .186, 171G, 488 AB,
91 H (1953-54 stats)**

Baumgartner spent four seasons behind the plate in the girls professional league.

The Fort Wayne native played softball, volleyball, and basketball in high school. She gave up a job to join the league in 1950.

Baumgartner's most exciting moment in the league was hitting a home run during the 1952 championship. She also contributed four dingers during the 1954 campaign.

After the league folded in 1954, Baumgartner went on to become a physical education teacher.

**George "Eaglebeak" Beck
(Ernest George B.)
Born: Feb. 21, 1890, South
Bend
Died: Oct. 29, 1973, South
Bend
5'11", 162, Pitcher
Cleveland, AL, 1914
TR, BR, 0-0, 0.00 ERA, 1 G**

**Ollie Bejma (Aloysius
Frank)
Born: Sept. 2, 1907, South
Bend
5'10", 165, Outfielder, in-
fielder
St. Louis, AL, 1934-36
Chicago, AL, 1939
TR, BR, .245, 316 G, 906 AB,
222 H**

Bejma (pronounced Bay-ma) played nearly every position with two major league teams during his fourteen-year professional career.

The South Bend native began his professional career in 1929 at Bloomington. He moved up to Indianapolis the following year and made stops in Quincy, Milwaukee, Wichita Falls, and San Antonio, before he finally made it to the big leagues in 1934 with the St. Louis Browns.

Manager Rogers Hornsby used Bejma at many different positions during the year, and the twenty-six-year-old Hoosier hit .271 in ninety-five games. During a July 28 doubleheader the following season, the Polish Falcon Society of St. Louis honored him with a day. In the second game of the doubleheader that day, the umpire was overcome by heat, so Manager Hornsby let Bejma fill in for the overheated umpire.

The Browns released the utility player after the 1936 season. The Chicago White Sox picked him up and assigned him to St. Paul for the year.

1939 found Bejma as the starting second baseman for the Southsiders. He responded to the promotion by hitting eight homers and batting .251. On July 23, he was honored with his own day and received a car and trophy for being named the MVP of the American Association in 1938.

The White Sox sent him back to St. Paul in 1940. He spent three more seasons in the minors before retiring from baseball in 1943. He did play

Mary Baumgartner played with the South Bend Blue Sox for four seasons.

semipro with a Michigan City team for a few years.

Andy Benes (Andrew Charles)
Born: Aug. 20, 1967, Evansville
6'6", 235, Pitcher
San Diego, NL, 1989-93
TR, 59-54, 3.44 ERA, 143 G, 5 SHO
BR, .096, 146 AB, 14 H, 2 HR

The first player taken in the June 1988 amateur draft, Benes earned a spot on the 1988 Olympic Team. He became the Number One starter for the San Diego Padres in 1992 and more than quadrupled his salary in arbitration before entering his fifth year in the majors. He also pitched in the 1993 All-Star Game.

Benes first began playing baseball when he was five in a T-Ball League. He played with boys he didn't know because he attended a parochial school. "The most important thing is that I wanted to get into it. I wasn't pushed into it," he recalled.

At nine he joined a rural Little League, playing short and pitching. Then he played in Pony League at age thirteen. He became an All-Star and the team traveled to Nashville, Louisville, and Indianapolis to play.

"I was a lot better pitcher in Little League and Pony League then I was in high school," Benes said. He attended Evansville Central High School, where he lettered in football, basketball, and baseball. At six-foot-five he was well equipped to play forward and center in basketball. He also was the quarterback for the football team. On the baseball diamond, the Evansville native played short and third when he wasn't on the mound, where he was the third best hurler on the team. Although his team was ranked first in the state, it never won the sectionals.

The 1985 graduate wasn't picked in baseball's amateur draft and decided to attend the University of Evansville. As a freshman, he continued to play in all three sports while studying organic chemistry. In his sophomore year he ended up as the quarterback when others got injured. He dropped out of basketball and married Jennifer Byers of Evansville during his sophomore year. In the summer he played in the Jay Hawk League, a summer league. "I was throwing hard and got a lot of exposure," he said.

In his junior year, Benes compiled a 16-3 record, along with a couple of saves. He became the first player picked in the 1988 amateur draft. Three weeks later he signed a contract with the San Diego Padres for $235,000. "It was a tough decision. If I hadn't gone number one, I probably wouldn't have signed," said the pre-med student.

Instead of going to the minor leagues, he went to the U.S. Olympic Team. Baseball was a demonstration sport in the Summer Olympics, which was played in Soeul, South Korea. Cuba, probably the best team in the world, boycotted the games. That left the door wide open for the American team, which won

"If I hadn't gone Number One, I probably wouldn't have signed."
Andy Benes

Andy Benes

B

Andy Benes made his first All-Star performance in 1993.

the Gold Medal. Benes pitched in one game and beat the Australian team. While the Olympics was a pleasure for Benes, the birth of his son, Andrew II, meant more to the new father.

After spring training in 1989, Benes was assigned to Class AA Witchita, Kansas. He played there for three months. "I did real well there. It was almost too easy. I just threw fastball after fastball," he explained. His excellent performance there earned him a promotion to Triple A Las Vegas. Benes didn't pitch as well there and his ERA was "over 8" when the Padres called him up less than a month later.

He remembered being called up on a Wednesday and pitching in his first major league start on Friday. The first hit he allowed was a home run to Darrell Evans. Then Dale Murphy took him deep. By the time he was pulled in the sixth inning, he had given up six runs. "It was like a blurr; I was so nervous," he explained. "It was a big relief just to get it out of the way." Benes finished the season with a 6-3 record and 3.51 ERA after such a rocky start. Benes gave up seven homers on the year and knocked one out himself against Philadelphia in San Diego.

In his first full year in the majors in 1990, Benes started in thirty-one games. He had his ups and downs and finished with a 10-11 record. He had good control of his fastball, slider and change, but when he grooved the pitches down the middle he was rocked for home runs.

1991 was a better year for the Hoosier. He out-pitched Tom Glavine of the Atlanta Braves three out of the four games to earn him some fame. He also had some good luck against the Philadelphia Phillies and hit another dinger against them.

Benes' best game so far in the majors came against the St. Louis Cardinals in the middle of the 1991 season. He had a lot of his family members at the game, since Evansville was just a few hours drive away. Their nervous relative gave up only one hit in a game that came down to the last pitch, as the Padres won 1-0. The victory was especially sweet, because he had been a Cardinal fan when he was growing up.

The victory over the Cardinals helped turn Benes' season around after a poor 4-10 start. It also helped him to a ten-game win skeen in which his ERA was a miniscule 1.50. The winning streak ended against the Los Angeles Dodgers, a big rival of the Padres. The big right hander finished the season with a 15-11 mark and a 3.03 ERA. As a hitter, he didn't perform very well. In fact, he was going for the longest non-hitting streak after he went 0-for-50.

As the Number One starter for the Padres in 1992, Benes got a start every fifth day. He had quality starts and gave up fewer homers (14) than in the previous season, but ended up with a 13-14 record. "There are a lot of variables for starters. You've got to be good and lucky," Benes said. San Diego hasn't given him much support.

Benes summed up his career so far: "I've learned a lot. That's going to make me a lot better.

Mentally, I know exactly what I'm going to do."

Benes would like to win twenty games in a season. He made $475,000 in 1992, so when it came time for arbitration in 1993, he asked for $2 million. The team offered $1.55 million. He won out.

During the 1993 season, the Padres unloaded several high-salary players and Benes expressed his displeasure. He said he would like to be traded to a Midwest team, so he could return to his native Indiana. He went 15-15 on the season.

After his baseball career is over, he'd like to finish his degree in organic chemistry. His son is already interested in sports, but the father won't push him into baseball. Benes' brother, Alan, may be a major league pitcher some day, as he was drafted in the first round in 1993 by the St. Louis Cardinals.

Joe "Butcher Boy" "Blitzen" Benz (Joseph Lewis)
Born: Jan. 21, 1886, New Alsace
Died: April 22, 1957, Chicago, Ill.
6'2", 190, Pitcher
Chicago, AL, 1911-19
TR, 76-75, 3 SV, 2.43 ERA, 250 G
BR, .138, 441 AB

The spitball and knuckleball pitcher tossed a no-hitter during his nine-year stint in the majors.

Benz made his debut with the Chicago White Sox on Aug. 16, 1911. He led the league in losses (19) in 1914 despite a no-hitter against Cleveland. He also beat the famed Walter Johnson

with a one-hitter that year.

"Butcher Boy" had his best season the following year with a career-best 15-11 record and 2.11 ERA. Then he had two more winning seasons: 9-5 in 1916 and 7-3 in 1917.

Al "Dutch" Bergman (Alfred Henry)
Born: Sept. 27, 1890, Peru
Died: June 20, 1961, Fort Wayne
5'7", 155, Second baseman
Cleveland, AL, 1916
TR, BR, .214, 8 G, 14 AB

Bergman was a September callup in 1916 with the Indians.

He earned letters in baseball, football, basketball, and track at Notre Dame, where he graduated in 1916. He was later with Peoria of the Three-I League before retiring from the game in 1919.

Claude "Admiral" Berry (Claude Elzy)
Born: Feb, 4, 1880, Losantville
Died: Feb. 1, 1974, Richmond
5'7", 165, Catcher
Chicago, AL, 1904
Philadelphia, AL, 1906-07
Pittsburgh, FL, 1914-15
BR, TR, .219, 245 G, 753 AB

Berry spent four of his professional seasons in the majors. He was a good defensive catcher, but couldn't hit well enough to stay in the majors.

The Hoosier began his professional career at Dallas in 1902. Then he went to Baton Rouge, Louisville, and Columbus. In 1904 he was drafted by the Chicago White Sox and

B

played three games before being sold to Indianapolis.

Berry played for Cedar Rapids of the Three-I League in 1905. Philadelphia of the American League drafted him in 1906 and he finished the season with the Americans. In one game he twice threw out the great base-stealing Ty Cobb. He considered it his greatest feat in baseball.

Berry played another eight games with Philadelphia in 1907 before going to Williamsport. He was sold to San Francisco where he played for five seasons and was named an All-Star each year.

When the Federal League formed in 1914, he hooked on with Pittsburgh as the team's full-time catcher. The league lasted only one more year.

Berry finished up his baseball career with Kansas City of the American Association.

Monte Beville (Henry Monte)
Born: Feb. 24, 1875, Dublin
Died: Jan. 24, 1955, Grand Rapids, Mich.
5'11", 180, Catcher, First baseman
New York, AL, 1903-4
Detroit, AL, 1904
BL, TR, .203, 145 G, 454 AB

Charlie Biggs (Charles Orval)
Born: Sept. 15, 1906, French Lick
Died: May 24, 1954, French Lick
6'1", 185, Pitcher
Chicago, AL, 1932
TR, 1-1, 6.84 ERA, 6 G
BR, .111, 9 AB

Emil "Hill Billy" Bildilli
Born: Sept. 16, 1912, Diamond
Died: Sept. 16, 1946, Hartford City
5'10", 170, Pitcher
St. Louis, AL, 1937-41
TL, 4-8, 5.84 ERA, 41 G
BR, .178, 45 AB

Inducted into the Delaware County Hall of Fame in May 1981, Bildilli saw limited action as a pitcher for the St. Louis Browns before World War II. The 5-foot-10-inch southpaw was described by the Browns as "a colorful little fellow with a great big heart." He had a great curveball, but his "fast ball (sic) could be faster."

Bildilli's organized baseball career began in 1936 when he played for several semipro teams: Sheppardsville, Blanford, Rushville, and the Indianapolis Rockwood Pulley Company. During a stint on an All-Star team, he impressed National League President Ford Frick with his performance.

In 1937 he joined a St. Louis Brown's farm club, the Terre Haute Tots of the Three-I (Indiana, Illinois and Iowa) League. When the majors expanded rosters in the fall, Bildilli was called up. In his major league debut on Aug. 24, he lost to the Washington Senators, 9-6. He appeared in relief roles in three other games and ended the year with a 10.13 ERA.

The Tots disbanded, and the lefty was sent to Johnston, Pa., to pitch for the Johnnies. He went 7-3 before the Browns called him up again. In five appearances in 1938 with the

Browns, he compiled a 1-2 record with an improved 6.95 ERA.

It was off to Springfield, Ill., in 1939 — his best in the minors with a 22-9 record. The trip to the Browns that fall resulted in a 1-1 record with a 3.32 ERA. That performance must have impressed the Browns, because 1940 became Bildilli's rookie season in the majors. He made the most of his first start on April 29 — a game he wasn't scheduled to start. "It wasn't my turn to pitch. It was Howard Mills turn, but he came up sick," a newspaper quoted him. The game against the New York Yankees began with the rookie hurler giving up a game opening triple to Frankie Crosetti. The next batter, Red Rolfe, drove in the run with a single. It was the last run the Yankees would score; the little fellow with the big curve allowed no more hits and only three runners to reach base. The Browns scored twice to win 2-1 and he became an instant hero. A Yankee Killer! A telegram to Drach's Restaurant read: CAN YOU HOLD GRACE LIKE BILDILLIE (sic) HELD YANKEES — signed Chicago customers.

The runt from Diamond also shutout the Yankees on Sept. 16 for his only two wins on the year against four losses. He appeared in a total of twenty-eight games during his rookie season and had a 5.57 ERA.

His career suffered a severe setback the following year when he was injured in a freak accident. "He was shagging flyballs in batting practice in Detroit and fell over a rail. He really got busted up," said his brother, Victor Bildilli, of Terre Haute.

He was sent to San Antonio and came back to the Browns for just two more games in 1941. Then he reportedly left the club over a salary dispute and came back to Indiana to play for the Muncie Citizens.

Baseball Commissioner Kenesaw Mountain Landis suspended him from Major League Baseball for breaking his contract with the Browns. When the two finally settled the matter, Bildilli reported to the Toledo Mudhens, but he soon jumped that team as well and never returned to the majors again.

"Hill Billy" played for the Muncie Fire Department from 1944-46. Then he went to Fort Wayne, a semipro team, in 1946 and pitched several exhibition games against major league clubs. Several teams talked to him about returning to the majors.

After a game the day before

B Emil Bildilli

Emil Bildilli played with Fort Wayne before his untimely death.

B

his birthday, he was returning to Muncie in his twelve-cylinder Chrysler when he fell asleep at the wheel and crashed. He died the next day on his thirty-fourth birthday.

Harry "Pree" Billiard (Harry Pree)
Born: Nov. 11, 1883, Monroe
Died: June 3, 1923, Wooster, Ohio
6', 190, Pitcher
New York, AL, 1908
Indianapolis, FL, 1914
Newark, FL, 1915
TR, 8-8, 3 SV, 3.96 ERA, 51 G
BR, .204, 49 AB, 10 H

Billiard pitched in five games in 1908 with the New York Giants. He was 8-7 with the Indianapolis Hoosiers of the Federal League in 1914.

Rae Blaemire (Rae Bertram)
Born: Feb. 8, 1911, Gary
Died: Dec. 23, 1975, Champaign, Ill.
6', 178, Catcher
New York, NL, 1941
BR, TR, .400, 2 G

Blaemire was an outfielder in his semipro days with a soap company in Hammond before becoming a catcher. His professional career began in 1935 with Nashville. He hit .317 in 1940. After his one month in the majors, he went to Jersey City, Columbus, St. Paul, and Grand Forks. He spent a total of twelve years in pro baseball.

Ray Blemker (Ray)
Born: Aug. 9, 1937, Huntingburg

5'11", 190, Pitcher
Kansas City, AL, 1960
TL, BR, 0-0, 27.00 ERA, 1 G

George Boehler (George Henry)
Born: Jan. 2, 1892, Lawrenceburg
Died: June 23, 1958, Lawrenceburg
6'2", 180, Pitcher
Detroit, AL, 1912-16
St Louis, AL, 1920-21
Pittsburgh, NL, 1923
Brooklyn, NL, 1926
TR, 7-13, .475 ERA, 60 G
BR, .233, 60 AB

Boehler had much more success in the minor leagues with 210 wins over eighteen years. His best professional season was in 1922 with Tulsa when he went 38-13. His best year in the majors came in 1914 when he was 2-3 in eighteen appearances with Detroit.

Tim Bogar (Timothy Paul)
Born: Oct. 28, 1966, Indianapolis
6'2", 198, Utility infielder
New York, NL, 1993
TR, BR, .244, 76G, 205 AB, 3 HR

A versatile player who can competently handle any position on the field, Bogar made his way onto the New York Mets squad after spring training in 1993. He received the Webster Award in 1989 for his outstanding contributions both on and off the field.

Born a Hoosier, he moved to Buffalo, Ill., and was graduated from Buffalo High School in 1984. He attended Eastern Illinois University, where he hit .408 with seventeen homers to

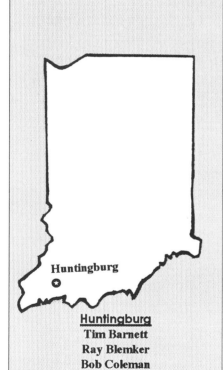

Huntingburg

Huntingburg
Tim Barnett
Ray Blemker
Bob Coleman

earn All-Conference honors in 1987. Bogar's numbers helped him earn a ninth-round selection by the Mets in the June 1987 draft.

Bogar spent the rest of the summer at Class A Little Falls, hitting .234, and the following year started at Class A Columbia before going to St. Lucie of the Florida State League, another Single A team. He shared the Doubleday Award with Kevin Brown as the top two players on the team. It earned him a promotion to Double A at Jackson, Miss., where he hit .266 in 1989.

Bogar started the 1990 season at Class AAA Tidewater, but struggled with a .162 average and was sent back down to Double A Williamsport. 1991 found him at Tidewater again this time mastering Triple A pitching and hitting .257 on the year with eleven doubles. In the last game of the season, he played all nine positions against Richmond.

The versatile player performed at all four infield positions during the 1992 season at Tidewater again, also pitching in three games. During the middle of the season, Bogar put together an eleven-game hitting steak. His best game of the season was a four-hit game on Aug. 26 against Pawtucket. He finished the season with a .279 average and thirty-two doubles. The Mets sent him to the Arizona Fall League.

At spring training in 1993 he hit .324 and made the team. His first at bat in the majors didn't come until April 21 when he struck out pinch-hitting for Doc Gooden in a 10-0 victory over the San Francisco Giants. His best game of the season was a two home run and two double performance in a 9-5 victory over Philadelphia. His season ended early when he suffered ligament damage in his left hand while sliding into home plate on Aug. 14.

His father, Jo Bogar, was a part-time scout for the Mets in 1992. Bogar is married and has a son named T.J.

Luther "Bonnie" Bonin (Ernest Luther)
Born: Jan. 13, 1888, Green Hill
Died: Jan. 3, 1966, Sycamore, Ohio
5'9", 178, Outfielder
St. Louis, AL, 1913
Buffalo, FL, 1914
BL, TR, .182, 21 G, 77 AB

Bonin had two seasons in the majors, including one year in the Federal League.

"Bonnie" began his professional career with Canton, Ohio, in 1910 where he was paid $125 a month. In 1911 the Green Hill native went to Columbus for the next three seasons. He was called up by St. Louis in 1912, but did not play.

After playing for St. Louis in 1913, he violated his contract by jumping to the newly formed Federal League. He played for Buffalo in 1915, and was married the same year to Dora Scott.

Bonin returned to Columbus in 1916 and also played for Muskegon, Mich.

Cy Bowen (Sutherland McCoy)

Ray Boyd

B

Born: Feb. 17, 1871, Kingston
Died: Jan. 25, 1925, Greensburg
6', 175, Pitcher
New York, NL, 1896
TR, 0-1, 6.00 ERA, 2 G

Ray Boyd (Raymond C.)
Born: Feb. 11, 1887, Hortonville
Died: Feb. 11, 1920, Hortonville
5'10", 160, Pitcher
St. Louis, AL, 1910
Cinncinnati, NL, 1911
TR, 3-4, 1 SV, 3.10 ERA, 10 G

Phil Bradley (Philip Poole)
Born: March 11, 1959, Bloomington
6', 185, Outfielder
Seattle, AL, 1983-87
Philadelphia, NL, 1988
Baltimore, AL, 1989-90
Chicago, AL, 1990
BR, TR, .286, 1022 G, 3695 AB, 78 HR

Bradley set several team records while he roamed the outfield for the Seattle Mariners. During his college days, he had been a quarterback for the University of Missouri.

After breaking into the majors in 1983, he hit over .300 and took the role of lead-off hitter the next three seasons.

1985 was his best year in the majors, as he hammered out twenty-six home runs and drove in eighty-eight runs.

The Mariners dealt him to Philadelphia in 1988 because of his constant complaining, although he held team season records for batting average, hits, total bases, and on-base percent-

age when he was traded.

He stayed with the Phillies for only one season and was traded to Baltimore. The Orioles sent Bradley to the Chicago White Sox in 1990, his last season in the majors.

The one-time Hoosier now resides in Columbia, Mo.

Bill Brandt (William George)
Born: March 21, 1915, Aurora
Died: May 16, 1968, Fort Wayne
5'8", 170, Pitcher
Pittsburgh, NL, 1941-43
TR, 5-3, 3.60 ERA, 34 G
BR, .133, 15 AB, 2 H

Elmer "Shook" Brown (Elmer Young)
Born: March 25, 1883, Southport
Died: Jan. 23, 1955, Indianapolis
5'11", 172, Pitcher
St. Louis, AL, 1911-12
Brooklyn, NL, 1913-15
TR, 9-11, 1 SV, 3.49 ERA
BR, .136, 59 AB

Mordecai "Three Finger" "Miner" Brown (Mordecai Peter Centennial)
Born: Oct. 19, 1876, Nyesville
Died: Feb. 14, 1948, Terre Haute
5'10", 175, Pitcher
St. Louis, NL, 1903
Chicago, NL, 1904-12
Cincinnati, NL, 1913
St. Louis, FL, 1914
Brooklyn, FL, 1914
Chicago, FL, 1915
Chicago, NL, 1916
TR, 239-127, 49 SV, 2.06

ERA, 481 G
BR, .206, 1143 AB
WS, 5-4, 63 IP

"Three Finger" was the first Hoosier to be enshrined into the National Baseball Hall of Fame in 1949 and the Indiana Baseball Hall of Fame in 1979. He still holds the all-time National League record for lowest ERA in a season — 1.04 in 1906. He also is considered the first great relief pitcher, leading the Chicago Cubs to four pennants and two world championships.

Brown acquired his nickname as a youngster when he lost part of his right index finger in a corn grinder. The seven year old further complicated his injury tumbling into a rain barrel while chasing a rabbit. When the cast was removed, his second finger was found broken and the little finger had a permanent crook to it. Instead of ending a possible baseball career, the injury made his pitching much better. It gave him a natural sinker and curveball.

"Miner," as he was also nicknamed, started playing semipro ball before the turn of the century. Then he played in the bush leagues for Terre Haute, Omaha, and St. Louis. His major league career began with St. Louis in 1903 where he went 9-13 for the last-place Cardinals. After the season, the Cardinals traded him with Jack O'Neill to Chicago for Jack Taylor and Larry McLean. His career took off after that.

Brown helped the Cubs to pennants in 1906, 1907, 1908, and 1910. In 1908, the ace of the staff won three of his last four games to allow the Cubs to win the pennant. He was untouchable in the 1907 and 1908 World Series, compiling a 3-0 record and 0.00 ERA! In 1909 he led the league in wins (27), saves (7), complete games (32), games pitched (50), and innings pitched (343).

In an era where pitchers were expected to finish a game they started, Brown was called into many games to relieve the starter and "save" the game. Three Finger was way ahead of his time, because the term "save" wasn't created until fifty years later. He led the league in saves from 1908 to 1911 and was the first pitcher to gain more than ten saves in a season. He won two World Series games in relief.

A couple of factors helped Three Fingers in Chicago. Behind him was the best double-play combination in the game — Tinkers to Evers to Chance. It was still the "dead-ball" era of baseball; not many balls went over the fence.

By 1912 Brown was thirty-five and age was beginning to take its toll on him. He was 5-6 on the year and the Cubs released him. The following year he went to Cincinnati and was 11-12 for the Red Stockings.

In 1914 Brown jumped to the new Federal League, as several of his veteran ball players did. He managed and pitched for St. Louis until going to Brooklyn halfway through the season, leading the Chicago team to the Federal League pennant with a 17-8 record in 1915. When the league folded, he was sold to the Cubs with ten other players.

Donie Bush played with the Detroit Tigers for sixteen years and was long-time owner of the Indianapolis Indians.

Brown's last game in the majors was one of his most memorable. He and Christy Mathewson agreed to pitch one last game at Weeghman Park, later renamed Wrigley Field. It was tabbed the "Greatest Treat of the Year for Baseball Fans." The Cubs led early, but the Reds bounced back and Brown lost the game.

After retiring from the majors after the 1916 season, Miner played and managed in the bush leagues. He once managed Terre Haute of the Three-I League, a team he had played on early in his career. He also played for the Indianapolis Indians in 1919.

Later on in life, when he was finished with baseball, he owned and operated a service station in Terre Haute. He was once quoted as saying, "All I know is that I had all the fingers I needed."

Brown's name still dots the record books. He pitched six one-hit games and fifty-six shutouts during his stellar career. His career ERA (2.06) ranks third in the history of the game. He still holds six Cubs' records: winning percentage (.649), ERA (1.80) and shutouts (50) in a career; wins (29), ERA (1.04), and shutouts in a season (10).

His hometown of Nyesville began building a monument to honor the great pitcher in 1993.

Sheldon Burnside (Sheldon John)
Born: Dec. 22, 1954, South Bend
6'5", 200, Relief Pitcher
Detroit, AL, 1978-79
Cincinnati, NL, 1980
TL, 2-1, 6.00 ERA, 19 G
BR, .000, 1 AB

Burnside got three shots at the majors, but struck out on staying there. He played a couple of seasons in Indianapolis.

The Hoosier was optioned to Indianapolis from Detroit in 1979. He turned out to be a valuable addition to the Indians as he was 6-4 with a 3.00 ERA.

Burnside was one of the four pitchers involved in a no-hit game on Aug. 29 against the Evansville Triplets. It was only the second time in baseball history that four pitchers no-hit another team.

The following season the reliever was 3-0 with a 0.50 ERA in nineteen appearances when he was called up to the Reds. 1980 was his last season in the majors.

Donie "Ownie" Bush (Owen Joseph)
Born: Oct. 8, 1887, Indianapolis
Died: March 28, 1972, Indianapolis
5'6, 140, Shortstop
Detroit, AL, 1908-21
BB, TR, .250, 1945 G, 7206 AB, 9 HR

Bush spent sixty-five years in professional baseball as a player, manager, scout, and club president. He was inducted into the Indiana Baseball Hall of Fame in 1979.

The fiesty little player began his professional career in 1905 with Sault Ste. Marie. He played for Saginaw, Dayton, South Bend, and Indianapolis before joining Detroit in 1908.

"Ownie" had an excellent eye for pitches and led the league in walks from 1909 to 1912 as the lead-off hitter. His best year in the majors came in 1917 when he hit .281 and led the league in runs scored with 112.

The Hoosier institution's playing career ended in 1923, and he began a twenty-year managing career. He managed the Indianapolis Indians from 1924-26. In 1927 Bush led the Pittsburgh Pirates to the World Series, but the team was swept by the Yankees. He managed the Chicago White Sox, Minneapolis, Cincinnati, and Louisville.

In 1942 he became president and chief executive officer of the Indianapolis club and headed the team until the late 1960s. Victory Field was renamed Bush Stadium in his honor.

In the 1950s he scouted for the Boston Red Sox and later for the White Sox.

Mary Butcher
Born: Berne
AAGPBL, 1945

Bill Butland (Wilburn Rue)
Born: March 22, 1918, Terre Haute
6'5", 185, Pitcher
Boston, AL, 1940, 42, 46-47
TR, 9-3, 3.90 ERA, 32 G
BR, .051, 39 AB

Butland's blossoming playing career was interrupted by World War II and after the war, he never returned to pre-war form.

The Terre Haute native began playing baseball in grade school. He played baseball in high school and for the local American Legion team. "I just loved to play ball," he said.

Butland nearly quit high school to play ball full time for a semipro team, but former major leaguer Paul Trout convinced him otherwise.

After he graduated, he played semipro and was first offered a contract for $125 a month by a scout from Minneapolis. He didn't know what to do, so he asked Hoosier Hall of Famer Mordecai "Three Finger" Brown. Brown told him to send the contract back unsigned. A few weeks later it came back with a $25 raise. Butland signed.

He played Class D ball at Eau Claire, Wisc., and Crookston, Minn., for three years and remembers one game in which he went 5-for-5, his best game ever as a hitter.

In 1939 Butland was promoted to Minneapolis, a Class A team, posting a 19-10 record that year. "I had fantastic luck. I hit a home run at midnight one game," he recalled. The next day the newspaper dubbed him "Burglar Bill," because the ball went out of the stadium and crashed through a retail store window, setting off the alarm.

In the fall of 1939, he was sold to the Boston Red Sox, where, in Butland's first major league start, his team helped the to an 11-2 victory over the Philadelphia Athletics. "You're nervous as hell, but once you get the ball in your hand, you're in good shape," Butland explained.

He was sent back to the minors and spent the next year in Louisville. In one game he

Bill Butland relaxes at his home in Terre Haute these days.

B pitched against his old friend Harry Taylor, who also made it to the majors. "We agreed not to throw curves against each other. He got the only hit," he said.

Boston brought Butland up to the majors again in 1942 as a middle reliever. He came out of the bullpen every couple of days until one day manager Joe Cronin ran out of pitchers and decided to start him. Cronin probably wishes he had made the move earlier, as the sidearm sinkerballer went on to a record-breaking seven straight victories — one against each team in the American League. Butland ended the season with a team-best 2.51 ERA.

By late 1942 the world was at war, and Butland was drafted by the Army and sent to Fort Benjamin Harrison in Indianapolis for a spell. In 1943 while playing some baseball at Fort Sill, Okla., the manager of the team, a sergeant, ordered him to slide during practice. Butland refused. The sergeant tried, unsuccessfully, to court-martial him over the incident.

After the war, Butland reported for spring training in 1946. "The arm didn't feel too good," he admitted. He pitched a few games for Boston in 1947 and 1948 before being released when a doctor diagnosed his problem as a ripped muscle in the upper arm, Butland decided to retire from baseball.

Butland still lives in Terre Haute and celebrated his fiftieth wedding anniversary with his wife, Margie Smith of Terre Haute, in 1993.

Bill "Big Bill" Byers (James William)
Born: Oct. 3, 1877, Bridgeton
Died: Sept. 8, 1948, Baltimore, Md.
5'7", 175, Catcher
St. Louis, NL, 1904
BR, TR, .217, 19 G, 60 AB

Byers had a cup of coffee with the St. Louis Cardinals. He was released at the end of the 1904 season and his contract was picked up by Brooklyn.

Byers spent the rest of his career in the bush leagues at Baltimore, Minneapolis, Winona, and Trenton. He played professionally until 1912.

Wes Callahan (Wesley LeRoy)
Born: July 3, 1888, Lyons
Died: Sept. 13, 1953, Dayton, Ohio
5'7", 155, Shortstop
St. Louis, NL, 1913
BR, TR, .286, 7 G, 14 AB

Callahan made his debut Sept. 7, 1913, and finished out the season with St. Louis in his only major league appearance.

Dave "Chopper" Campbell (David Alan)
Born: Sept. 3, 1951, Princeton
6'3", 210, Relief Pitcher
Atlanta, NL, 1977-78
TR, 4-10, 14 SV, 3.82 ERA, 118 G
BR, .083, 12 AB, 1 H

Campbell had thirteen saves for the last-place Atlanta Braves in his rookie season. The following season, his last in the majors, he developed arm problems and struggled to a 4.80 ERA.

Chet Carmichael (Chester Keller)
Born: Jan. 9, 1888, Muncie
Died: Aug. 23, 1960, Rochester, N.Y.
5'11", 200, Pitcher
Cincinnati, NL, 1909
TR, 0-0, 0.00 ERA, 2 G
BR, .000, 2 AB

Max "Scoops" Carey (Max George)
Born: Jan. 11, 1890, Terre Haute
Died: May 30, 1976, Miami, Fla.
5'11", 170, Outfielder
Pittsburgh, NL, 1910-26
Brooklyn, NL, 1926-29
BB, TR, .285, 2476 G, 9363 AB, 69 HR
1 WS, .458, 2 RBI

As one of the best base stealers and defensive center-fielders of his era, Carey set several records during his days — some of which stood for decades. He was named to the National Baseball Hall of Fame in 1961 and the Indiana Baseball Hall of Fame in 1979.

Carey played amateur baseball at Concordia College in Fort Wayne from 1903 to 1909. After graduating, he signed with South Bend of the Central League and played shortstop, third base, and the outfield. Carey hit a measly .158 during his first season, but he learned to switch hit. His average rose to .293 the following season at South Bend, which earned him a September call-up to Pittsburgh.

1911 became his rookie season with the Pirates, who put the fleet-footed Hoosier in centerfield. Carey hit .258 and established himself as a starter for the team. The following year he raised his average to .302 and led the league in putouts.

Leading the National League in steals for ten of thirteen seasons beginning in 1913, he set a career mark of 738 thefts, which ranks him among career leaders. He also led the league in putouts nine times from 1912 to 1924. His fielding ability led to his nickname "Scoops." Four times Carey led the league in assists, and his 339 outfield assists is the modern NL record. He also has the switch-hitting record for most runs in a season, which he set in 1922.

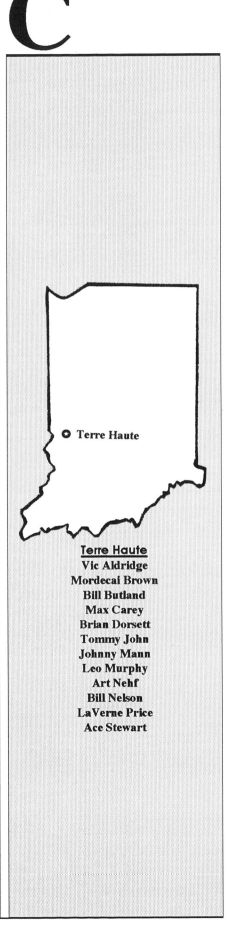

Terre Haute
Vic Aldridge
Mordecai Brown
Bill Butland
Max Carey
Brian Dorsett
Tommy John
Johnny Mann
Leo Murphy
Art Nehf
Bill Nelson
LaVerne Price
Ace Stewart

21

C

Darrel Chaney played with the Atlanta Braves for four seasons.

One of his best games came in 1922 in an eighteen-inning contest against the New York Giants. He went 6-for-6 and stole three bases, including home. The leadoff man scored forty-two percent of the time he reached base in his career.

In 1925 the Hoosier helped the Pirates to a World Series victory despite playing with two broken ribs. In Game Seven his four hits and three runs scored beat the Washington Senators and the great Walter Johnson.

Carey was made the team captain in 1926, which led to his demise at Pittsburgh. When player-manager Fred Clarke urged manager Bill McKenie to bench the slumping slugger, Carey called a team meeting. The Pirates responded by selling him to Brooklyn for $4,000 and outrighting two of Carey's supporters.

After twenty years as a player, Carey began a long coaching and managing career. He coached with the Pirates in 1930 and managed the Dodgers in 1932 and 1933. As a manager his record was 146-161. He also went on to manage Miami, Fla., in 1940; Cordele, Ga., in 1955; and Louisville in 1956.

During the 1940s he was a manager and president in the All-American Girls Professional Baseball League.

Scott "Red" Cary (Scott Russell)
Born: April 11, 1923, Kendallville
5'11", 168, Relief Pitcher
Washington, AL, 1947
TL, 3-1, 5.89 ERA, 23 G

BL, .077, 13 AB

Cary pitched most of 1947 as a reliever for the seventh-place Senators. He did get three starts and allowed five homers in fifty-four innings pitched.

Eli Cates (Eli Eldo)
Born: Jan. 26, 1877, Green-stork
Died: May 29, 1964, Richmond
5'9", 175, Pitcher
Washington, AL, 1908
TR, 4-8, 2.50 ERA, 19 G

Cates spent a summer with Washington and started ten games for his only season in the majors.

Darrel "Nort" Chaney Dar-rel Lee)
Born: March 9, 1948, Hammond
6'2", 188, Utility infielder
Cincinnati, NL, 1969-75
Atlanta, NL, 1976-79
BB, TR, .217, 915 G, 2113 AB, 14 HR

Used mainly as a utility infielder for the Big Red Machine, Chaney earned a World Series ring in 1975 with Cincinnati. During his major league career he played at every position except pitcher.

When Chaney was eight he announced to his parents that he was going to be a major league baseball player. Of course his parents didn't take him seriously. Because Cubs player Ernie Banks was his idol, Chaney chose to play shortstop. He also pitched and started throwing breaking balls. "I developed a slider at ten and got Little League elbow," he said. At his Little League banquet that year was none other than the superstar Banks. "Ten years later I was playing against Banks," he noted.

Chaney was an All-Star player in Little League and Babe Ruth. At Oliver P. Morton High School in Hammond, he lettered in baseball, basketball, and football. In the summer he played baseball for American Legion Post 232 in Hessville.

In his senior year the quarterback led Hammond Morton to a state championship and *Parade Magazine* honored him as the best high school quarterback in the country. He was showered with football scholarships from Notre Dame, every Big-10 school, and many other universities. "I thought about it, but no Big-10 team would let me play both football and baseball," he said. Only Ball State University would allow him to play both, so Chaney signed a letter of intent with them. However, college took a back seat two weeks later as the Reds drafted him in the second round.

Chaney graduated in June 1966 and went straight to the Rookie League at Sioux Falls, South Dakota. The following year he went to Knoxville, Tenn., a Class AA team, but lasted only two weeks there, as his Army Reserve unit called him up for duty. The Vietnam War interrrupted his baseball career for the rest of that year. In 1969 Chaney was back in the Southern League with Ashville, N.C. In the second half of the season the manager put him at cleanup in the batting order "I

had the responsiblity of hitting the ball, so I choked down on the bat and started swinging for power," he explained. The added responsibility worked, as he started hitting home runs. "The ball just traveled in the Carolina air. They had a short porch in right field," he said. On his way to twenty-three homers that year, the best in the league, he hit two grand slams, which caught the attention of the Reds. "It helped me to get to the big leagues."

During Double A ball he picked up the nickname "Nort," short for Norton, the television character. "They thought I looked like Art Carney of The Honeymooners. I even dressed like Carney," he admitted.

After a good spring training in 1969, the Reds brought him up and he became the backup shortstop to Woody Woodward.

The following year Dave Concepcion became the regular shortstop and Woodward the backup. That made Chaney a utility infielder. His batting average rose to .232, as he helped the Reds to the Western Division title. Chaney rode the bench in the playoffs. In the World Series against Baltimore, Chaney was put in three of the five games for defensive purposes. He batted only once with no hit, as the Orioles prevailed.

The Big Red Machine sputtered the following year, and so did Chaney's career. He was sent back down to Indianapolis to play for the Class AAA Indians. He felt right at home, however, and helped lead the Indians to an American Association title. At the end of the

C
Darrel Chaney

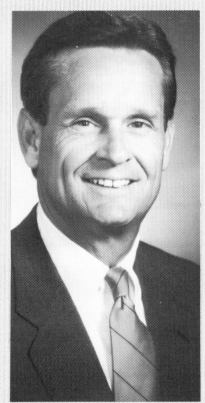

Darrel Chaney traded his uniform in for a suit and is on the Board of Directors for the Major League Alumni Association.

Darrel Chaney

C

season he was called back to the Reds for the rest of the year.

Chaney bounced back to the Reds in 1972, and Manager Sparky Anderson decided to use Chaney more at short. "Sparky decided to platoon us. I played against righties and he (Concepcion) against lefties," he explained. His batting average increased to .250. In the League Championship Series, Chaney started at short and played in all five games, going 3-for-16 and scoring three runs. The Reds won the series in five games.

In the World Series, Chaney and Concepcion took turns playing short, but in the seventh game Concepcion was called on to face "Blue Moon" Odom, a right hander. "It kind of ticked me off," Chaney said. But Chaney got his chance at redemption as a pinch hitter in the bottom of the ninth against Rollie Fingers with Oakland ahead 3-2. "I fouled the first pitch off. Then Rollie Fingers hit me in the knee. I was looking for the home run ball. [Pete] Rose lined out next to end the game."

In 1973 Chaney played more because Concepion suffered a broken ankle just before the All-Star Game and was out the rest of the season. However, Chaney was barely hitting above his weight and ended the season at a paltry .181. In the LCS he split shortstop duties with Dennis Menke. Chaney was hitless in nine at bats and the Reds lost the series to the New York Mets.

Concepicion was healthy in 1974 and hit fourteen homers the first half of the season, so Chaney was back to being a

utility infielder. He played in 117 games and hit .200. The following year his average rose to .219 and the Reds won the pennant easily. Chaney sat on the bench in the playoffs. In the World Series against Boston, he was used as a pinch hitter twice.

"My idol [Banks] never got to the World Series, but I did. It's really gratifying to play in the World Series," he reflected.

In the off-season the Reds traded Chaney to the Atlanta Braves for Mike Lum. "Atlanta was the worst team in baseball at the time. Had I stayed in Cincinnati, I never would have had a chance to play," he said. So Chaney invited the trade and his chance to play every day. Playing every day gave him a chance to hit more and he had his best season in the majors — .252, twenty doubles, eight triples, and fifty RBI. One distinction he didn't like earning that year was the most errors in the National League with thirty-six. "That was misleading. Most of those were throwing errors," he said, putting some of the blame on first basemen Willie Montanez and Darrell Evans.

During spring training in 1977 Chaney had bone spurs in both heels — a condition known as a stone bruise — and had to wear casts on both feet. He was on the shelf until the second week of the season. "I struggled the whole season," he said. He was used in a utility role the rest of his career.

Nowadays Chaney lives near Atlanta and sells real estate. He's also a part owner in Baseball Heaven, which runs baseball fantasy camps for the Braves, Reds, and Cleveland Indians. Chaney also is on the board of directors for the Major League Alumni Association. He and his wife, Cindy, have raised another ball player, their son Keith. The Braves signed him as a non-draft pick and he played rookie ball. When he asked to be released from the Braves, they refused and he retired from baseball. "He gave it a shot," Chaney said.

Glenn "Pete" Chapman (Glenn Justice)
Born: Jan. 21, 1906, Cambridge City
Died: Nov. 5, 1988, Richmond
5'11", 170, Outfielder
Brooklyn, NL, 1934
BR, TR, .280, 67 G, 93 AB, 1 HR

Oscar "The Black Ruth" Charleston (Oscar McKinley)
Born: Oct. 14, 1896, Indianapolis
Died: Oct. 5, 1954, Philadelphia, Pa.
6'1", 185, Outfielder
Indianapolis, NNL, 1915
Detroit, NNL, 1919
American Giants, NNL, 1919
Indianapolis, NNL, 1920
St. Louis, NNL, 1921
Indianapolis, NNL, 1922-23
Harrisburg, NNL, 1924-27
Philadelphia, NNL, 1928-29
Homestead, NNL, 1930-31
Pittsburgh, NNL, 1932-34
Chicago, NNL, 1934
Pittsburgh, NNL, 1935-38
Toledo, NNL, 1940-41
BL, TR, .357, 821 G, 2992 AB

Charleston is ranked among the greatest Negro players and managers of all time. He led the Negro Leagues in many categories and was inducted into the National Baseball Hall of Fame in 1976 and the Indiana Baseball Hall of Fame in 1981.

"The Hoosier Comet," as he was called by his fans, first played baseball in the U.S. Army in 1913. The following year he became the only black player in the minor leagues. In 1915 he returned to Indianapolis to join the ABCs and played for the Detroit Stars and American Giants in 1919 before returning to the ABCs again in 1920.

In 1921 with the St. Louis Giants, "The Black Ruth" hit .430 and led the Negro National League in doubles, triples, and homers. He reportedly hit four homers in an exhibition game against the St. Louis Cardinals. A great outfielder and base stealer because of his gazelle-like speed, Charleston returned to the ABCs, leading the league in home runs again. During the Roaring '20s, people learned a dance called the Charleston, while the player with same name was playing in Harrisburg and Philadelphia.

Charleston continued to be one of the best players in the Negro leagues well past his prime. At age forty he hit .450 for the Pittsburgh Crawfords. He began managing in the 1930s and took it up full time in the 1940s. He also scoured the Negro leagues for the Brooklyn Dodgers, who signed Jackie Robinson, the first black player in the majors. Charleston man-

C

aged his hometown ABCs then crowned his career managing the Indianapolis Clowns to a Negro World Championship in 1954.

Dorothy Christ
Born: LaPorte
South Bend, AAGPBL, 1948
1 G, 0 AB

Rich Coggins (Richard Allen)
Born: Dec. 7, 1950, Indian-apolis
5'8", 170, Outfielder
Baltimore, AL, 1972-74
Montreal, NL, 1975
New York, AL, 1975-76
Chicago, AL, 1976
BL, TL, .265, 342 G, 1083 AB, 12 HR
2 LCS, .200, 5 G

Coggins was runner-up to the American League Rookie of the Year in 1973 when he hit .319 for the Orioles. A thyroid condition ended his promising career early.

Coggins made his major league debut with Baltimore on Aug. 29, 1972, and hit .333 in sixteen games. In his rookie season the following year, he finished behind teammate Al Bumbry for the rookie award. He put up some good numbers: nineteen doubles, nine triples, seven home runs, and seventeen stolen bases.

The sophomore jinx struck the Hoosier in 1974 when he managed only a .243 batting average. Then to make matters worse, he went 0-for-11 in the LCS. The Orioles promptly traded him to Montreal.

During spring training in 1975, Coggins' health problems began. Montreal shipped him to the Yankees for cash. He hit just .224 as an outfielder and with New York in 1975.

The following season he was traded to the White Sox. After hitting .156, the Sox dealt him to Philadelphia for Wayne Nordhagen. Coggins never played for the Phillies and his career ended at age twenty-five.

Bob Coleman (Robert Hunter)
Born: Sept. 26, 1890, Hunt-ingburg
Died: July 16, 1959, Boston, Mass.
6'2", 190, Catcher
Pittsburgh, NL, 1913-14
Cleveland, AL, 1916
BR, TR, .241, 116 G, 228 AB

Coleman was a backup catcher for three seasons in the majors. After his playing days, he managed Evansville of the Three-I League for some thirty years and won several pennants in that time. He also managed in Fort Wayne. Coleman was inducted into the Indiana Baseball Hall of Fame in 1980.

Bill Collins (William Shirley)
Born: March 27, 1882, Ch-esterton
Died: June 26, 1961, San Bernardino, Calif.
6', 170, Outfielder
Boston, NL, 1910-11
Chicago, NL, 1911
Brooklyn, NL, 1914
Buffalo, FL, 1914
BB, TR, .223, 228 G, 775 AB, 3 HR

Orth "Buck" Collins (Orth Stein)

Born: April 27, 1880, Lafayette
Died: Dec. 13, 1949, Ft. Lauderdale, Fla.
6', 150, Outfielder
New York, AL, 1904
Washington, AL, 1909
BL, TR, .250, 13 G, 24 AB

Roy "Irish" Corhan (Roy George)
Born: Oct. 21, 1887, Indianapolis
Died: Nov. 24, 1958, San Francisco, Calif.
5'9", 165, Shortstop
Chicago, AL, 1911
St. Louis, NL, 1916
TR, BR, .211, 135 G, 426 AB

The graduate of Indianapolis Manual Training School in 1905 played semipro ball for the local Tuxedos in 1905. His professional career began in 1907 and lasted twelve years.

Phil Corridan (Philip)
Born: Unknown, Fort Wayne
Second baseman, outfielder
Chicago, UA, 1884
.143, 2 G, 7 AB

John "Red" Corriden (John Michael Sr.)
Born: Sept. 4, 1887, Logansport
Died: Sept. 28, 1959, Indianapolis
5'9", 165, Shortstop, third baseman
St. Louis, AL, 1910
Detroit, AL, 1912
Chicago, NL, 1913-15
BR, TR, 222 G, .205, 640 AB, 6 HR

Corriden spent more than forty years in professional baseball as a player, scout, coach, and manager. In his first year in the majors, he was involved in an incident that resulted in the manager of the St. Louis Browns being banned for life. His son, John Jr., also played professional ball.

As a boy, Corriden delivered newspapers to Judge Kenesaw Mountain Landis, who later became the first commissioner of baseball. "Red," so named after his flaming red hair, first became involved with organized baseball in his late teens with Logansport Auto. The following year he played with another semipro team in nearby Frankfort.

In 1908 he signed a major league contract with the St. Louis Browns and was assigned to Class D Keokuk, Iowa, of the Central Association. He played third base for two years with the club and hit .282 in 1909. He was moved up to Class C Omaha, Neb., in 1910, where he played well and raised his average to .308.

At the end of the 1910 season, the Browns called him up to play both at third and shortstop. In a game against the Chicago White Sox, he was batting against "Big Ed" Walsh, when the pitcher threw a ball under his chin, his son related. Corriden ran up to the mound and Walsh asked him, "What's the matter young man? Did that ball come up there fast enough?" The smaller infielder thought better of trying to fight the six-foot pitcher. On the next pitch, Walsh hit Corriden on the wrist. He went to first, stole second and scored on a hit. The Browns

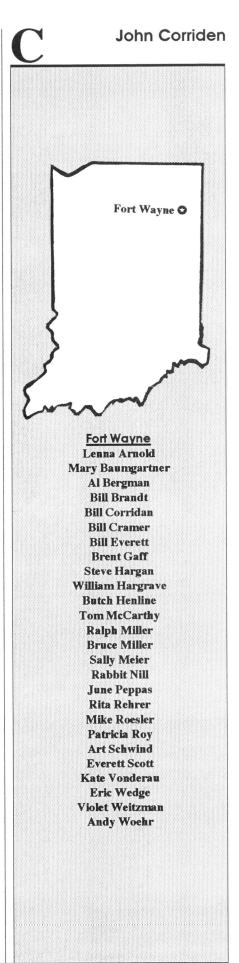

Fort Wayne
Lenna Arnold
Mary Baumgartner
Al Bergman
Bill Brandt
Bill Corridan
Bill Cramer
Bill Everett
Brent Gaff
Steve Hargan
William Hargrave
Butch Henline
Tom McCarthy
Ralph Miller
Bruce Miller
Sally Meier
Rabbit Nill
June Peppas
Rita Rehrer
Mike Roesler
Patricia Roy
Art Schwind
Everett Scott
Kate Vonderau
Eric Wedge
Violet Weitzman
Andy Woehr

John Corriden

beat Walsh 1-0.

In the last two games of the season, the Browns were playing the Cleveland Indians. Indians player Nap Lajoie was battling Ty Cobb for the batting crown and a new car. Manager Jack O'Connor told Corrriden to play back at third base when Lajoie came to bat. "Why don't you let the best man win," Corriden told O'Connor, according to his son. The manager told Corriden to do what he was told. So, Corriden played back and Lajoie picked up six bunt hits in going 8-for-9 in two games. The streak allowed him to win the battting title by a single percentage point over Cobb. After the season, American League President Ban Johnson called Corriden to his office to find out what happened. As a result, Johnson gave the batting title and car to Cobb and banned O'Connor from baseball for life.

The nest season the Browns sent Corriden to Kansas City of the American Association. He began 1911 by getting married to Ethel Shumm, then played the whole year at Kansas City and hit .247. The next year he was hitting .318 when he was sold to Detroit for $15,000. He hit just .203 for the Tigers, so he was sold for cash to Cincinnati in November 1912. The Reds turned right around and dealt him to the Chicago Cubs in a multi-player trade.

Corriden played short for the Cubs and hit a paltry .175. But he found his batting stroke in 1914 and hit .230 in 107 games. He played in just six games in 1915 for the Cubs before he was released. His days as a major leaguer were over and he played in the bush leagues until 1924.

Then Minneapolis of the American Association hired him as a coach for three years. In 1928 he returned to his home state to coach for the Indianapolis Indians for three-and-a-half years. During the 1931 season he was hired as a scout for the Chicago Cubs and scouted for the Cubs for nearly a decade before being released in late 1940.

The Brooklyn Dodgers signed him as a coach less than a month later. He coached with the Dodgers for five seasons before going across town to coach for the Yankees. Ironically, the Yankees ended up beating the Dodgers in 1947 to earn Corriden a World Series ring.

John and Red Corriden were one of the few father-son combinations from Indiana.

In 1950 the White Sox hired Corriden as a coach. When Manager Jack Onslow compiled 8-22 record, he was fired and Corriden reluctantly took the job. He guided the Sox to a 52-72 record the rest of the way. At the end of the season he told his son, "I wouldn't really mind managing next year." It was not to be; he was released. After forty-two years of baseball, Corriden decided to retire.

John Corriden Jr. (John Michael Jr.
Born: Oct. 6, 1918, Logansport
5'6", 160, Outfielder
Brooklyn, NL, 1946
RB, TR, 1 G, 1 R

Corriden tried to follow in the footsteps of his father, but he only enjoyed a cup of coffee in the majors. He did spend nearly a decade in the minor leagues.

At age ten Corriden began hanging around his dad, a coach at the time for the Indianapolis Indians, who played in a stadium on West Washington Street. Corriden learned the game by watching and practicing with the bush league players. He didn't play baseball in high school, because Cathedral High School didn't have a team. Then he went to Indiana University in Bloomington. However, he wasn't really ready for academics and signed a contract for $500 with the Brooklyn Dodgers, who assigned him to Class D Ontario, N.Y. His father may have influenced the decision, because he was a scout for the Dodgers at the time. Corriden signed as an outfielder, because

he had taken a grounder in his right eye and suffered retina damage when he was a youngster.

The outfielder moved up to Class C in 1942 with Dayton, Ohio. He was hitting about .280 at the time and progressing well, so the Dodgers moved him up to Class AA Montreal in the International League. He played for two months there before he was sent down to Class A New Orleans for the rest of 1943. Then he was sent back up to Montreal. In one season the team wore satin uniforms, he remembered. "Boy, they were hot," he said. Probably his best game in baseball came one night in a game in Montreal. Not known as a power hitter, the small Corriden stroked two home runs against Buffalo in Offerman Stadium.

He was invited to the major league spring training camp in 1946. Afterwards, he was assigned to Mobile, Ala., a Class AA team in the Southern League. Then he was called up to the Dodgers where he spent time on the bench. Finally he was called on to pinch run for Billy Herman, another Hoosier. Corriden ended up scoring the winning run in the game, as the Dodgers beat the New York Giants. "I didn't go to bat. Maybe it's just as well that I didn't," he explained. "The odds of making it to the big leagues are remote. If I could have been an infielder, I might have made it."

Corriden was soon sent back down to the minors and he spent the rest of the season with Fort

"The odds of making it to the big leagues are remote. If I could have been an infielder, I might have made it." John Corriden Jr.

C

Worth in the Texas League. Then it was on to St. Paul and Jersey City before he decided to go play in the "Outlaw" League in Canada in 1948. "There were some good players there, such as Sal Maglie," he said. Maglie had been suspensed by Major League Baseball for playing in the Mexican League.

In 1949 Corriden returned to Indiana to play semipro ball with Lafayette. After that he settled down to a career as a traffic dispatcher for two moving companies in Indianapolis. He retired from Wheaton Van Lines in 1981 and settled down in Indianapolis with his wife, Lucille. They have two sons, Kevin and John, and two daughters, Sheila and Sharon.

In 1991 he received a letter from a woman in Washington who wanted to know if he was interested in purchasing a 1919 watch from the St. Paul team. His father's name was inscribed on the inside. "I sent $125 to get that watch back," he said. He cherishes his father's watch and the World Series ring his father passed on to him.

Bill Cramer (William Wendell)
Born: May 21, 1891, Bedford
Died: Sept. 11, 1966, Fort Wayne
6', 175, Pitcher
Cincinnati, NL, 1912
TR, 0-0, 0.00 ERA, 1 G

James "Doc" "Otey" Crandall (James Otis)
Born: Oct. 8, 1887, Wadena
Died: Aug. 17, 1951, Bell, Calif.
5'10", 180, Pitcher, infielder
New York, NL, 1908-1913
St. Louis, NL, 1913
New York, NL, 1913
St. Louis, FL, 1914-15
St. Louis, AL, 1916
Boston, NL, 1918
TR, 102-62, 2.92 ERA, 25 SV, 302 G
BR, .285, 500 G, 887 AB, 9 HR
3 WS, 1-0, 1.69 ERA, 10 IP

Crandall became one of the first relief pitchers in the majors, as he had more relief appearances than starts. The versatile player also filled in at infield positions and had a lifetime .285 batting average with nine home runs — good power during the dead-ball era.

When Crandall came up to the majors in 1908 with the majors, he was primarily a starter. The following season he was used more in relief and picked up six saves at a time when pitchers were expected to start and finish a game. He picked up the nickname "Doc" for coming into a game and being "the physician of the pitching emergency."

For the next four seasons he led the league in relief appearances and relief victories in helping the Giants to pennants, 1911-13.

Crandall was traded to St. Louis in 1913, but after two games he was re-purchased. The following season he was lured to the new Federal League, where he took the role of a starter. The following year he enjoyed his best season in the majors with a 21-15 record. He led the league in relief wins with six, too.

After the Federal League folded, he had brief appearances with the St. Louis Cardinals and Boston Braves.

Ken Crawford (Kenneth Daniel)
Born: Oct. 31, 1894, South Bend
Died: Nov. 11, 1976, Pittsburgh, Pa.
5'9", 145, First baseman, outfielder
Baltimore, FL, 1915
TL, TR, .244, 23 G, 82 AB

Lou Criger (Louis)
Born: Feb. 3, 1872, Elkhart
Died: May 14, 1934, Tucson, Ariz.
5'10", 150, Catcher
Cleveland, NL, 1896-98
St. Louis, NL, 1899-00
Boston, AL, 1901-08
St. Louis, AL, 1909
New York, AL, 1910
St Louis, AL, 1912
BR, TR, .221, 1012 G, 3199 AB, 11 HR
1 WS, .231, 8 G

Criger was best known for being the receiver for the famed Cy Young and caught most of his victories. He turned down a $12,000 bribe in the first World Series.

Criger broke into the majors at the end of the 1896 season with Cleveland. He began catching Young the following season and became his favorite receiver. Then he followed Young to St. Louis in 1899 and Boston in 1901. At the turn of the century Criger was considered the best catcher in baseball.

In the first World Series,

Criger was offered the bribe to allow a few extra runs to come in. He refused and received threats for his denial. He said nothing about the offer until years later. He helped the Boston Puritans to victory in the first World Series.

Young and his best catcher parted ways in 1909 when Criger went to St. Louis. His last season in the majors came in 1910 with the New York Highlanders. He also played a game for St. Louis in 1912.

Criger's batting average, which had dropped below .200 for good after the 1904 season, is probably the reason he was never inducted into the Baseball Hall of Fame. He still holds the Red Sox record for putouts with 156 in 1903.

Clyde "Bucky" Crouse (Clyde Ellsworth)
Born: Jan. 6, 1897, Anderson
Died: Oct. 23, 1983, Muncie
5'8", 158, Catcher
Chicago, AL, 1923-30
BL, TR, .262, 470 G, 1306 AB, 8 HR

Crouse shadowed Hall of Fame catcher Ray Schalk during his eight-year career with the Chicago White Sox. In 1937 Crouse was named as Most Valuable Player with the International League. He has been inducted into the Indiana Baseball Hall of Fame and Buffalo, N.Y., Hall of Fame.

Crouse began playing semi-pro ball in Muncie in 1918. In 1920 he played for Hawkins Furniture Factory in Connersville.

Bucky Crouse was a backup catcher with the Chicago White Sox.

George Crowe

C

In 1921 he signed with the White Sox and played in Jackson, Mich. Then in 1922 he was promoted to the Muskegon, Mich., team. The White Sox called him up in 1923 and he was the back-up left-handed hitting catcher. He played in twenty-two games that season and hit .257.

Schalk was in a slump in 1924, so Crouse was the receiver for ninety games and hit .259. Crouse was back to a back-up role the next two years.

In 1926 he shared the catching duties nearly equally with Harry McCurdy when Schalk became the manager of the team.

The following year he shared the spot with Moe Berg. He reportedly told the scholarly Berg, "Moe, I don't care how many of those degrees you got, they ain't learned you to hit the curveball no better than me." Crouse out-hit Berg by six percentage points.

Crouse had to share catching duties with Berg and Martin Autry in 1929. Then, the White Sox obtained Bennie Tate, another left-hander, in a trade in 1930. The Sox decided to go with the younger Tate and sent Crouse to Indianapolis Indians until he was sold to Buffalo of the International League.

The Hoosier played at Buffalo for the next six seasons and played in two International League playoffs.

In 1937 he became the player/manager for Baltimore in the same league. He was named MVP for the season. He managed Baltimore again in 1938. 1939 found him at Little Rock,

Ark., and Montgomery, Ala.

Crouse returned to his home state in 1940 to coach the Indians. During the war, from 1940 to 1944, Crouse played semipro for the Muncie Citizens. He retired from baseball and became a night superintendent for Acme Lees in Muncie for twenty-one years.

He was once asked who he thought was the best baseball player of the Roaring '20s when he was in the majors. Crouse didn't hestitate in answering, "Babe Ruth."

George "Big George" Crowe (George Daniel)
Born: March 22, 1923, Whiteland
6'2", 210, First baseman
Boston, NL, 1952
Milwaukee, NL, 1953, 55
Cincinnati, NL, 1956-58
St Louis, NL, 1959-61
BL, TL, .270, 702 G, 1727 AB, 81 HR

Crowe began his professional baseball career in the Negro Leagues. He also was a center for Dayton of the National Basketball League in 1948-49.

The Hoosier broke into the majors with Boston Braves in 1952. The following season he was the backup for Joe Adcock and was used primarily as a pinch hitter. After a year away from the majors in 1954, he was put in the starting role when Adcock suffered an injury. He responded with fifteen homers.

The Braves traded him to Cincinnati where he was backup to Ted Kluszewski. He helped contribute ten homers to the league record-tying 221 homers

"Moe, I don't care how many of those degrees you got, they ain't learned you to hit the curveball no better than me." Bucky Crouse

32

in 1956. Crowe filled in adequately for the injured Kluszewski in 1957 when he clouted a team-high thirty-one home runs.

Crowe's numbers diminished in 1958 and he was traded to St. Louis the following year, where he became a backup to Hall of Famer Stan Musial. He led the league in pinch hits (17) in 1959.

Nig Cuppy (George Joseph)
Born: July 3, 1869, Logansport
Died: July 27, 1922, Elkhart
5'7", 160, Pitcher
Cleveland, NL, 1892-98
St. Louis, NL, 1899
Boston, NL, 1900
Boston, AL, 1901
TR, 161-100, 5 SV, 3.49 ERA, 302 G
BR, .235, 945 AB, 222 H

Cuppy was one of the first, best relief pitchers in the game after the mound was moved to 60 feet, 6 inches. He went 8-0 in relief in 1894 for the Cleveland Spiders. His best year in the majors was the first when he compiled a 28-13 record.

Chad Curtis (Chad David)
Born: Nov. 6, 1968, Marion
5'10", 175, Outfielder
California, AL, 1992-93
TR, BR, .273, 291 G, 1024 AB, 16 HR

The chances of a late-round draft pick making the majors is astonishing, but Curtis beat all the odds and made it to the majors after just three years in the minors. The forty-fifth round draft pick in June 1989 estab-lished himself as one of the best centerfielders and basestealers in the American League during the 1993 season.

Curtis learned to play hard when he was in Little League in Marion. After attending his freshman year at Centerville High School, he moved with his family to Arizona. He was graduated from Benson High School and was selected All-State in baseball and football twice.

After graduation, Curtis began his collegiate career at Yavapai Community College and hit .360 in 1987. He transferred to Cochise Community College in 1988 and hit .407 with fifteen home runs. In 1989 he switched to Grand Canyon College in Phoenix and slugged nineteen homers in hitting .369. He established an NAIA record by scoring six runs in one game on April 15. He was named to the NAIA All-American team.

The California Angels drafted the Hoosier and he went to Mesa where he hit .303. That earned him a promotion to Class A Quad City for the remainder of the season.

He played all of 1990 in Quad City. On May 7 he decided to get married — in his baseball uniform! The ceremony was at 1:30 p.m. and he had a 2 p.m. game, so he wore his uniform to save time. By the end of season, Curtis had racked up some impressive numbers. He was first in the Midwest League in hits, total bases, and on-base percentage. He was second in the league in batting average (.307) and stolen bases (64).

C

AA — American Association
AAGPBL — All-American Girls Professional Baseball League
AB — at-bats
BB — bats both
BL — bats left
BR — bats right
ERA — earned-run average
FL — Federal League
G — games
IP — innings pitched
K — strikeout
LCS — League Championship Series
NA — National Association
NL — National League
NNL — Negro National League
PL — Player's League
SHO — shutouts
TL — throws left
TR — throws right
UA — Union Association
WS — World Series

He made the jump to Triple A Edmonton in 1991 and continued to rack up good numbers. The outfielder was selected to the Triple A All-Star team. By the end of the year his average was .316 with forty-six stolen bases, third best in the league. He went to the Venezuelan Winter League where he was named as the MVP for hitting .338.

1992 became Curtis' rookie season in the majors. He began the season on the Opening Day roster. He singled on the first major league pitch by Chicago's Greg Hibbard. His first major league home run came a month later off of Toronto's Todd Stottlemyre. Curtis had a solid rookie season and led American League outfielders with sixteen assists, which tied the club record. He hit .259 on the season with ten homers and forty-six RBI.

Curtis avoided any sophomore jinx in 1993 by improving on his rookie numbers. He raised his average to .285 and swiped forty-eight bases, one of the leaders in the league. He was second in the league in assists (13).

In the off-season he and his wife, the former Candice Reynolds, live in Middleville, Mich.

Cliff "Shanty" Daringer (Clifford Clarence)
Born: April 10, 1885, Hayden
Died: Dec. 26, 1971, Sacramento, Calif.
5'7", 155, Shortstop
Kansas City, FL, 1914
BL, TR, .263, 64 G, 160 AB

Rolla Daringer (Rolla Harrison)
Born: Nov. 15, 1889, North Vernon
Died: May 23, 1974, Seymour
5'10", 155, Shortstop
St. Louis, NL, 1914-15
BL, TR, .148, 12 G, 27 AB

Hooks Dauss (George August)
Born: July 27, 1889, Indianapolis
Died: July 27, 1963, St. Louis, Mo.
5'10, 168, Pitcher
Detroit, AL, 1912-28
TR, 221-182, 41 SV, 3.32 ERA, 538 G
BR, .189, 1124 AB, 212 H, 6 HR

Dauss holds the Detroit record for most wins by a pitcher (221). He acquired the nickname "Hooks" for his sharp-breaking curveball. Sometimes the pitch got away from him and he led the league in hit batsmen three times. He won more than twenty games in a season three times during his fifteen-year career — all with the Tigers.

Bill Davidson (William Simpson)
Born: May 10, 1884, Lafayette
Died: May 23, 1954, Lincoln, Neb.
5'10", 170, Outfielder
Chicago, NL, 1909
Brooklyn, NL, 1910-11
BR, TR, .235, 225 G, 808 AB

Nancy DeShone (Nancy Rockwell)
Born: March 22, 1932, Osceola
5'3", 120, Outfielder
South Bend, AAGPBL, 1948
Fort Wayne, AAGPBL, 1948
.000, 1 G, 2 AB

DeShone was the chairman for the 50th Reunion of the All-American Girls Professional Baseball League in August 1993 in South Bend.

The tomboy began playing baseball before she attended school. "I played baseball with the boys," she explained. In her teens she played for Miles, a fast-pitch softball factory team. The aggressive base stealer recalled one game in which a second baseman took exception to her stealing. "I was going into second and she was going to cleat me. I put my right foot up and spiked her, and slid in safely with my left foot," she recalled.

The strong hitter helped lead Miles to a South Bend championship. This got her noticed by the South Bend Blue Sox and she was drafted in 1948. DeShone didn't see much action — was put in one game — since she was being primed as a pitcher. The league went to overhand pitching and a smaller ball in 1948. The teen got $50 a week for sitting on the pine.

"At an away game, one of the players from the other team

— AAGPBL —

Nancy DeShone hands out this baseball card to interested fans.

came up to me and said, 'When did the Blue Sox start carrying their bat girl.'" The sixteen-year-old DeShone told the player in no uncertain terms she was a player. Later in the season, she was sent to the Fort Wayne Daisies by the league, which shifted players around at will.

After one season in the league, she decided to go back to high school and finish her diploma. Then she married Rocky Rockwell in 1950, which ended her baseball days. She remained interested in baseball and coached women's softball and Little League over the years.

The chairman of the 50th Reunion coordinated events for more than 200 former players at the five-day event. DeShone is now in sales with a local glass company. Her husband died in 1992. She has four daughters: Debbie, Sherry, Jacki, and Conni.

Dick Dietz (Richard Allen)
Born: Sept. 18, 1941,
Crawfordsville
6'1", 195, Catcher, first
baseman
San Francisco, NL, 1966-71
Los Angeles, NL, 1972
Atlanta, NL, 1973
BR, TR, .261, 646 G, 1829 AB,
66 HR

Dietz was named to the All-Star Team once during his eight years in the majors.

After getting a $90,000 bonus from San Francisco, Dietz spent time at Artesia, Fresno, El Paso, Tacoma, and Phoenix before getting the call in June 1966 with the Giants.

His best season came in 1970

when he hit .300 with twenty-two homers and thirty-six doubles. He was named to the All-Star squad and hit a home run in the game. The following season he hit nineteen homers.

Dietz was cut during spring training in 1972 and went to the Dodgers the day before the season began for the waiver price. He was sent to the Braves the following spring.

Dutch Distel (George
Adam)
Born: April 15, 1896, Madison
Died: Feb. 12, 1967, Madison
5'9", 165, Infielder, outfielder
St. Louis, NL, 1918
BR, TR, .176, 8 G, 17 AB

Brian Dorsett (Brian Richard)
Born: April 9, 1961, Terre Haute
6'3", 215, Catcher
Cleveland, AL, 1987
Calfornia, AL, 1988
New York, AL, 1989-90
San Diego, NL, 1991
Cincinnati, NL, 1993
BR, TR, 70G, .221, 154 AB, 3 HR

Injuries and a low batting average have hampered Dorsett's ability to become a full-time catcher in the majors. However, he made his way back to the majors with the Cincinnati Reds in 1993.

Dorsett began tossing a ball around when he was two, his parents told him. "When I got to be five or six, I told my parents that I was going to be a major

"When I got to be five or six, I told my parents that I was going to be a major league baseball player," he said. "And I felt it was God-given dream." Brian Dorsett

league baseball player," he said. "And I felt it was God-given dream."

He was a Little League All-Star shortstop and didn't start fooling around behind the plate until he was twelve. He went on to Babe Ruth and at age thirteen traveled to the semi-state finals were he played against another Hoosier who would eventually make it to the majors — Don Mattingly. "He pitched left handed and when he was playing shortstop, he played right handed. He was ambidextrous!" said Dorsett, who played for American Legion Wayne Newton Post 346.

In high school at Terre Haute North Vigo, Dorsett played baseball only three years, because there was no freshman team. The school had an incredible baseball team in his sophomore year — were rated third in the country at the time. Unfortunately, the team was beat in the semi-state playoffs. Dorsett also lettered in basketball for three years and played football in his senior year. After a great start in baseball in his senior year, he tired and his numbers went down. Still, the catcher was named to All-State team. However, the distinction wasn't good enough to earn him a draft pick by a major league team.

Since he wasn't drafted, the 1979 high school graduate attended Indiana State University in his hometown and continued playing baseball. In his senior year, he was drafted in the tenth round by the Oakland A's. He was given a $14,000 signing bonus in 1983.

The A's sent him to a mini-camp for three weeks in Medford, Ore. He passed that little test and was moved up to Class A ball at Madison, Wisc., in the Midwest League. At the end of the season he was sent to an instructional league in Arizona.

After spring training in 1984, he was assigned to Class A Modesto, in the California League. "We had some kind of team. He won the whole thing," he remembered. Also on that team were Jose Canseco and Mark McGwire.

In 1985 Dorsett started off in Madison again for five weeks before jumping to Double A at Huntsville, Ala. After the season ended, he went on to winter ball in the Dominican Republic. He missed his new wife and had an incident there that could have ended his career, if not his life. "Jimmy Jones (San Diego Padres) was in the back seat. I'm in the passenger side. Terry Leach (New York Mets) is driving. We hit a horse head on — didn't see it. After that it looked like I was in a war," he explained. Fortuantely, he suffered just cuts and bruises, but it curtailed his stay in the winter league.

He started 1986 as he ended 1985, with an injury. He damaged the cartilage in his knee and missed most of spring training. "It really didn't heal during the year," he said. "I had surgery again the next year." When he was good enough to play, he was assigned to Class AAA Tacoma, Wash. He played the whole season there and went to Puerto

D   **Brian Dorsett**

Brian Dorsett played with the Indianapolis Indians in 1993 until mid-season.

Brian Dorsett

D

The Indianapolis Indians scoreboard lights up Dorsett's name and numbers.

Rico for winter ball again. But he didn't stay long because his knee was bothering him again. In the off-season he had surgery on the knee.

1987 found him back in Tacoma. Halfway through the season in July he was traded with Darrel Akerfelds, a pitcher, to the Cleveland Indians for veteran Tony Bernazard. Cleveland sent Dorsett to Buffalo, N.Y., for more Triple A ball. At the end of the season the Indians called him up. He gained his first hit off Gene Nelson and his old teammates, the A's. "That was nice," he said laughing. Dorsett also slammed his first major league homer of his career, a shot off Don Sutton of the California Angels. He caught in just four games that September and had three hits in eleven at bats.

The next spring bone chips in his elbow prevented him for an early call up. He had surgery and was put on the disabled list. The day after coming off DL, he was traded to California. "George Bradley had liked me and got me to the Angels," Dorsett explained. He went to Edmonton and played the entire season in Canada before being called up with the Angels in September. He caught in seven games and had one hit in eleven at bats.

The Angels dealt him to the New York Yankees in the off season, so now he hoped to play with Mattingly, instead of against him, as he had as a child and with other teams in the league. The Yankees sent him to Class AAA Columbus, Ohio. His numbers were good there and he

was selected for the All-Star team. At the end of the season Dorsett got his usual fall callup, like a Canadian Goose going south for the winter. He showed he could hit, as averaging .364 in twenty-two at bats.

He began 1990 in the minors again, but was called up in July when Mattingly was injured. He played in the designated hitter position several times and was with the Yankees for fourteen days until Mattingly returned. At the end of the season he was called up again and caught in nine games but hit just .143 on the season.

The Yankees acquired Rick Cerone in the off-season, so they released Dorsett. He felt the release was the greatest setback in his career, "because everyone had in their mind: why is this guy getting released?" Still, he found a home in San Diego, but Benito Santiago was the starter. He had a good spring, but was the last man cut before the team started the season. San Diego assigned him to Triple A ball in Las Vegas. Injuries on the Padres paved the way for him to take a trip to San Diego in June, but he didn't play much and wasn't even used behind the plate.

At the end of the season Dorsett ran out of options on his contract. The Padres took him off the forty-man roster, which meant they were getting ready to trade him to Pittsburgh. They asked him, "Will you take the trade or do you want to leave?" Since he had been in the minor leagues for six years, he had the option of becoming a free agent.

He decided on the trade, because he liked playing in Buffalo and he wouldn't lose his pay level.

The Hoosier receiver played well during the 1992 season, still Pittsburgh failed to call him at the end of the season. The Pirates were about to win the pennant again and had plenty of support behind the plate with Mike LaValliere and Don Slaught, whom Dorsett had played behind in the Yankee organization. "I guess they didn't want to make a roster spot for me," he assumed.

Because the Pirates didn't call him up, his agent began looking elsewhere for the 1993 season. The agent talked a lot with the new expansion Florida Marlins, but no deal was set. Finally, Dorsett settled on a contract that would allow him to shop around during spring training while he trained with the Cincinnati Reds. After spring training he signed a minor league contract with the Reds to play in Indianapolis for the Triple A affiliate. He liked coming to Indianapolis because it was only an hour and a half from home.

At the beginning of the 1993 season he had the best game of his baseball career, as he hit three home runs in one game. He ended the day with six RBI and four runs scored in a 11-1 victory over the Oklahoma City 89ers. "I never had that much power before. The last time I did that was in T-ball," he explained while he iced his knees after a game. Two days later he hit two homers in a game against the same team, hoping the Reds

were reading the headlines. "I'm not going to make a career out of this. I want to make a career of the majors," he said a few days after the five dingers.

Dorsett made the right choice by picking the Reds — he was called up on July 1 when catcher Joe Oliver cut his hand while cleaning out a dishwasher. He ended up playing the rest of the season with the Reds and hit .254 in twenty-five games, including two home runs.

Dorsett is just about finished with a bachelor's degree in business administration. During the off season, he goes to college and works in his hometown of Terre Haute. He also is a Christian and is interested in the ministry. In December 1992, he traveled to Bangkok with other players to teach baseball and religion to 500 youngsters. Thailand plans to have a baseball team in the 2000 Summer Olympics.

Dorsett is married to the former Gina Mascari of Terre Haute. They have three children: Abigail and twins Brittany and Brandon.

Red Downey (Alexander Cummings)
Born: Feb. 6, 1889, Aurora
Died: July 10, 1949, Detroit, Mich.
5'11", 174, Outfielder
Brooklyn, NL, 1909
BL, TR, .256, 19 G, 76 AB

Dorothea Downs
Born: South Bend
South Bend, AAGPBL, 1945

Elmer "Mer" Duggan

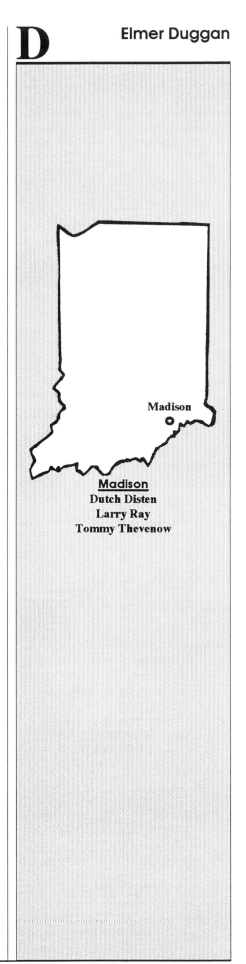

Madison

Madison
Dutch Disten
Larry Ray
Tommy Thevenow

Dan Dumoulin

D

(James Elmer)
Born: June 3, 1884, White-land
Died: Dec. 5, 1951, Indian-apolis
5'10", 165, First baseman
St. Louis, AL, 1911
BL, TL, .000, 1 G, 4 AB

Dan "Dummy" Dumoulin
(Daniel Lynn)
Born: Aug. 20, 1953, Kokomo
6'0", 175, Relief Pitcher
Cincinnati, NL, 1977-78
TR, 1-0, 8.10 ERA, 8 G, 10 IP
BR, 0-0, .000

With a fastball clocked over ninety-five mph, Dumoulin's bright major league future was cut short by elbow problems. He won one major league game, but had much more success in the minors.

Dumoulin's baseball career began when he was eight years old in the Little League minors. He quit the minors to play softball the rest of the summer. The following year he joined the Kokomo Northside Little League as an outfielder and catcher. He didn't begin pitching until he was eleven. At twelve he was named to the All-Star Team, which went on to win the State Championship. In the first round the Little League World Series at Dayton, Ohio, Dumoulin pitched and hit a home run, but his team lost 4-2 to Kankakee, Ill. He credits his Little League coach, Fred Wilson, as the most helpful person in his career.

At thirteen he joined Babe Ruth baseball and didn't start pitching until halfway through the season. He caught some until he got hit in the right shoulder on a foul tip. His manager decided against him catching anymore. "They said I was too valuable as a pitcher. That was the last time I caught," he said.

He was selected to the Babe Ruth All-Star team at fifteen. His team got beat at the State Championship.

As a freshman in high school, he did double duty on the freshman and varsity teams. When he wasn't on the mound, he was playing outfield. He played high school baseball through his junior year. In the summer he played American Legion ball for Post 6 in Kokomo. Instead of finishing his senior year, Dumoulin quit school to get married and go to work on the auto assembly line at the local Chrysler plant. He took classes at night to get his diploma.

Cincinnati drafted him in the nineteenth round and offered him $2,000, but he declined. For the next two seasons he played for the semipro Kokomo Highlanders. Then he was invited by the Reds to a tryout camp at Riverfront Stadium in June 1974. Dumoulin wanted to try out for the outfield as well; however, he changed his mind when he found out that pitching was the fastest way to get to the majors. Of the 156 players who tried out that rainy day, he was the only one offered a contract. Ironically, he was offered the same amount he had been offered two years earlier. "They gave me tickets to the Reds game that night, but we (his family) decided to go to Kings Island instead," Dumoulin

Dan Dumoulin played three seasons with the Indianapolis Indians.

said.

Dumoulin signed as a free agent on June 6, and was assigned to the Rookie League in Billings, Mont., going 4-2 on the year with a 3.33 ERA.

In spring training the next year, he decided he'd have a better chance at making the majors as a relief pitcher than a starter. He was promoted to Tampa, Fla., in the Class A League after training, and he relieved all season ending up with a 2.04 ERA and 7-3 mark. During the year his scout, Clifford Alexander, died. "Once he was gone, I was lost," he explained.

He must have felt lost the next season as he was shipped from warm Florida to cool Canada at Three Rivers near Quebec. Dumoulin attributed his tendinitis problems there to the weather. He did just as well though in the AA League with a 2.02 ERA.

Announcers didn't know how to pronounce his last name; thus, they called him "Dummy" for short.

In late 1976 he went to Winter Ball in Tampa. "It was probably the best experience I got," the by-now experienced player admitted. The Reds added him to their forty-man major league roster rather than losing him to another team. He was promoted to the Indianapolis Indians. During spring training he had one outing with the parent club. During the 1977 season though he impressed Indians Manager Roy Majtyka with his fastball and was one of four called up by the Reds at the end of the season.

In his first Major League appearance against Houston, Dumoulin struck out the first two batters before being lifted by Manager Sparky Anderson. "Sparky wasn't big on giving younger kids a chance," Dumoulin said. His other four appearances that September weren't as impressive.

At spring training the next year, he again was given only one appearance. He went to the Indians again where Majtka worked him hard. "I was warming up all the time," Dumoulin explained. The excessive work began to take its toll on the twenty-four-year-old fireballer. In September he was again called up to the Reds, along with his roommate Ron Oester.

Dumoulin earned his solo Major League victory when George Foster clouted his fortieth homer of the season in the thirteenth inning. Foster was given the game ball that Dumoulin thought he should have received. So Foster gave him the bat he used to hit the homer. He made two other appearances that fall, as the Reds finished second behind Los Angeles. Instead of a World Series, the Reds went to Japan on a goodwill tour with Dumoulin on the squad. He pitched only once during the tour. "I got a cortisone shot before we left for Japan. When it wore off, I couldn't turn a door knob. They wouldn't give me another," he said.

In 1979 he went to spring training, where he got his usual one appearance. He was sent to

Dan Dumoulin holds the bat given to him by George Foster.

Mike Dunne

D

Indianapolis again and he began to develop elbow problems. He couldn't straighten his arm. He was in a lot of pain from the bone chips and spurs in the elbow, yet the Reds didn't want to perform surgery on the arm. He finally convinced them it was necessary, so a team physician performed elbow surgery in Cincinnati rather than sending him to the best in the business in Los Angeles. The surgery didn't correct all the problems. "The therapist said it (the elbow) wasn't even in the right place!"

The Reds took him off the forty-man roster, which meant he'd make minor-league pay if he wanted to continue to play at Indianapolis. The team refused any further surgery on him, and since Dumoulin had no health insurance, he couldn't afford the surgery himself. He went to a surgeon in Indianapolis who told him he'd need surgery right away if he ever wanted to pitch again. Cincinnati tried selling his contract to the Mexican League. He refused. Baltimore and the White Sox wanted to buy his contract, but the Reds weren't interested. Dumoulin had no choice but to quit under the circumstances.

Besides not getting a fair shake from the Reds, Dumoulin feels the other pitchers weren't very helpful either. "The big league pitchers didn't want to help you out, because you were going to be taking their job. Nobody wanted to help you out except the infielders or catchers," he complained.

Because his arm problems were publicized locally,

Dumoulin had a hard time getting a job after baseball. He will still need surgery on the elbow some day. Now he is a plant operator at Kokomo Glass and Fuel. He built himself a large house on the northside of Kokomo for his family of five. His wife, Joan, is a policewoman. They have a son, Danny II, and three daughters: Wendy, Kasey, and Kiley.

Mike Dunne (Michael Dennis)
Born: Oct. 27, 1962, South Bend
6'4", 190, Pitcher
Pittsburgh, NL, 1987-89
Seattle, AL, 1989
San Diego, NL, 1990
TR, 23-30, 4.07 ERA, 81 G
BR, .101, 109 AB

A member of the 1984 U.S. Olympic Team, Dunne was the first draft pick of the St. Louis Cardinals in the June 1984 free-agent draft. He was dealt to the Pirates and broke into the majors in 1987. After an excellent rookie season — led league in winning percentage (.684) with a 13-6 record — his career went south.

"The therapist said it (the elbow) wasn't even in the right place!"
Dan Dumoulin

Scott "Scottie" Earl (William Scott)
Born: Sept. 18, 1960, Seymour
5'11", 165, Second baseman
Detroit Tigers, AL, 1984
14 G, .114, 35 AB

Scottie was beamed up to the majors just once during his nine years in the minors. He was named to several minor league All-Star teams, but couldn't crack the majors.

Earl was seven years old when he began playing baseball. That summer he joined the North Vernon Little League, playing mainly third base and pitching some. "I was a good player, but I wasn't head and shoulders above everyone else," he admitted.

After Little League, Earl played Pony League ball for two years. At Jennings County High School his coach moved him around the infield. "I didn't really blossom into a good player until my junior year," he said. In his senior year he battled with another player for the batting title and ended up hitting .361 on the year.

During the summer, the emerging pitcher played in the Babe Ruth League. He was a member of the Columbus Babe Ruth All-Stars that won the state championship in 1979, which was his first exposure to pro scouts.

After graduation Scott attended Glen Oaks Junior College. In June 1980 he went to a pre-draft tryout in Cincinnati with the Reds. Unable to impress the scouts, he impressed the college coaches enough get a partial baseball scholarship from Eastern Kentucky.

The Detroit Tigers drafted him in 1981 in the fourteenth round. "Six teams called me the day before the draft. I was kind of disappointed I was drafted in the fourteenth round," he said. He received a $12,500 signing bonus and was sent to Bristol, Va., a Rookie League team. "It was the first time I'd ever used a wooden bat," he said. Earl hit around .260. He was one of three players invited to participate in the Instructional League in St. Petersburg, Fla.

In 1982 after being assigned to Class A Lakeland, Fla., he was called to the office during spring training and told that he was going to the major league spring training team to play in a game against Boston. He didn't get into the game until the eighth inning, but he was happy for the opportunity. His performance in the A League that summer earned him a spot on the Florida State All-Star Team. After he was again invited to the Instructional League, the newspapers began calling him "Scottie" after the engineer in the television series Star Trek.

For spring training in 1983 he was put on the Triple A roster, but afterwards was assigned to Class AA Birmingham, Ala. His season mirrored his performance of the year before as he made the All-Star team and went to the Instructional League. At the end of the year he had been added to the major league roster and was being called the "cream of the crop" in 1983.

1984 was his best year yet in

Scott Earl

Scott Earl got to wear the Tigers uniform for a month.

E baseball. After spring training he was assigned to the Class AAA Evansville Triplets. The Hoosier felt more at home in Evansville and played well enough to make the All-Star Team for the third consecutive year. "Baseball America moved me to top rookie at second base," he recalled. At the end of the season he was called up to the Tigers, who had been leading the American League East all season. The Tigers had jumped out to a big lead early, winning their first nine out of ten games and by May had compiled a 35-5 record. "They were way ahead, but hadn't clinched it," Earl said.

By the time Earl reported to the Tigers, the players were so loose and assured of the league championship that the players decided to have some fun with the rookie. When he reported to the stadium the guard wouldn't let him in. "I never heard of Scott Earl," the guard said. He finally made it to the locker room only be turned down for admittance by the guard there. When he finally made it to the locker room, players were "laughing their heads off."

A day later he wasn't suppose to report until 5 p.m., but he was at the stadium about 12:30. He just hung out in the dugout until 5. About a minute before practice, Jack Morris asked him to go to his locker to get a letter. "I ran to the clubhouse, got the letter and ran back. It was about 5:02 and all the Tigers were on the field. Sparky Anderson came over to me and asked, 'Scott, what time is it?' It's 5:02, I said," he said. Earl explained

why he was late and Sparky replied, "Who is running this team? Me or Jack Morris?" Then everyone on the field laughed.

The Tigers clinched the pennant on Sept. 17, the day after Earl was inserted into the roster. In his second at bat against Tom Candiotti of Milwaukee he lined a 3-2 pitch into left center field for a triple. At the end of the season, the Tigers flew to Kansas City to get ready for the playoffs. Earl flew home for a couple of weeks before going to the Domincan Republic to play winter ball.

At the end of major league spring training camp, Earl was sent to Class AAA Nashville, Tenn. "It was one of the biggest disappointments of my career. I expected to make the team," he said. The Tigers brought up Chris Pittaro from Class AA instead of Earl. The Tigers had Lou Whitaker at second, so they didn't need a second baseman. Earl had a steady year in Nashville, hitting around .250. In September he didn't get called up and took the winter off.

After spring training the next year, he was again assigned to Nashville. "At that point I was ready to move on. There was no backup for Whitaker if he got hurt. I was an insurance policy," he said. The year passed and he wasn't called up in September. The following spring he went to the Toledo Mudhens to play Triple A again. Early in the season he broke his left tibia. "I was fielding a grounder and my spikes got stuck in the ground," he explained. The injury put him out for two months.

At the end of the season he became a six-year minor league free agent, deciding then to say goodbye to the Tigers and signed with the Reds. "Pete Rose was my all-time favorite player. Now he was the manager," Earl said.

He had his best spring ever in 1988 and thought he had a chance at making the team. The team decided to use Jeff Treadway at second instead of Earl and sent him to Class AAA Nashville. But just a couple of days before the season began, the Reds called for him because they were going to put Buddy Bell on the Disabled List to start the season. Earl got to play in two exhibition games with the Reds against the St. Louis Cardinals. On Opening Day a call came from the traveling secretary of the Reds at his hotel room. The team had decided not to put Bell on the DL. That left Earl off the team back in the minors. Soon into the season Bell was put on the DL after all and Luis Quinones was called up instead of him. Earl had a better batting average than Quinones, but he wasn't a switch hitter.

After the 1989 season ended, he was released. Several teams called him about playing, but none would assure him he would play in the majors. "I wanted to play in the big leagues or do something else," he said.

He put baseball behind him and married Stacia Jordan of Muncie in 1990. His wife is an athlete, too, and was named to the Delaware County Hall of Fame in 1993 for her volleyball career at Ball State University. Earl is now a sales representative for an apparel company and lives in Indianapolis.

Bill Edgerton (William Albert)
Born: Aug. 16, 1941, South Bend
6'2", 185, Pitcher
Kansas City, AL, 1966-67
Seattle, AL, 1969
BL, TL, 1-2, 4.95 ERA, 17 G

Edgerton spent parts of three different seasons in the majors, but never landed a steady job. The left-handed pitcher's best game in professional baseball was a two-hitter in Triple A.

Edgerton remembered throwing the baseball around when he was six and played sandlot ball with older boys in his younger days around South Bend. Then, at Thomas Jefferson Junior High School, he began to take the sport more seriously. "I was fortunate to have a good coach, " he said about Alan Vincent, who helped him and another boy eventually make it to the majors.

His family moved a few times during his high school playing days, with Edgerton ending up at Penn High School in Mishawaka his last two years and lettering in basketball and baseball. During the summers he played semipro and traveled around the Midwest. The pro scouts spotted him, but he wasn't interested. "I was undecided of whether to go to college or play baseball," he recalled.

Graduating in 1961, he didn't decide until the next year then signed a contract with the New York Mets, a new expan-

> *"Pete Rose was my all-time favorite player. Now he was the manager." Scott Earl*

Bill Edgerton

E sion club at the time. The Mets gave him a "slight" bonus and sent him to Quincy, Ill., a Class A team. When his contract was up at eighty-nine days, the Mets released him. "I had one of those ninety-day contracts," he said. He signed five days later with the Kansas City A's and played against the Mets team he had just left.

The following year he was sent to Lewiston, Idaho, another Class A team. Then he moved up to Class AA in 1964 and was assigned to Birmingham, Ala. At the end of the 1965 season he was sent to Triple A Fort Worth, Texas. "That was the worst team I ever played for," he said. The team lost over 100 games that year.

However, Edgerton threw his best game ever in professional baseball at Fort Worth. In a game against the Louisville Cardinals he gave up but two hits, because batters couldn't hit his curveball, his best pitch. Unfortunately, the other pitcher, John Morris, threw a no-hitter and Edgerton lost the game. "I was proud of that game. That proved I could do it," he explained.

In 1966 he pitched at Class AAA Vancouver, British Columbia. After the season ended he was called up to the A's. His first game was a relief appearance against Baltimore. In another game he was given the start against the Cleveland Indians and went six innings with no decision. In all Edgerton appeared in six games with a 0-1 record and 3.38 ERA.

Going to spring training with the big club in 1967, he was again assigned to Vancouver. Edgerton was called up to the A's in mid-season and earned his only major league win off Detroit. His seven appearances were all in relief.

The A's didn't protect the left hander in the expansion draft and the Seattle Pilots picked him first. Since the Pilots lacked a spring training site, he was sent to the California Angels camp. After spring training he was "farmed out" to several minor league teams during 1969. "The people that organized the team went into it backwards," he said.

The Hoosier got a cup of coffee with Seattle and gained one loss. Seattle then went bankrupt and Edgerton was sold to Baltimore. "I lost a couple of years off my career because of them. The whole thing was weird," he said.

Edgerton played in Rochester, N.Y., in 1970. Baltimore sent him to Los Angeles. He played with the Dodgers in Spokane, Wash., in 1971 before they released him. He then signed with the Milwaukee Brewers, who had bought the Seattle franchise. The Brewers sent him to Evansville, where he finished out the season. He quit baseball after that season.

"I never got a chance to show what I could do," he explained. "But I'm not crying about it."

Today he works at the Hummer Plant in Mishawaka. Now single, he has a daughter, Julie Plummer, from a previous marriage. When he isn't working, he helps out Little Leaguers

"I never got a chance to show what I could do," he explained. "But I'm not crying about it."
Bill Edgerton

become baseball players.

Stump Edington (Jacob Frank)
Born: July 4, 1891, Roleen
Died: Nov. 29, 1969, Bastrop, La.
5'7", 180, Outfielder
Pittsburgh, NL, 1912
BL, TL, .302, 15 G, 53 AB

Hod Eller (Horace Owen)
Born: July 5, 1894, Muncie
Died: July 18, 1961, Indianapolis
5'11", 185, Pitcher
Cincinnati, NL, 1917-21
TR, 60-40, 5 SV, 2.62 ERA, 160 G
BR, .221, 308 AB, 68 H, 1 HR
1 WS, 2-0, 2.00 ERA

Eller held a World Series record against the Chicago White Sox in the tainted 1919 World Series until he died in 1961. In the first game of the series, he fanned six straight players. He won two games in the series, which was thrown by eight White Sox players who were later banned from baseball.

Eller began his professional career in 1913 with Champaign, Ill. He tried out for the White Sox in 1916, but the Sox had no room on the roster for him. The Muncie native came up with the Reds in 1917.

1919 was Eller's best season in the majors as he hurled a no-hitter and compiled a 19-9 record with his famed "shiner" ball to help the Reds to a world championship.

After baseball, he became a policeman in Indianapolis.

Rowdy Elliott (Harold B.)

Born: July 8, 1890, Kokomo
Died: Feb. 12, 1934, San Francisco, Calif.
5'9", 160, Catcher
Boston, NL, 1910
Chicago, NL, 1916-18
Brooklyn, NL, 1920
BR, TR, .241, 157 G, 402 AB, 1 HR

Carl "Oisk" Erskine (Carl Daniel)
Born: Dec. 12, 1926, Anderson
5'10", 165, Pitcher
Brooklyn, NL, 1948-57
Los Angeles, NL, 1958-59
TR, 122-78, 13 SV, 4.00 ERA, 14 SHO
BR, .156, 588 AB, 1 HR
5 WS, 2-2, 5.83 ERA

Erskine pitched in five World Series for the Brooklyn Dodgers and hurled two no-hitters during his twelve-year career. His best year was in 1953 when he led the National League in winning percentage (.769) and set a World Series record of fourteen strikeouts against the New York Yankees in Game Three. He was named to the Indiana Baseball Hall of Fame in Jasper in 1979.

Erskine remembers playing catch with his father, a sandlot player, when he was three. He didn't begin playing organized baseball until he was nine with the local Parks Department. His first game was at Westvale Park, now the site of a school where he frequents as a speaker to tell the children to stay away from drugs.

An excellent student himself, Erskine advanced to Anderson

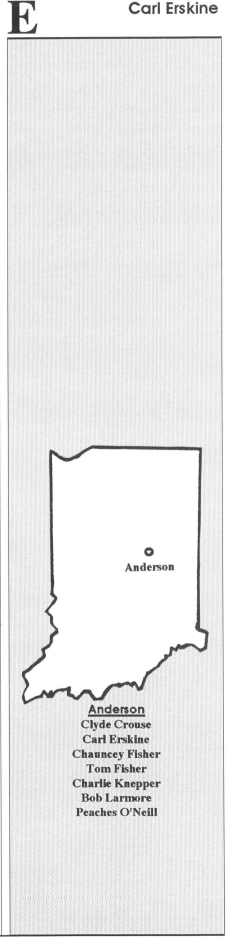

Anderson

Anderson
Clyde Crouse
Carl Erskine
Chauncey Fisher
Tom Fisher
Charlie Knepper
Bob Larmore
Peaches O'Neill

E

Carl Erskine threw two no-hitters during his career.

High School midway through eighth grade. One spring day the school's baseball coach, Archie Chad, ordered a petrified Erskine to report to his office. "He gave me my first uniform and I didn't know how to put it on," he admitted. He was able to practice with the team that year, but wasn't allowed to play.

The next four years he lettered in basketball and baseball. During the summers he played American Legion ball, which is where scouts first caught a glimpse of him. The Chicago Cubs were the first to approach him about playing professional ball. Then Brooklyn Dodgers scout Stanley Feezle from Indianapolis took an interest in Erskine and two of his classmates, Jack Rector and Johnny Wilson. After the trio graduated, Feezle gave them first-class train tickets and a $100 bill, a lot of money in those days, to go to Brooklyn and tryout for the Dodgers. Owner Branch Rickey wined and dined the three Hoosiers for a week. Rector was the only player to sign a Class D contract, because Erskine had an invitation to play elsewhere — the U.S. Navy. He was drafted as was Wilson.

Erskine was shipped to Sampson Naval Air Station in New York and was in boot camp when the atomic bomb was dropped on Hiroshima. His orders to report to an aircraft carrier in the Pacific were changed to the Boston Naval Yard. "I wanted to play for the Navy, but they wouldn't let me tryout. They had enough players," he said in disbelief.

Since he really wanted to play ball, he sought a local semipro team in nearby Milton. The manager asked Erskine to throw a few balls for him. "I threw a fastball and it went right through his (the catcher) hands and two blocks down," he explained. A few more pitches and the manager was convinced. The manager told Erskine that he reminded him of pitcher Johnny Beazeley of the St. Louis Browns.

During his weekly pitching performances for Milton, Erskine was spotted by the Boston Braves, who offered him a bonus of $2,500 to sign a contact, an unheard of amount at that time. The Braves also offered to bring his mom and dad to Boston for the All-Star Game. The Dodgers said they would do better. When all were assembled in town, Rickey called for Erskine and his folks to come to his suite. "What do you want?" Rickey asked. "I remember looking at my dad, who couldn't help me," he recalled. He turned to Rickey and asked for $3,000. Rickey was known to be a tight wad, but he wasn't about to be outdone by the Braves or Erskine. He gave him $3,500.

After getting out of the Navy, Erskine went to Class B Danville, Ill. He won three games before losing three in the Three-I League. At the end of the season, Baseball Commissioner Happy Chandler declared Erskine a free agent because Brooklyn had signed him to a contract while he was still in the Navy. Boston had blown the whistle. Chandler gave Erskine the option of signing with any team, including Brooklyn. The Philadelphia Phillies, Boston Red Sox and the Pirates offered him bonuses of $10,000. Yet Erskine still wanted to play in Brooklyn and told his scout he'd sign again with the Dodgers for another $5,000. "In a year when nobody was getting bonuses, I got two!"

Brooklyn took him back and assigned him to Danville again for the 1947 season. During the year he married his wife, Betty, and picked up twenty-one victories and led the league with 233 innings pitched. At the end of the season, he went to Cuba to play winter ball.

After spring training in 1948, he was promoted to Triple A Fort Worth in the Texas League, posting a 15-6 record by mid-July resulting in the Dodgers calling for him. He remembered vividly the day he joined the Dodgers. He arrived at Ebbets Field and didn't know where to get in, so he went to the fans entrance. He was carrying a duffle bag that had Fort Worth printed on it, so the fans recognized the rookie right away. One fan yelled out, "Hey, there's Oiskine from Fort Worth." They also called him "Oisk" for short. "It was an abberation of my name," Erskine said.

His first major league game came as a reliever in Pittsburgh and he got the victory. His first start came in Wrigley Field against the Cubs. The defense was porous that day and the Dodgers committed five errors, yet Erskine held Chicago to four runs and the Dodgers won 6-4.

Winning his first major league start was a thrill, but he was concerned about his arm. "I threw a high fastball to Big Bill Nicholson — they called him 'Swish' — and I had a sharp pain in my shoulder. It was a pain I had never had before. I thought I pulled a muscle," Erskine said.

The next day he couldn't lift his pitching arm. A few days later he started against the Phillies. After five innings his arm was killing him and he told Manager Burt Shooton about the pain. Shooton told him, "You're pitching a shutout and doing fine." The rookie went back out on the mound and completed the game. His record was now 4-0. Still in pain, Erskine's next start was against the Phillies again. The Dodgers breezed to an 8-1 victory. He was 5-0.

The injury finally took its toll on Erskine, who was staying at the YMCA. Still, he completed the year with a respectable 6-3 record and a 3.23 ERA.

Spring training was no joy for Erskine the following year. His arm still hurt. The club decided to send him back to Fort Worth. Erskine complained of the move, but he never mentioned the pain. "When you're a rookie, you had to act like a rookie. One thing you didn't do was hang around the trainer's room," he said.

Erskine nursed the arm as best he could at Fort Worth. By mid-year he had won ten games and the Dodgers called him back to join a pennant race with St. Louis. He won eight straight games, all in relief before he

"When you're a rookie, you had to act like a rookie. One thing you didn't do was hang around the trainer's room." Carl Erskine

E

finally lost a game. The Dodgers won the dogfight with the Cardinals for the pennant by a mere game. He was still in pain, but he wouldn't confide in anyone — not even his wife!

In the World Series, the Dodgers faced their crosstown rivals, the Yankees. Erskine made two relief appearances in the last two games of the series. In both situations the Yankees held big leads and athough Erskine gave up two runs, it didn't matter. The Dodgers lost the series in five games.

After 6-3 and 8-1 seasons, Erskine thought he had earned a spot on the team. Not with the Dodgers. After a poor spring, he was sent to Montreal where Walter Alston was the manager, Tommy LaSorda was the star pitcher, and Chuck Connors, who would later become a television star, played first base. Erskine thought he was going to get a rest. "Alston saw me coming and said, 'You're pitching tonight! I need you!'" He shutout Buffalo.

In Montreal, Erskine finally sought professional help with the club doctor, because his shoulder problems were leading to neck and back spasms. Physical therapy helped in making the shoulder feel better. "I could still throw, but I was in misery," he commented. "The good Lord gave me a fantastic arm."

Rickey came to Montreal to see him pitch three separate times before he bought him up again. This time it was for good. Erskine finished the year in Brooklyn with a 7-6 mark for the second-place Dodgers.

Oisk was both a starter and reliever for the Dodgers in 1951. He recorded nineteen starts among his forty-six appearances. As the youngest starter on the staff, Erskine compiled a 16-12 mark with four saves. The Dodgers and New York Giants battled all season and tied for the pennant, which the Giants won in a three-game playoff.

One of Erskine's finest pitching performances came during the 1952 campaign. It was a rainy day on June 19. "We had a 5-0 lead and we were trying to get the game in before the rain," recalled Oisk. In the third inning he walked a batter before the rains came. The players retired to the locker room to get in a game of bridge, since a long delay was evident. Erskine's luck on the field poured over to the bridge game as well. Not only did he have a no-hitter going on the field, he pulled off a hand with four hearts in the locker room. After about a forty-minute delay, Erskine resumed his power over Cub hitters. He recorded his first no-hitter. The bridge game was written about as well the next day by the local writers. Bridge expert Charles Gorman read about the game and called Erskine in the clubhouse about the hand. Gorman then wrote about it in his own column. The Hoosier credits the no-hitter as the game that finally earned him some fame.

Erskine's 14-6 record in 1952 helped the Dodgers to the pennant. He was called on to start Game Two of the World Series against the Yankees. He pitched well until the fifth inning. The Yankees won 7-1, and he was credited with the loss. Calling on Erskine again to start Game Five, the Dodgers spotted him a 4-0 lead before the Yankees jumped on Oisk for five runs in the fifth. But Manager Chuck Dressen stayed with Erskine, who shut out the Yankees for six more innings as the Dodgers won 6-5 in eleven frames. He also got a relief call in the seventh game of the series with the Yankees ahead. He stopped the bleeding, but the patient died anyway. The Yankees won 4-2.

1953 started off rocky for the Hoosier, who was having trouble loosening up the arm. But he was a different pitcher after the All-Star break and went 15-2. He finished the season with a 20-6 record — the best win-loss ratio in the National League. Erskine clinched the pennant for the Dodgers in Milwaukee in the mid-September. He was pitching so well that Dressen decided to start him in Game One against the Yankees. Unfortunately, Oisk didn't have his best stuff that day and he promptly loaded the bases in the first inning. Billy Martin tripled to clean them. It was the only frame Erskine would pitch that day.

After losing the first two games of the series, Dressen decided to go with Erskine in Game Three. "I went out there so determined. I was going to pitch like no tomorrow." And he did.

Going into the top of the ninth, the Dodgers led 3-2, as Erskine struck out thirteen. A nemisis of his, Johnny Mize, was called on to pinch hit. Mize had hit a homer off Erskine in the '52 series. "Mize had sat on the bench all day and was telling all the guys how to hit me. He had everyone irritated. I struck him out and the crowd went crazy because they had announced I had tied the record before that," he recalled. His fourteen strike-outs eclipsed the record and, more importantly, gave the Dodgers some breathing room. He had gunned down Mickey Mantle and Joe Collins four times in the game. The record was broken some years later by Dodger great Sandy Koufax. Erskine got the start in Game Six, too. He pitched four shutout innings before being lifted in the fifth. The Yankees went on to win the game and the series.

Erskine was the leading starter for the Dodgers in 1954, and began thirty-eight games. He was 18-15 on the year, and the Dodgers finished second.

The following year Erskine started twenty-nine games and compiled an 11-8 record, taking the Dodgers to the pennant. In the series against the Yankees again, Erskine didn't get the call until the fourth game. He started and gave up two runs in three innings. He left with the Yankees ahead 2-1, but the Dodgers rallied and won 8-5. The Dodgers also won the series in seven games to earn Erskine a World Series ring, although he pitched in only one game.

In 1956 Erskine had his usual winning record, 13-11, in aiding the Dodgers to another pennant. On May 12 he fired the

Carl Erskine wears a business suit these days as a bank president.

second no-hitter of his career against the Giants. As in the year before, he started Game 4 in the series against the usual opponent, the Yankees. The Dodgers lost the game, 6-2, and Erskine was nabbed for the loss.

The years of pitching with a continual sore arm finally caught up to Hoosier hurler in 1957. He started in only seven games that year and the Dodgers sent him to the bullpen. He still had a winning mark, 5-3, during the Dodgers last year in Brooklyn. Ebbets Field would become part of history and only a memory. "I personally had my best days at Ebbets Field," he said of the park. He enjoyed the fans, too.

The following year in Los Angeles, Manager Alston honored Erskine by starting him in the opener at the LA Coliseum. Oisk responded with a win. The rest of the year he was used mainly in long relief and posted a 4-4 record for the lowly seventh-place Dodgers.

In 1959 Erskine knew he was on the bubble and his arm was spent. "I pitched three or four bad games. I must have quit twelve times in my mind before I finally decided to quit," he said.

The end came in Pittsburgh. After striking out Bill Virdon, he couldn't get anyone else out. Alston finally came out to get him. Erskine told him, "This will be the last time you come to get me." It was. He burned that moment in his mind so that he wouldn't regret it later.

Erskine stayed with the team as a batting practice pitcher. "It was a pleasure because I didn't have to get loose," he said. He taught Maury Wills how to hit and the Dodgers went from fifth to first place during the year to win the pennant in a three-game playoff with the Braves. The Dodgers whipped the Chicago in the World Series to give Erskine his second series ring.

Since retiring from baseball, Erskine has stayed in touch with Dodgers on special assignments and goes to the Dodgers Fantasy Camp every year with his severly retarded son, Jimmy, who was born after his baseball career ended. He chose a banking career in his hometown of Anderson. He's now the president of Star Financial Bank and vice president of the Major League Baseball Players Alumni Association. The white-haired senior citizen doesn't plan on retiring soon.

John "Honest John" Eubank (John Franklin)
Born: Sept. 9, 1872, Servia
Died: Nov. 3, 1958, Bellevue, Mich.
6'2", 215, Pitcher
Detroit, AL, 1905-07
TR, 8-13, 2 SV, 3.13 ERA, 42 G
BL, .196, 102 AB

Bill "Big William" "Wild Bill" Everett (William L.)
Born: Dec. 13, 1868, Fort Wayne
Died: Jan. 19, 1938, Denver, Colo.
6', 188, First and third baseman
Chicago, NL, 1895-00
Washington, AL, 1901
BL, TR, .320, 697 G, 2839, 535 AB, 11 HR

Howard Farmer (Howard Earl)
Born: Jan. 18, 1966, Gary
6'3", 185, Pitcher
Montreal, NL, 1990
TR, 0-3, 7.04 ERA, 6 G
BR, .400, 5 AB

Farmer was with the Indianapolis Indians in 1990 prior to his call to the Expos in July that year. His lackluster performance in Montreal resulted in his return to the minors.

Bill "Dutch" Fehring (William Paul)
Born: May 31, 1912, Columbus
6', 195, Catcher
Chicago, AL, 1934
BB, TR, .000, 1 G, 1 AB, 1 SO

George Ferguson (George Cecil)
Born: Aug. 19, 1886, Ellsworth
Died: Sept. 5, 1943, Orlando, Fla.
5'10", 165, Pitcher
New York, NL, 1906-07
Boston, NL, 1908-11
TR, 29-46, 8 SV, 3.34 ERA, 142 G
BR, .188, 218 AB, 1 HR

Joel Finch (Joel D.)
Born: Aug. 20, 1956, South Bend
6'2", 175, Pitcher
Boston, AL, 1979
BR, TR, 0-3, 4.87 ERA, 15 G

Chauncey "Peach" "Whoa Bill" Fisher (Chauncey Burr)
Born: Jan. 8, 1872, Anderson
Died: April 27, 1939, Los Angeles, Calif.
5'11", 175, Pitcher
Cleveland, NL, 1893-94
Cincinnati, NL, 1896
Brooklyn, NL, 1897
New York, NL, 1901
St. Louis, NL, 1901
TR, 21-26, 3 SV, 5.37 ERA, 65 G
BR, .216, 176 AB

Chauncey was the older of the Fisher Brothers who played in the majors about the turn of the century. He first broke into the majors with the Cleveland Spiders. His best season came in 1896 with Cincinnati when he was 10-7. He pitched for the Chicago White Sox in 1900 before the American League achieved major league status.

Maury Fisher (Maurice Wayne)
Born: Feb. 16, 1931, Uniondale
6'5", 210, Pitcher
Cincinnati, NL, 1955
TR, 0-0, 6.00 ERA, 1 G
BR, .000, 1 AB

Fisher tossed ten no-hitters in high school, but his success didn't carry over to the majors.

After their son was born in Indiana, his parents moved to the Cincinnati area early in his life. Fisher began playing baseball at eight in a community league. The first game he ever pitched at age twelve turned out to be a no-hitter. His greatest thrill as a youth came in an American Legion All-Star game. The game was held in old Crosley Field and Babe Ruth threw out the first pitch.

At Greenhills High School in Cincinnati, Fisher lettered in football, basketball, and base-

F

Indianapolis

Indianapolis
Bill Barnes
Paddy Baumann
Tim Bogar
Elmer Brown
Donie Bush
Oscar Charleston
Rich Coggins
Roy Corthan
John Corriden
Hooks Dauss
Elmer Duggan
Hod Eller
Charlie French
Jeff James
John Kerins
Ron Keller
Matt Kinzer
Chuck Klein
Don Leppert
Marshall Locke
Joe McCabe
Al McCauley
Don Miles
Dennis Musgraves
George Orme
Bill Owens
Ray Oyler
Jeff Parrett
Todd Ramsey
Charlie Reising
Rodney Scott
Steve Senteney
Joe Slusarski
Ed Summers
Gary Thurman
Frank Warfield
Bill Whaley
Jack White

Tom Fisher

ball. Among his ten no-hitters was a perfect game — a game in which he had eighteen Ks! He was All-State in basketball and was offered a scholarship by the University of Kentucky, but he chose baseball.

"I graduated on Friday night, and I had appointments with ten agents on Saturday. It was the most confusing day of my life," he remembered. He signed for $10,000 with his hometown Reds in 1949.

After several years in the minors, the Reds put him on the forty-man roster in 1953 and signed him to a major league contract. He went to major league spring training for three years in a row. "I never gave up an earned run in spring training," he explained.

Cincinnati finally called the former Hoosier on April 16 in 1955. His only appearance came in relief against the Milwaukee Braves. The Uniondale native gave up a couple of runs. "I played against Henry Aaron, and he didn't get anything off of me," he said.

The Reds relegated Fisher to the minors again shortly after his only appearance. By mid-July he had eighteen saves at Triple A Seattle. He continued to play in Class AAA ball in 1956. In 1957, the Reds moved him to Double A ball. "I was stuck in the minor leagues. That's why I got out of baseball," he said. Cleveland and St. Louis were interested in the hurler, but the Reds wouldn't release him.

Fisher is retired from General Motors and lives in Fredericktown, Ohio, with his wife, the former Shirley Rawlings of London, Ky., and their two boys: Dwayne and Randy.

Tom "Red" Fisher (Thomas Chalmers)
Born: Nov. 1, 1880, Anderson
Died: Sept. 3, 1972, Uniondale
5'11", 175, Pitcher
Boston, NL, 1904
TR, 6-15, 4.25 ERA, 31 G
BR, .212, 99 AB, 2 HR

Tom was the younger brother of Chauncey Fisher, another right-handed pitcher. The younger Fisher played for the Detroit Tigers in 1902, the year before the American League was recognized as a major league. Then he had one season with the lowly Boston Braves.

Freddie "Fat Freddie" Fitzsimmons (Frederick Landis)
Born: July 28, 1901, Mishawaka
Died: Nov. 18, 1979, Yucca Valley, Calif.
5'11", 185, Pitcher
New York, NL, 1925-37
Brooklyn, NL, 1937-43
TR, 217-146, 3.51 ERA, 513 G
BR, .200, 1155 AB, 14 HR

Fitzsimmons was inducted into the Indiana Baseball Hall of Fame in 1992 for being a consistent pitcher during his nineteen major league seasons. He twice led the league in winning percentage and set a Brooklyn Dodgers record. He also managed and coached until retiring in 1966.

The chunky pitcher with the corkscrew windup broke into professional baseball in 1920 with Muskegon. From 1922-25 he pitched for the Indianapolis Indians. He was 14-6 in 1925 for the Indians before breaking into the majors at the end of the season.

In 1930 he led the National League in winning percentage with a 19-7 mark (.731). He had a winning mark every season until 1935 when he suffered an arm injury.

Fitzsimmons was traded to Brooklyn in 1937 for pitcher Tom Baker. It was one of the worst trades ever; Baker won a single game and then dropped out of sight.

After a losing mark of 7-9 in 1939, Fitzsimmons set a Dodger record when he went 16-2, which led the league with a .889 winning percentage.

During the 1941 World Series, Fat Freddie was shutting out the New York Yankees when he was hit by a savage liner in the seventh inning. He was carried off the field on a stretcher.

From 1943 to 1945 he managed the Philadephia Phillies to a 102-179 record. Then in 1949, as a coach with the Giants, he was involved in a tampering uproar that resulted in his being fined by Commissioner Happy Chandler.

In addition to his career in baseball, the Mishawaka native was the general manager for the National Football League Brooklyn Dodgers for three years.

Gene "Suds" Fodge
(Eugene Arian)
Born: July 9, 1931, South Bend
6', 175, Pitcher
Chicago, NL, 1958
TR, 16 G, 1-1, 4.73 ERA
BR, 7 AB, .000

Fodge spent one season with the Chicago Cubs before he quit baseball. He hurled three one-hitters during his best season in the minors. He also earned an unusual nickname.

Fodge first picked up a baseball when he was four and played with his uncles. As a youth he played in sandlot leagues in his hometown of South Bend.

At South Bend Central High School, Fodge played both baseball and basketball. He helped his roundball team to the state finals in 1948 in Indianapolis before South Bend lost to Madison. The team also did well in 1949 and made it to the semi-state round. But he was an even better baseball player, and during the summers he played ball for American Legion Post 50 and Northern Indiana Transit, a semipro team.

After Fodge graduated in 1950, the Boston Braves offered him a contract as an outfielder. He declined. When the Cubs offered him a contract later in the summer, he accepted. He received a conditional bonus of $500. "You had to be with the club for thirty days before they gave you the bonus," he explained.

Fodge didn't receive his bonus until the following year because he signed too late in

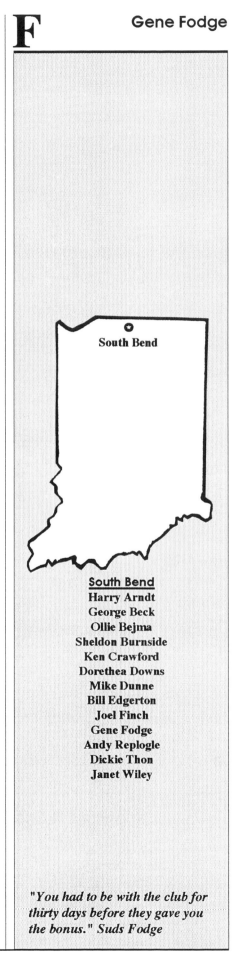

South Bend
Harry Arndt
George Beck
Ollie Bejma
Sheldon Burnside
Ken Crawford
Dorethea Downs
Mike Dunne
Bill Edgerton
Joel Finch
Gene Fodge
Andy Replogle
Dickie Thon
Janet Wiley

"You had to be with the club for thirty days before they gave you the bonus." Suds Fodge

55

F

1950 to play. He was assigned to Janesville, Wisc., a Class D team. In December that year he was drafted by the U.S. Marine Corp for the Korean Conflict. He spent the next two years in the military.

When Fodge came out of the service, the Cubs assigned him to Class A Des Moines, Iowa. He was used more in middle relief than as a starter and went 4-5 on the season.

The following year the South Bend native stayed at Des Moines and was moved into the starting rotation. He responded by leading the league in ERA (2.25) and completing twenty games for a 16-10 record. He also tossed three one-hitters and nine shutouts! "I lost six games by a run," he explained. His excellent record resulted in the Cubs buying his contract and putting him on the forty-man roster.

After spring training with the Cubs in 1956, he was sent to the Los Angeles Angels of the Pacific Coast League. There he went 19-7. "We won the pennant by sixteen games," he said.

Fodge called 1957 the "year of traveling." He began the season at Fort Worth in the Texas League. After experiencing elbow problems, he was sent to Portland, Ore. There he went 8-14 before the Cubs sent him down to Memphis, Tenn., a Class AA team.

It was during his minor-league career that Fodge picked up his nickname. "Johnnie Briggs and me were roommates and we used to sip a few (beers). One day he called me 'Suds,'"

he explained. The name stuck.

In 1958 Fodge found himself on the opening-day roster of the Cubs. During the first month of the season he picked up his only victory in the majors. He started a game in the LA Coliseum, the new home of the Dodgers. Only about 10,000 fans showed up to watch the game in the 102,000-seat stadium. "I didn't attract too many people," he said kiddingly. Fodge had his knucklecurve and sinker working well that day and limited the Dodgers to just two runs. Meanwhile, the Cubs scored fifteen.

In June the Cubs sent Suds back to Fort Worth to make room for another pitcher. Then they recalled him in July and he pitched mainly in relief until August. The Cubs ran out of options on his contract, so he was sold outright to Fort Worth. After the season, his contract was sold to Denver, a Yankee farm club. "I decided it wasn't worth it. I needed to get a job with more security for my family," he explained.

Two years later the Houston Astros, a new expansion club, invited him to a tryout. Fodge told them that he would come for the tryout but only for a guaranteed contract of $10,000. Houston declined.

He hasn't had much to do with baseball since then and quit drinking altogether. He was on the South Bend White Sox Board of Advisors for awhile. Today he works at the University of South Bend alongside his wife, Eileen Major of South Bend. They have four children: Curt, Scharm, Laurie, and Stacy.

Pete Fox (Ervin)
Born: March 8, 1909,
Evansville
Died: July 5, 1966, Detroit,
Mich.
5'11", 165, Outfielder
Detroit, AL, 1933-40
Boston, AL, 1941-45
BR, TR, .298, 1461 G, 5636
AB, 65 HR

Fox set a World Series record for hitting six doubles in a seven-game series in 1938. He made only two errors during the 1938 season. His best season at the plate came in 1937 when he hit .331. He was inducted into the Indiana Baseball Hall of Fame in 1980.

Charlie French (Charles Calvin)
Born: Oct. 12, 1883, Indianapolis
Died: March 30, 1962, Indianapolis
5'6", 140, Second baseman, shortstop, outfielder
Boston, AL, 1909-10
Chicago, AL, 1910
BL, TR, .207, 105 G, 377 AB

French began playing professionally at Vincennes in 1905. He went to Clinton and Evansville before breaking into the majors with the Red Sox in 1909.

Bob "Warrior" Friend (Robert Bartness)
Born: Nov. 24, 1930, Lafayette
6', 195, Pitcher
Pittsburgh, NL, 1951-65
New York, AL, 1966
New York, NL, 1966
TR, 197-230, 11 SV, 3.58
ERA, 602 G, 36 SHO

BR, .121, 1137 AB, 2 HR
1 WS, 0-2, 6 IP, 13.50 ERA

Friend became the first pitcher in the history of the game to lead the league in ERA while playing with a last-place team. His durability on the mound was evident in that he led the league in starts from 1956-58. He is one of the Major League leaders in most shutout losses (45) in a career. The Purdue graduate was inducted into the Indiana Baseball Hall of Fame in 1979.

Friend started playing the game when he was six years old. "Baseball was it. That's all we had to do in those days," he said. He played in a junior league in West Lafayette, which was sponsored by the American Legion. There was no Little League.

He played four years of baseball at West Lafayette High School, starting mainly at third base or the outfield in his early years and didn't start pitching seriously until his senior year. "I always had a good arm at a young age and played all the time," he explained. In high school he also played football and basketball.

Scouts from nine teams tendered offers to the young phenom and he finally decided on the Pittsburgh Pirates, who offered him $17,500 in 1950. "That was a decent bonus," he said. After spring training he was assigned to Waco, Texas. Halfway through the season he was brought up to Triple A Indianapolis and played out the year with the Indians.

After spring training the following year he made the club at

Bob Friend was a consistent performer for the Pittsburgh Pirates.

Bob Friend

"After I was released by the Mets I decided not to pursue baseball."
Bob Friend

age twenty. He was used both as a starter and reliever and ended his first year in the majors with a 6-10 record and 4.26 ERA. The next year his ERA was about the same, but he ended with a 7-17 record for the last-place Pirates. 1953 was similar and he had an 8-12 mark. The Pirates continued their losing ways in 1954 and Friend took a beating as well with a 7-12 mark. In his first four years his record was 28-51.

Things began to happen for the better in 1955. He was more mature and he had better control of his pitches. Batters were finding it harder to hit his sinkerball. Friend had his first winning season in the majors with a 14-9 mark and led the league in ERA (2.84). The Pirates, however, were still mired in last place.

Friend became the Number-One starter for the Pirates in 1956, and his hot start resulted in his getting picked for the All-Star Game. He started the game and ended up with the victory, something he's still very proud of today. His season record was 17-17 and the Pirates didn't finish last.

He continued to pitch well in 1957, but he didn't get much help from his team and ended up with a losing record (14-18). The Pirates were last again, but he wasn't discouraged by the lack of run support. "That's part of the game," he reflected.

The Pirates dug themselves out of their last-place hole in 1958 with Friend's help. He was named to the All-Star Team, but this time he got pinned with the loss. The Pirates finished second behind Milwaukee and Friend

tied Braves' pitcher Warren Spahn with the most victories on the season (22).

Friend's ERA and record fell off the next season, as did the Pirates' performance. He finished 8-19 on the year and the Pirates finished fourth. His best game of the season was an unusual twelve-hit shutout against St. Louis.

"Warrior" bounced back in 1960, as did the Pirates. He was selected for the All-Star Game and picked up his second victory, which tied a record for most victories in All-Star games. The steady performer helped the Pirates to a first-place finish with his 18-12 record. He didn't have much luck against the New York Yankees in the World Series and was tabbed with two losses. He relieved in Game Seven, but couldn't stop the Yankees. However, Bill Mazerowski's famous ninth-inning homer won it all for the Pirates.

"Old Reliable," as he was sometimes called, continued being a workhorse for the Pirates. He had a 14-19 mark in 1961, 18-14 in 1962, 17-16 in 1963 and 13-18 in 1964. But he had a losing year again in 1965 and Pirates decided to trade him to the Yankees in the off-season for Pete Mikkelsen.

After going 1-4 for New York, the Yankees sold him to the New York Mets for cash on June 15. He finished the year with a 5-8 record for the Mets. The Mets let him go. "After I was released by the Mets, I decided not to pursue baseball," he explained.

He became the only pitcher

to have lost more than 200 games while winning less than 200. He twice topped the National League in hits allowed. But also threw three one-hitters. He recalled a game in Chicago where he had a no-hitter going until two outs in the bottom of the eighth inning.

Now he is an insurance broker and lives in Fox Chapel, Pa., with his wife, the former Patricia Kovam of Washington, Pa. His son, Bobby, is a golfer on the PGA Tour. He also has a daughter, Mary Ellen Alexander. Friend still does some promotion work for the Pirates.

Larry Fritz (Lawrence Joseph)
Born: Feb. 14, 1949, East Chicago
6'2", 220, First baseman
Philadephia, NL, 1975
TL, BL, 1 G, 1 AB, .000

Fritz played in the Major Leagues for two weeks and pinch hit once. The home-run swinger once led the Mexican League in batting before his knees gave out to end his baseball career.

Growing up in Whiting, Fritz was an All-Star player in Little League. "I was noted more for pitching than anything else," he said.

After a year of Babe Ruth ball, he started playing in an American Legion League at fourteen. He helped his Legion team win a state championship and aided his high school baseball team to a conference championship. At Whiting High School, Fritz lettered in baseball, football, and basketball. He was named All-State in football.

Knee problems began in his junior year. "I hurt my arm in my senior year and couldn't throw as hard as I used to," he explained. He began concentrating on hitting and playing first.

When Fritz graduated in 1967, the Detroit Tigers selected him as a late draft pick because he had a football scholarship to Arizona State. He ignored the offer and opted for college. He played both baseball and football as a freshman, but he didn't see eye-to-eye with coach Bobby Winkles and quit the baseball team, which went on to win the College World Series in his sophomore year. Despite not playing, he was picked by the New York Mets in the second round of the 1969 amateur draft. He signed for a $10,000 bonus and went to the Rookie League in Marion, Va.

The following year he was promoted to Class A Vislia, Calif. Fritz was leading the league in homers when he was drafted by the U.S. Army for the Vietnam War. He avoided the draft by going into the National Guard. His season was over.

In 1971 Fritz was elevated to Class AA Memphis and led the league in homers. That winter he went to play in the Mexican League for the first time. "It was a learning experience. The conditions weren't the greatest," he admitted.

The Mets tried him at Triple A to start the 1972 season, but Fritz wasn't up to it and was sent back to Double A Memphis less than a month later. After two weeks of Guard duty, he came

"I hurt my arm in my senior year and couldn't throw as hard as I used to." Larry Fritz

Abbreviations

AA — American Association
AAGPBL — All-American Girls Professional Baseball League
AB — at-bats
BB — bats both
BL — bats left
BR — bats right
ERA — earned-run average
FL — Federal League
G — games
IP — innings pitched
K — strikeout
LCS — League Championship Series
NA — National Association
NL — National League
NNL — Negro National League
PL — Player's League
SHO — shutouts
TL — throws left
TR — throws right
UA — Union Association
WS — World Series

back five pounds overweight and Manager Whitey Herzog disciplined him by sending him back to Class A. Between seasons he went to the Mexican League again.

Fritz spent all of 1973 at Class AAA Tidewater, Va. The next year the Mets were deep at first base, so he was dealt to Philadelphia. The Phillies put him at Class AA Reading, Penn. He hit around .300 and was promoted to the Toledo Mudhens.

1975 began with Fritz hitting a dozen dingers at Reading to earn him a quick promotion to Toledo. Then in July, Larry Bowa broke his thumb and Fritz got his call. "They wanted a left-handed pinch hitter," he said.

The Hoosier made his only Major League appearance in the ninth inning against the Houston Astros. He lined out to left field. "I felt like I was floating above the clouds looking down. It was the ultimate high!"

Fritz was sent back down two weeks later when Bowa returned. He finished the year at Toledo.

During the winter he went back to the Mexican League again. Going into the last day of the season, he led the league in hitting. The closest contender was a Mexican on his own team. In the first game of a double-header, the Mexican player bunted for singles every time he was up. Fritz became suspicious. "I didn't get wind of it until he laid down four bunts in a row. He never bunted for singles before," he explained. Fritz's manager sent him to his hotel for

the second game in order not to jeopardize his chances at winning the batting title. Fritz watched the last game from his hotel and won the title with a .355 average. "They didn't want to see an American win the title."

A double knee operation the following season limited his play and spelled the end of his career. In 1990 he had knee replacement surgery.

Fritz is an electrician these days and works for Calumet Coach. He lives in Highland with his wife, the former Jean Benkl of Whiting, and two children, Natalie and Douglas. He's beginning to teach his son how to play baseball.

Brent Gaff (Brent Allen)
Born: Oct. 5, 1958, Fort Wayne
6'1", 195, Pitcher
New York, NL, 1982-84
TR, 4-5, 1 SV, 58 G, 4.06 ERA
BR, .000, 17 AB, 0 H

Shoulder and elbow injuries dealt a fatal blow to Gaff's short major league career. He was a player who went from nearly getting cut in Class A ball all the way to making it to the majors.

Gaff grew up across the street from a baseball field, so he began playing in pickup games at an early age. He became a Little Leaguer at eight. "I started pitching right away," he recalled. The park he played at in Churubusco, where he grew up, was one of the first lighted fields in the state.

All the youngster did during the spring and summer was play ball. He remember being in five different leagues at age fifteen. In high school he was an all-conference basketball star until his senior year. "I got kicked off the team for chewing tobacco," he explained. Of course he lettered in baseball and hurled a no-hitter in the snow during his senior year.

Gaff also won MVP honors during a Connie Mack Tourna-ment, which he thought would increase his worth in the 1977 amateur baseball draft. The New York Mets signed the young hurler in the sixth round and offered him a $10,000 contract. He declined because he felt he and his knucklecurve was worth more, so he went to Central Arizona on a baseball scholar-ship. However, the Mets contin-ued to hound him and college didn't interest him. "I never went to class," he said.

He signed with the Mets and went to Class A Wausau, Wisc. He lost thirteen games before he won the last game of the season. The Mets thought of releasing him, but sent him back to Wau-sau the following season with a co-op team of misfits. "I was given one last chance," he explained.

Gaff turned the last chance into a 10-1 record by mid-season and was named to the All-Star team. However, after that he hurt his back and went home for the rest of the season.

The following year the Mets put him on their forty-man roster and sent him to Class AA Jackson, Miss. He went 8-9 on the season. He was 5-1 the following season at Jackson when the Mets moved him up to Triple A Tidewater, Va.

In 1982 Gaff pitched his way to a 5-1 mark at Tidewater when he got the call from the Mets in late June. He made his major league debut on July 7, starting against San Francisco. He started the game and had a shutout going into the eighth when Reggie Smith hit a three-run homer to give him a loss. Gaff was sent back to Tidewater until September, when he was called up again.

During spring training in 1983 he was 4-0. "I should have made the club after spring training," he surmised. Instead, he was traded to the Milwaukee Brewers, but the trade didn't go through. "I was mad and booked," he said. The club was

61

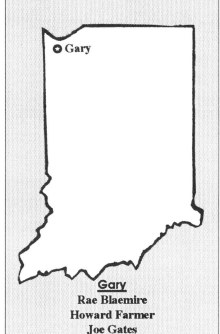

G

going to fine him $5,000, but thought better of it when he returned to Tidewater.

"I never got called up and got an attitude problem," he explained. He turned his attitude around and finally got called up again at the end of the season.

1984 became his rookie and only full season in the majors. He was 4-5, mostly in relief. In the last game of the year he injured himself. "I popped something in my shoulder," he explained.

He rested over the winter, but couldn't throw when he went to spring training. He had surgery on the shoulder and spent 1985 rehabbing the shoulder. Then the Mets released him.

Gaff signed with the Brewers and went to spring training in 1986. Again he hurt his shoulder. The Brewers released him. He tried to come back again after another surgery. He spent one spring training with the Indianapolis Indians and thought he had a chance with the Montreal Expos, but he never made it back and retired.

Gaff now runs a home improvement company and makes ice fishing rods for Canadians from his home in Albion. He is married to the former Shelly Wright or Churubusco, and they have two boys: Chase and Elliott. He thinks they may be baseball players someday.

Joe Gates (Joseph Daniel)
Born: Oct. 3, 1954, Gary
5'8", 175, Second and third baseman
Chicago, AL, 1978-79
BL, TR, .175, 24 G, 40 AB

George Gick (George Edward)
Born: Oct. 18, 1915, Dunnington
6', 190, Pitcher
Chicago, AL, 1937-38
TR, 0-0, 1 SV, 0.00 ERA, 2 G

Doc Gill (Warren Darst)
Born: Dec. 21, 1878, Ladoga
Died: Nov. 26, 1952, Laguna Beach, Calif.
6'1", 175, First baseman
Pittsburgh, NL, 1908
BR, TR, .224, 27 G, 76 AB

Claral Gillenwater (Claral Lewis)
Born: May 20, 1900, Sims
Died: Feb. 26, 1978, Pensacola, Fla.
6', 187, Pitcher
Chicago, AL, 1923
TR, 1-3, 5.57 ERA, 5 G
BR, .000, 6 AB

Len "Meow" Gilmore (Leonard Preston)
Born: Nov. 3, 1917, Clinton
6'3", 175, Pitcher
Pittsburgh, NL, 1944
TR, 0-1, 7.88 ERA, 1 G
BR, .000, 2 AB

Bob Glenalvin (Robert J.)
Born: Jan. 17, 1867, Indianapolis
Died: March 24, 1944, Detroit, Mich.
Second baseman
Chicago, NL, 1890, 93
.283, 82 G, 311 AB

Harry "Husky" Glenn (Harry Melville)
Born: June 9, 1890, Shelburn

Died: Oct. 12, 1918, St.
Paul, Minn.
6', 185, Catcher
St. Louis, NL, 1915
BL, TR, 6 G, 16 AB

Jot Goar (Joshua Mercer)
Born: Jan. 31, 1870, New
Lisbon
Died: April 4, 1947, New
Castle
5'9", 160, Pitcher
Pittsburgh, NL, 1896
Cincinnati, NL, 1898
TR, 0-1, 15.85 ERA, 4 G
BR, .167, 6 AB

George Goetz (George)
Born: 1865, Greencastle
Died: Unknown
6'2", 180, Pitcher
Baltimore, AA, 1889
1-0, 4.00 ERA, 1 G
.000, 4 AB

Harley Grossman (Harley
Joseph)
Born: May 5, 1930,
Evansville
6', 170, Pitcher
Washington, AL, 1952
0-0, 54.00 ERA, 1 G

Grossman has one of the highest ERAs in major league history (54.00), but that's because he pitched only one-third of an inning and gave up two runs.

The Evansville native didn't start playing organized baseball until he was in high school in 1945. At Reitz High School he played all four years of baseball and graduated in 1948.

In 1948 Washington Senators scout Ivan Kuester signed him to a contract. He received no bonus. He went to Fulton, Ky., to play in a Class D league for $150 a month in 1949. In 1951 he moved up to Charlotte, N.C. "I hurt my back throwing. My back was giving me trouble for half a year," he said.

After spring training in 1952, the Senators kept him on the opening-day roster. On April 22, which was his father's birthday, he was called in to pitch relief against Boston in Fenway Park. He allowed a two-run homer to Matt Dropo and got only one batter out before being relieved.

The Senators sent him back to Chattanoga, Tenn., a Class AA League. Grossman continued heading the wrong way and dropped to Class A Scranton the next year. Then in 1954 he ended up with a semipro team in Minnesota. He dropped out of baseball and went to Evansville University.

In 1978 he suffered a stroke that paralyzed his right side, so he has trouble remembering many parts of his baseball career. He still lives in Evansville today with his wife Gertrude Whitaker of Ambridge, Pa. They have five children: Karen, Keith, Kim, Kathy, and Krista. Keith played baseball at Indiana State University. Kim, who married former major league Harry Spillman, was once pitcher Nolan Ryan's secretary.

"I hurt my back throwing. My back was giving trouble for half a year." Harley Grossman

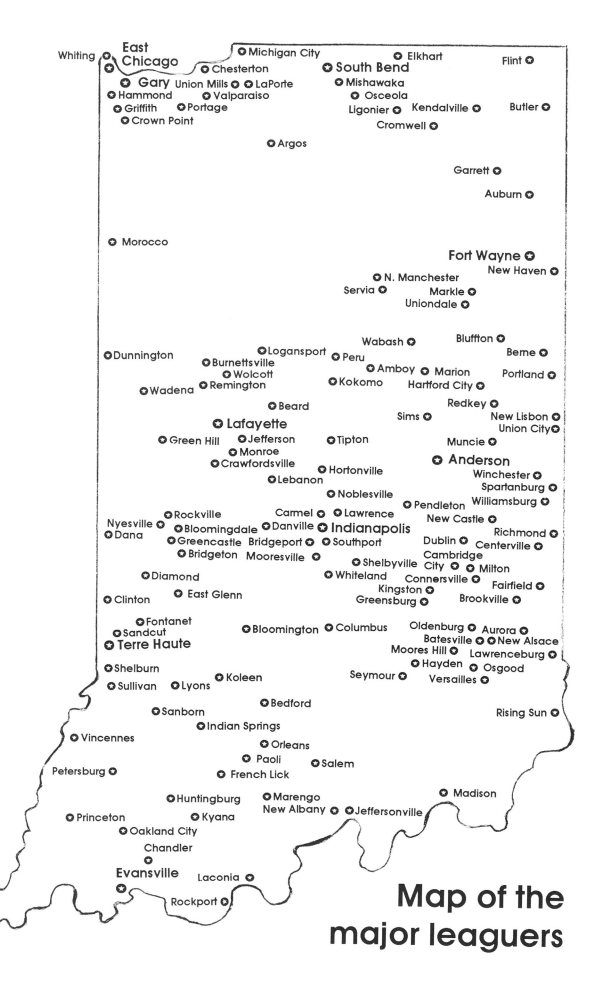

Map of the
major leaguers

Don Hankins (Donald Wayne)
Born: Feb. 9, 1902, Pendleton
Died: May 16, 1963, Winston-Salem, N.C.
6'3", 183, Relief Pitcher
Detroit, AL, 1927
TR, 2-1, 2 SV, 6.43 ERA, 20 G
BR, .143, 7 AB

Don Hanski (Don Thomas Hanyzewski)
Born: Feb. 27, 1916, LaPorte
Died: Sept. 2, 1957, Worth, Ill.
5'11", 180, Pitcher, first baseman
Chicago, AL, 1943-44
TL, 0-0, 9.00 ERA, 3 G
BL, .227, 11 G, 22 AB

Hanski was the cousin of crosstown Chicago Cubs pitcher Ed Hanyzewski. He contracted with the White Sox under his surname and appeared only briefly with the club. He retired from baseball in 1947. He was graduated from Washington High School in South Bend.

Ed Hanyzewski (Edward Michael)
Born: Sept. 18, 1920, Union Mills
6'1", 200, Pitcher
Chicago, NL, 1942-46
TR, 12-13, 3.30 ERA, 58 G
BR, .062, 65 AB

Hanyzewski was used mainly in relief during the war years with the Cubs. His best year was in 1943 when he was 8-7 with a 2.56 ERA. His cousin, Don Hanski, pitched for the White Sox during the same time span.

Steve Hargan (Steven Lowell)
Born: Sept. 8, 1942, Fort Wayne
6'3", 175, Pitcher
Cleveland, AL, 1965-72
Texas, AL, 1974-76
Toronto, AL, 1977
Texas, AL, 1977
Atlanta, NL, 1977
TR, 87-107, 4 SV, 3.92 ERA, 354 G
BR, .129, 325 AB, 1 HR

Bubbles Hargrave (Eugene Franklin)
Born: July 15, 1892, New Haven
Died: Feb. 23, 1969, Cincinnati, Ohio
5'10", 174, Catcher
Chicago, NL, 1913-15
Cincinnati, 1921-28
New York, AL, 1930
BR, TR, .310, 852 G, 2533 AB, 29 HR

The older Hargrave had the best average of the two brothers and led the National League in average one season, although it wasn't recognized.

Bubbles broke into professional ball in 1911 with Terre Haute. After hitting .309 in 1913, he was called up by the Cubs. Batting just .207 in parts of three seasons, he caused the Cubs to give up on him and ship him back to the minors for more work.

After six seasons in the bush leagues, Cincinnati bought his contract from the Cubs for $10,000 in 1920. It turned out to be a solid investment, as Hargrave began hitting major league pitching at a .300 clip. He was good behind the plate as well

Chuck Harmon was the first black player with the Cincinnati Reds.

and led the league in double plays in 1924.

1925 was Hargrave's banner year and he hit .353. He's not credited now as the batting leader, because he didn't have enough at-bats — 326.

Hargrave hit .300 for six straight seasons. He finished his major league career with the New York Yankees in 1930. After his playing days, he managed Cedar Rapids for a year.

Pinky Hargrave (William McKinley)
Born: Jan. 31, 1896, New Haven
Died: Oct. 3, 1942, Fort Wayne
5'9", 180, Catcher.
Washington, AL, 1923-25
St. Louis, AL, 1925-26
Detroit, AL, 1928-30
Washington, AL, 1930-32
Boston, NL, 1932-33
RB, TR, .278, 650 G, 1602 AB, 177 R, 39 HR

Pinky followed in the footsteps of his older brother, Bubbles, and came to the majors as a catcher, too. However, he didn't hit as well and was used mainly as a backup receiver. He acquired his nickname for his flaming red hair.

Chuck Harmon (Charles Byron)
Born: April 23, 1926, Washington
6'2", 175, Utility infielder
Cincinnati, NL, 1954-56
St. Louis, NL, 1956-57
Philadelphia, NL, 1958
TR, BR, 289 G, .238, 592 AB, 7 HR

Harmon was one of the first Blacks to sign a Major League contract. He also was the first African-American to play for the Cincinnati Reds. He has been named to the Indiana Basketball Hall of Fame.

Born and raised in Washington, Harmon began tossing around a baseball when he was "old enough to walk." He played in recreational leagues as a youngster, because no organized baseball leagues existed in his town during the Depression.

When he entered Washington High School, the tall boy was more fit for basketball than baseball. "Basketball was really the sport," he said. He helped his high school to state championships in 1941 and 1942.

After graduation he accepted a basketball scholarship with the University of Toledo. The all-Black squad made it to the NIT finals at Madison Square Garden in 1943.

In the spring of 1943 he joined the U.S. Navy. He was assigned to Great Lakes Naval Station near Chicago, then played on an all-Black Navy baseball team with Larry Doby, the first Black player in the American League. "We'd play against other service teams," he said. Paul Brown, who would later coach in the National Football League, finally got the Navy to integrate the baseball teams in 1945, according to Harmon.

Harmon never thought he would get a chance to play baseball in the majors because of his color. Then the Brooklyn Dodgers signed Jackie Robinson to a contract in 1946. Harmon

was finally offered a contract himself the following year by the St. Louis Browns. Bill DeWitt, who would later own the Cincinnati Reds, was scouting for the Browns and signed Harmon. "He saw me play and remembered me from the service," Harmon said.

Harmon's bonus was a pair of spikes, a baseball glove, and $225 a month to play in Gloversville, N.Y., a Class C team. "There was no such thing as a bonus. You'd go for years without a raise," he explained.

The following year the NCAA changed their rules and wouldn't allow college athletes to play any professional sports. So Harmon decided to drop out of professional baseball and play college basketball. He did play some semipro ball in 1948 with the Fort Wayne General Electric team.

Harmon returned to the Bush Leagues in 1949 and was assigned to Class D Olding, N.Y. before he earned a trip back to Gloversville. At the end of the season, the Browns folded up its minor league operations and released all its players, including Harmon. The citizens of Olding bought the team from the Browns and invited Harmon to play. The Hoosier played on the team in 1950. After the season ended, he was invited to tryout for the Boston Celtics. He didn't make the squad, but he went to play with Utica, N.Y., a farm team of Syracuse. Near the end of the season, he became the player/coach of the team, which made him the first Black to ever coach a professional basketball team.

1951 was great year for Harmon on the diamond. Again he played for Olding. He led the league in doubles (49) and hit .375 with 140 RBI. His impressive numbers caught the attention of the Cincinnati Reds, who bought his contract from Olding.

The Reds sent Harmon to Toledo to begin the 1952 season. He lasted just a couple of weeks there before being sent down to Class B, Burlington, Iowa. He hit .350 on the year. That earned him a promotion to Class AA Tulsa, Okla., the next year. He hit around .330 on the season, so the Reds bought his contract and put him on the forty-man roster. He went to Winter Ball in Puerto Rico. He played very well there. "I thought I had won the batting title, but the scorekeeper found another hit for a local player and I came in second," he explained.

Harmon cracked the opening day roster of the Reds in 1954. His best day in the majors came on the day the Reds honored him with "Charlie Harmon Day." He went 4-for-5 in front of family and friends. The third baseman and pinch hitter batted .238 on the season. His first major league home run came off of Hall of Famer Warren Spahn. "It was the first time my mother saw me play," Harmon said.

The following year he played third base and in the outfield. In ninety-six games he hit .253 with five home runs. The Reds finished in fifth.

At the beginning of 1955, the Reds used him mainly for defensive purposes and decided to trade him in May to St. Louis.

"There was no such thing as a bonus. You'd go for years without a raise." Chuck Harmon

H

Harmon went into a slump and went 0-for-15 before the Cardinals sent him to Omaha for the rest of the season. He hit about .360 there, but went hitless in the majors that year.

The Cardinals brought him back to the majors in 1956, and he appeared in nine games for the Cardinals before being traded to Philadelphia. The talented fielder played in fifty-seven games for the Phillies, hitting .265.

After spring training in 1958, Harmon was sent to Triple A Miami. In June he hurt his knee and went on the disabled list. "When I recuperated they didn't have room on the roster," he recalled. He was released.

He wrote Gabe Paul, who found him a spot with St. Paul, a Class AAA team of the Los Angeles Dodgers. He played two seasons with St. Paul until his release. "They were one of the first teams to fly everywhere. They had their own plane. That was first class," he commented.

He continued playing in the minors until hurting his knee again in 1961 in Hawaii. During the 1960s, he lived in Indianapolis and owned a gas station. He did some "bird-dog scouting" for the Reds and also scouted for the Indianapolis Pacers.

Nowadays he lives in Cincinnati with his wife, Charlene, from Gloversville. They have two children, Charles Jr. and Cheryl.

Grover "Slick" Hartley (Grover Allen)
Born: July 2, 1888, Osgood
Died: Oct. 19, 1964, Day-

tona Beach, Fla.
5'11", 175, Catcher, infielder
New York, NL, 1911-13
St. Louis, FL, 1916-17
New York, NL, 1924-26
Boston, AL, 1927
Cleveland, AL, 1929-30
St. Louis, AL, 1934
BR, TR, .266, 566 G, 1321 AB, 3 HR

Hartley spent fourteen years in the majors, mainly as a backup catcher. The only year he was the starting receiver was in St. Louis of the short-lived Federal League. He also was a minor league manager and coach in the St. Louis Browns and Pittsburgh Pirates organization.

John Heinzman (John P.)
Born: Sept. 27, 1863, New Albany
Died: Nov. 10, 1914, Louisville, Ky.
First baseman
Louisville, AA, 1886
.000, 1 G, 5 AB

Don Hendrickson (Donald William)
Born: July 14, 1915, Kewanna
Died: Jan. 19, 1977, Norfolk, Va.
6'2", 195, Pitcher
Boston, NL, 1945-48
TR, 4-9, 4.92 ERA, 5 SV, 39 G
BR, .158, 19 AB

Butch Henline (Walter John)
Born: Dec. 20, 1894, Fort Wayne
Died: Oct. 9, 1957, Sarasota, Fla.
5'10", 175, Catcher, out-

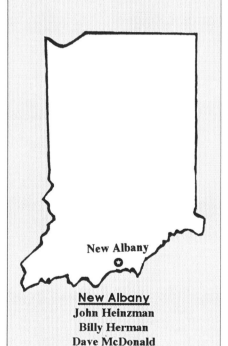

New Albany

New Albany
John Heinzman
Billy Herman
Dave McDonald
Jouette Meekin

fielder
New York, NL, 1921
Philadelphia, NL, 1921-26
Brooklyn, NL, 1927-29
Chicago, AL, 1930-31
BR, TR, .291, 740 G, 2101 AB,
40 HR

Henline came up with the New York Giants, but was traded after just one game to Phildelphia for veteran Irish Meusel. The Phillies were criticized for the trade, but Henline proved his worth and hit a career high .316 in 1922, leading National League catchers in fielding.

Pete Henning (Ernest Herman)
Born: Dec. 28, 1887, Crown Point
Died: Nov. 4, 1939, Dyer
6'1", 185, Pitcher
Kansas City, FL, 1914-15
TR, 14-25, 3.83 ERA, 4 SV, 68 G
BR, .196, 112 AB

Henning played in the Federal League during its two-year existence. He had the dubious distinction of leading the league in relief losses with eleven in 1914.

Billy Herman (William Jennings Bryan)
Born: July 7, 1909, New Albany
Died: Sept. 5, 1992, West Palm Beach, Fla.
5'11", 195, Second and first baseman
Chicago, NL, 1931-41
Brooklyn, NL, 1941-43, 46
Boston, NL, 1946
Pittsburgh, NL, 1947
BR, TR, .304, 1922 G, 7707

AB, 47 HR
4 WS, .242, 66 AB, 1 HR

Herman was one of the best hit-and-run men of all time. The ten-time All-Star player led the National League in several categories during many of his seasons. He was inducted into the Baseball Hall of Fame in 1975 and the Indiana Baseball Hall of Fame in 1979.

Herman began his professional career in 1928 at Vicksburg. He moved to Daytona in 1929 and was promoted to Louisville of the American Association near the end of the season. The New Albany native remained near his hometown at Louisville through 1931, hitting over .300 each season in the minors.

The Chicago Cubs called Herman up at the end of the 1931 season and he hit .327 in twenty-five games. His performance earned him the starting job at second base and his career took off the following season when he hit .314 with forty-two doubles.

H   Billy Herman

Billy Herman was one of the best-hit-and-run hitters in baseball.

On June 28, 1933, Herman tied the National League record for most second base putouts in a doubleheader (16). He also set the NL mark for leading the league in putouts for the most years with seven.

1934 marked his first performance on the All-Star Team. He was chosen for the squad for the next nine years. He holds the NL record for the highest batting average in All-Star games at .433 (18-for-33).

Herman had his career year in 1935 in helping the Cubs to the World Series. He led the NL in putouts, double plays, hits (227) and doubles (57), which still stands as the Cubs single-season record. He had a career-high .341 average and scored 113 runs. In 1939 he led the NL in triples with eighteen.

After a slow start in 1941, he was traded to Brooklyn on May 6 for two mediocre players — John Hudson and Charley Gilbert — and $65,000.

He joined the Navy after the 1943 season, thus missing two seasons. When he returned, the Dodgers traded him to Boston for another Hoosier, catcher Stew Hofferth. At the end of the 1946 season, the Braves sent him to Pittsburgh in a multi-player trade. He was a player-manager for the Pirates in 1947 and the Minneapolis, Minn., in 1948. Then he played a year at Oakland in the Pacific Coast League. Herman also managed Richmond in 1951, the Boston Red Sox from 1964 to 1966, Bradenton in 1968, and Tri-City in 1969. Coaching and scouting for several other teams rounded out his career.

After almost fifty years of baseball, Herman retired in Florida with his second wife, Frances Ann Antonucci, in 1975,

Lefty Hermann (Martin John)
Born: Jan. 10, 1893, Oldenburg
Died: Sept. 11, 1956, Cincinnati, Ohio
5'10", 150, Pitcher
Brooklyn, NL, 1918
TL, BL, 0-0, 0.00 ERA, 1 G

Walt "Reds" Herrell (Walter William)
Born: Feb. 19, 1889, Rockville
Died: Jan. 23, 1949, Front Royal, Va.
Pitcher
Washington, AL, 1911
0-0, 18.00 ERA, 1 G
.000, 1 AB

Jim Hicks (James Edward)
Born: May 18, 1940, East Chicago
6'3", 205, Outfielder, first baseman
Chicago, AL, 1964-66
St. Louis. NL, 1969,
California, AL, 1969-70
BR, TR, .163, 93 G, 141 AB, 5 HR

Hicks played with the Indianapolis Indians for three seasons. He contributed nineteen homers and sixty RBI in 1965 before going to the White Sox at the end of the season.

The following season Hicks had fifteen homers. Then in 1967 he was named as the Tribe's MVP for hitting twenty-one homers and eighty-seven RBI.

Oral Hildebrand (Oral Clyde)
Born: April 7, 1897, Bridge-
port
Died: Sept. 8, 1977, South-
port
6'3", 175, Pitcher
Cleveland, AL, 1931-36
St. Louis, AL, 1937-38
New York, AL, 1939-40
TR, 83-78, 13 SV, 4.36 ERA,
258 G
BR, .187, 513 AB

Hildebrand was a member of the first All-Star team in 1933. His best season in the majors came that same year as he was 16-11. He played basketball at Butler University before going into baseball.

Eric Hillman (John Eric)
Born: April 27, 1966, Gary
6'10", 225, Pitcher
New York, NL, 1992-3
TL, BL, 4-11, 4.33 ERA, 38 G,
1 SHO

Selected by the New York Mets in the 1987 free-agent draft, Hillman was called up three times with the club in 1992. 1993 became his rookie season in the majors. At 6-foot-10, he has the distinction of being the tallest player in the history of the game alongside Seattle pitcher Randy Johnson.

Hillman was born in Gary, but grew up in Illinois. He was graduated in 1984 from Home-wood-Flossmoor High School, where he tossed a no-hitter.

While he was selected by the Mets in seventeenth round of the 1987 draft, he didn't begin playing for the organization until the next year. He began the year at Class A Columbia of the South Atlantic League; then, after going 2-0 with a 1.19 ERA in April, he was promoted to St. Lucie in May.

In 1990 he was to begin at Double-A ball at Jackson of the Texas League, but he sustained an elbow injury while pitching in a exhibition game against the University of Mississippi. He was put on the disabled list and joined St. Lucie on May 18. He finally got to Jackson on June 13 were he went 6-5 on the year with a 3.93 ERA.

The following year he was promoted to Class AAA Tidewa-ter. He got off to a rocky start at Triple-A, as he went 0-8 with four no-decisions in his first twelve starts of the season. He didn't pick up his first win until June 13.

1992 went much better for the lanky lefty. He was called up to the Mets on May 18 and was used in several relief situations until May 14. At Tidewater he continued to dominate batters and won seven of eight starts between June 27 and Aug. 6. Then in mid-August he was called back again. In his initial big league start on August 11, he shut out the Pittsburgh Pirates on six hits in eight innings to pick up his first major league victory. The Mets sent him back to Triple A until August 26, when they called him up for the rest of the season. He marked his return to the big leagues with a 5-3 win over the San Francisco, finishing the season with a 2-2 mark.

In 1993 he began the season at Norfolk, where he pitched a complete game four-hit shutout on May 2. Eight days later the

Eric Hillman stands tall on the mound for the Mets.

H

Mets called him up. The last-place Mets didn't give him much run support during the year and he ended the season with a 2-9 mark with 3.97 ERA.

Hillman now resides in Citrus Heights, Calif.

Harley Hisner (Harley Parnell)
Born: Nov. 6, 1926, Naples
6'1", 185, Pitcher
Boston, AL, 1951
TR, 0-1, 4.50 ERA, 1 G
BR, .500, 2 AB

Oris "Brown" Hockett (Oris Leon)
Born: Sept. 29, 1909, Amboy
Died: March 23, 1969, Torrance, Calif.
5'9", 162, Outfielder
Brooklyn, NL, 1938-39
Cleveland, AL, 1941-44
Chicago, AL, 1945
BL, TR, .276, 551 G, 2165 AB, 13 HR

Hockett started off as an excellent football player, but ended up in baseball because he needed the money the minor leagues was paying during the Great Depression.

During his youth, his family moved to Dayton, Ohio, and he played football at Roosevelt High School. He was induced into going to Southern Military Academy in Greensboro, Ala., where he played halfback and scored 136 points in seven games. He went to a couple more colleges before he finally broke into baseball in 1936 because he needed the extra money. He employed the alias of Jim Brown in order to keep his college eligibility.

Hockett excelled in baseball and hit over .300 in the minors, which led him to a September callup in 1938. In his first game in the majors he belted out a triple and three singles in helping fellow Hoosier Fat Freddy Fitzsimmons to a victory.

He finally became a regular outfielder for Cleveland in 1942, as the war drained the league of its talented players.

Gil Hodges (Gilbert Ray)
Born: April 4, 1924, Princeton
Died: April 2, 1972, West Palm Beach, Fla.
6'2", 200, Catcher, first baseman, outfielder
Brooklyn, NL, 1943, 1947-57
Los Angeles, NL, 1958-61
New York, NL, 1962-63
BR, TR, 2071 G, .273, 7030 AB, 370 HR
7 WS, 39 G, .267, 5 HR

Hodges was an excellent fielder and hitter during his seventeen seasons in the majors. He hammered out twenty or more home runs for eleven straight years and set the National League mark for grand slams with fourteen. He appeared on eight All-Star teams, played in seven World Series, and earned three gold gloves. The New York Mets, whom he managed to a world championship in 1969, have honored him by retiring his number (14). He was elected to the Indiana Baseball Hall of Fame in 1979.

Hodges was an all-around athlete in high school, where he lettered in basketball, football, baseball, and track. The son of a

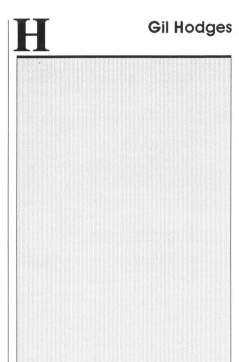

coal miner snubbed the mines and a Class D contract with Detroit when he graduated from Princeton High School in 1941. Instead, he chose to attend nearby St. Joseph's College on an athletic scholarship.

In college he studied physical education and continued playing four sports. In the summer he was involved in semipro ball near Indianapolis. Brooklyn Dodger scout Stanley Feezle saw Hodges and convinced him to go to a Dodger tryout camp. He was so impressive at the camp that he was sent to Brooklyn for a personal tryout before Dodger president Branch Rickey. Rickey signed Hodges as a catcher for $500.

The young Hoosier played in one game for the Dodgers in August 1943 before the war beckoned him. He spent the next two years in the Marines, as a gunner for an anti-aircraft battalion in the Pacfic. He spent some time on Iwo Jima, where the Marines hoisted Old Glory in honor when they took the island.

Upon Hodges discharge in the winter of 1945, Rickey presented another $500 bonus. He was sent to Newport News, Virginia, for the 1946 season. In the off-season he attended Oakland City College and played

Gil Hodges (standing far left) checks out the lumber with his St. Joseph College teammates in this 1942 photo.

H varsity basketball.

After spring training in 1947 Hodges made the Dodgers team as a third-string catcher. He played in twenty-eight games that season, but in that short time he impressed some players. Pitcher Harry Taylor, a fellow Hoosier, recalled throwing to Hodges when he first came up. "He was the best catcher I ever had, as far as I'm concerned. He knew what he was doing back there. He had potential sticking out all over him," Taylor said.

Manager Leo Durocher decided to make some player moves in 1948 and put Hodges at first base, so he could put Roy Campanella behind the plate. "When they switched him to first base, it was a great move," said former Dodger pitcher Carl Erskine, another Hoosier. "He was an intense player and kept things inside."

In his first full season with the Dodgers, Hodges struggled behind the plate, but still hit a respectable .249 with eleven home runs and seventy RBI — not bad for a rookie. He married Joan Lombardi of Brooklyn during the year.

In 1949 Hodges began to come of age. He was hitting and fielding well enough to be named to the All-Star Game. By the end of the season he had complied 115 RBI with twenty-three homers and a .283 average. In the World Series against the Yankees, he batted .235 with one home run.

Hodges' numbers were similar in 1950, and he was again named to the All-Star Team. On Aug. 31 he had probably the best game of his career. He hit four homers in one game at Ebbets Field! Few players have accomplished that feat. Unfortunately, Hodges couldn't lift the Dodgers to a pennant, as the season ended in the last inning of the last game in a loss to the Philadelphia "Whiz Kids."

An All-Star again in 1951, Hodges launched forty dingers, second in the league, and drove in 103 RBI, but he also struck out a league high ninety-nine times. The Dodgers again experienced a disheartening season when the Giants tied them for the pennant and beat them in a three-game playoff with Bobby Thompson's famous ninth-inning home run.

But the Dodgers were resilient and Hodges would help them to a pennant in 1952. Near the end of the season he began to slump badly. The slump continued into the World Series against the New York Yankees and he went 0-for-21. 1953 began the same way. Hodges couldn't hit the curveball. Manager Chuck Dressen had the team photographer take motion picture film to figure out his problem. The film showed how Hodges was stepping in the bucket. His stance was adjusted and Hodges began hitting again. The Dodgers again finished in first place and again faced the Yankees in the series. The big first baseman turned in a fine performance in the series, hitting .364 with one home run, but the Dodgers lost anyway in six games to their crosstown rivals.

In 1954 Hodges made the

All-Star Team and hammered out forty-two round trippers with 130 RBI, but the Dodgers finished second. His numbers dropped the following year, but he was named to his seventh straight All-Star team. He helped the Dodgers win the pennant. Again the opponent in the World Series was the Yankees. Hodges went 7-for-24 in the series and contributed a home run and five RBI, as the Dodgers got by the Yanks in seven games.

Hodges knocked out thirty-two homers during 1956 to help the Dodgers to their second straight pennant. Brooklyn again faced the Yankees in the series, which was highlighted by a perfect game by another Hoosier, Don Larsen. Hodges hit .307 in the series with one home run and eight RBI. The Yankees won the series in seven games.

1957 was an off-year for the Dodgers, but not for Hodges. He was named to the All-Star Team for the eighth time and earned a Gold Glove. He hit .299 on the year with twenty-seven home runs. He grabbed his second Gold Glove in 1958 when the Dodgers made the move to Los Angeles. With a left field foul pole at only 250 feet, Hodges had hoped for a great season. Instead it turned into his worst year, batting .259 with twenty-four homers and only 64 RBI. The Dodgers also had a bad year, finishing in seventh place.

Hodges rebounded in 1959, as did the Dodgers. In his last year as a regular first baseman for the Dodgers, he hit .276 with twenty-five home runs. He helped the team to a World Series victory over the Chicago White Sox by hitting .391. In his last two years with the Dodgers he was used mainly as a pinch hitter.

In the winter of 1961 the expansion New York Mets purchased Hodges from the Dodgers. He was thirty-eight years old and had an injured right knee. In the Mets first game of the season, Hodges became the first Met to hit a home run, but the Mets still lost the game. He played in fifty-four games that year.

In 1963 Hodges played in only eleven games before a knee operation became necessary. He retired after the operation to takeover as manager of the Washington Senators. One of his players was another Hoosier, Joe McCabe. "At Washington we had cast offs from the league. He had a tough time understanding it," explained McCabe. "I had a tough time with him. He was very knowledgeable. If you didn't keep up with his way of thinking, he didn't appreciate you. He didn't have the patience. He didn't know all the intracies of managing."

Hodges learned how to manage better year by year and improved the Senators from a last-place team to sixth place before he was traded to the Mets in the fall of 1967 for pitcher Bill Denehy. The Mets showed improvement right away, as he led them to their best season with seventy-three wins in 1968. He wasn't able to finish managing the season because of heart attack Sept. 24 during a game. He was hospitalized for a month.

Stew Hofferth

Stew Hofferth became a free agent when there wasn't any free agency.

Hodges' platoon system began to instill a sense of teamwork in 1969 and the Mets began to play championship ball despite being 100-to-1 shots in Las Vegas. He platooned four of eight starting positions so that every member of the team made a contribution — camaraderie. "The Amazin' Mets" won the pennant despite the odds and went on to win the World Series.

Hodges managed the Mets to third-place finishes the next two years. During spring training in 1973, Hodges died from a massive heart attack after a round of golf. He's remembered well in Petersburg. A sign greets visitors: "Welcome to Petersburg, Home Town of Gil Hodges." There's also a bridge named in his honor in northern Pike County.

Hodges put up some big numbers while he was in the majors, but he was overshadowed by teammates Roy Campanella, Duke Snider and Pee Wee Reese, all of who made the Hall of Fame. However, the Veterans Committee may someday look back at his career and reconsider.

Much of the information in this biography compiled with permission from "Gil Hodges: The Quiet Man" by Marino Amoruso, copyright 1991, Paul S. Eriksson Publisher.

Stew Hofferth (Steward Edward)
Born: Jan. 27, 1913, Logansport
6'2", 195, Catcher
Boston, NL, 1944-46
BR, TR, .216, 136 G, 408 AB,
4 HR

Hofferth was one of the few players to become a free agent in the 1940s. He was granted that status after he had been tricked into accepting an assignment to Toronto of the International League by the Brooklyn Dodgers. An All-Star player and Most Valuable Player at Indianapolis, the catcher couldn't master major league pitching.

Hofferth attended Kouts High School and played on the basketball team. At age seventeen the Chicago White Sox invited him to a tryout at Comiskey Park. After three weeks there, he became homesick and returned to Kouts without signing a contract. "I can remember seeing sixteen year olds being signed up. Now there are some rules and regulations stating they have to wait until graduation," he reportedly said.

The catcher went to work for Inland Steel after graduation and played baseball on the company's team. In 1936 he was given a contract by Nashville, Tenn., of the Southern Association. He was assigned to Tallahassee, where he played for several years. The best game of his career came during the 1937 season. He clobbered three home runs in one game!

In 1939 Nashville sold Hofferth to the Brooklyn Dodgers, who sent him to Montreal. He also played in Dayton, Ohio, that year. The Dodgers recognized his leadership abilities and made him a player-manager of the Class D Valdosta, Ga., team in 1940. He played there for two seasons.

Then in 1942 he got his big chance. The Dodgers called him up, but manager Leo Durocher assigned him to the bench. After Hofferth spent ten days on the pine, Dodgers President Larry MacPhail gave him a release and a ticket to Toronto. Hofferth just wanted to play, so he didn't question the move. However, Commissioner Kenesaw M. Landis got wind of the illegal deal. He let Hofferth finish the season in Toronto before declaring him a free agent. Landis ordered that the Dodgers couldn't sign him again for three years.

"My dad said,"Where do I go now that I'm a free agent?'" explained Ted Hofferth, his son. Free agency was still several decades away. Buzzie Bavasi helped Hofferth by calling Indianapolis owner Donie Bush, who agreed to give the catcher a $5,000 bonus and $600 a month—$200 more than he had been earning. Hofferth gladly accepted the offer back to his native state.

1943 became his best year in baseball. In mid-season he was named to the All-Star Team. Then, at the end of the season, the American Association named him MVP. Hofferth's stock rose after the honor and Bush took advantage by selling him to the Boston Braves for $18,500.

For some reason, he was late in reporting to spring training in 1944. Still, the Braves called him up as the third-string catcher behind Phil Masi and Clyde Kluttz. The thirty-one-year-old receiver caught in forty-seven games and hit .200. Hofferth improved his average to .235 the following year and he became the backup to Masi.

Hofferth got off to a poor start in 1947 and was hitting a paltry .207 when the Braves dealt him to the Brooklyn Dodgers for Hoosier Billy Herman. President Branch Rickey wanted to send Hofferth to Mobile, Ala., to help young pitchers develop. However, Hofferth didn't want to go to the minors so the two got into a heated argument over the matter. Hofferth quit on the spot!

He stayed out of baseball for a year before the Dodgers asked him to go to St. Paul, Minn. Hofferth agreed to play for the team, which had Walter Alston as its manager. The team also included a catcher that was tearing up the league—Roy Campanella. Hofferth's season ended early when he suffered torn ligaments in his throwing arm after a collision at first base.

The Dodgers gave him a managing position at Cambridge, Mass. Hofferth turned the club around and took them to the playoffs. Rickey sent him a congratulatory telegram at the end of the season.

Hofferth finished his career by playing semipro ball at Michigan City from 1949 to 1951. The retired steel worker suffered a stroke in 1992 and lost his ability to speak and write. He is married to the former Anna Bercellie of Tom's Creek, Va., and they live in Kouts. They have four children — Edward, Rita, Linda, and Ted — and four grandchildren. Ted played baseball for Valparaiso Univer-

I

sity and semipro in the Industrial League, like his father.

Fred "Lefty" Houtz (Fred Fritz)
Born: Sept. 4, 1875, Connersville
Died: Feb. 15, 1959, Wapakoneta, Ohio
5'10", 170, Outfielder
Cincinnati, NL, 1899
BL, TL, .235, 17 AB, 5 G

Emil "Hap" Huhn (Emil Hugo)
Born: March 10, 1892, North Vernon
Died: Sept. 5, 1925, Camden, S.C.
6', 180, Catcher, first baseman, outfielder
Newark, FL, 1915
Cincinnati, NL, 1916-17
TR, BR, .229, 184 G, 560 AB, 1 HR

Bert Inks (Albert Preston Inkstein)
Born: Jan. 27, 1871, Ligonier
Died: Oct. 3, 1941, Ligonier
6'3", 175, Pitcher
Brooklyn, NL, 1891-2
Washington, NL, 1892
Baltimore, NL, 1894
Louisville, NL, 1894-95
Philadelphia, NL, 1896
Cincinnati, NL, 1896
TL, 27-46, 5.52 ERA, 89 G
BL, .300, 250 AB

Hal "Grump" Irelan (Harold)
Born: Aug. 5, 1890, Burnettsville
Died: July 16, 1944, Carmel
5'7", 165
Philadelphia, NL, 1914
TB, TR, .236, 67 G, 165 AB

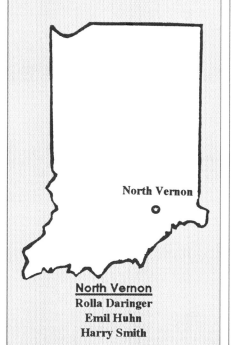

North Vernon

North Vernon
Rolla Daringer
Emil Huhn
Harry Smith

Henry Jackson (Henry Everett)
Born: June 23, 1861, Union City
Died: Sept. 14, 1932, Chicago, Ill.
6'2", 185, First baseman
Indianapolis, NL, 1887
BR, TR, .263, 10 G, 38 AB

Jeff "Jesse" James (Jeffrey Lynn)
Born: Sept, 29, 1941, Indianapolis
6'3", 195, Pitcher
Philadelphia, NL, 1968-69
TR, 6-6, 4.50 ERA, 35 G
BR, .135, 44 AB, 6 H

Nicknamed for the famous gunfighter, James earned a promotion to the Phillies after winning eleven straight games in the minors.

Loretta Janowsky
Born: Griffith
AAGPBL, 1951

Fran "Red" Janssen (Francis)
Born: Jan. 25, 1926, Remington
Pitcher
Grand Rapids, AAGPBL, 1948
Peoria, AAGPBL, 1950
Muskegon, AAGPBL, 1950
Kalamazoo, AAGPBL, 1950
Fort Wayne, AAGPBL, 1950-51
Peoria, AAGPBL, 1951
Battle Creek, AAGPBL, 1952
BR, TR, 11G, 20 AB, 5 H, .250
(1948 stats)

Janssen was moved around the league quite a bit in her four seasons, because the league had the power to move players at will to fill roster spots.

She was initially allocated to the South Bend Blue Sox in spring training at Opa Locka, Fla., but was sent to the Grand Rapids Chicks for the season. She pitched a few games for Grand Rapids before being released because she couldn't throw a curveball.

Janssen, whose name was misspelled frequently in the league records, spent 1949 with a rookie touring team to gain experience and develop a curve before rejoining the regular league in 1950. She was shipped to four different teams during the season and was used mainly in relief.

After she quit the league, she continued to play softball for the South Bend Rockettes and appeared on three national championship teams. She also played volleyball for the South Bend Turners in the 1960s.

Tommy John (Thomas Edward)
Born: May 22, 1943, Terre Haute
6'3", 200, Pitcher
Cleveland, AL, 1963-64
Chicago, AL, 1965-71
Los Angeles, NL, 1972-74, 76-78
New York, AL, 1979-82
California, AL, 1982-85
New York, AL, 1986-89
TL, 288-231, 4 SV, 3.34 ERA, 760 G, 46 SHO
BR, .157, 900 AB, 141 H, 5 HR

John's career spanned twenty-six seasons under seven U.S. presidents, second only to Nolan Ryan. He's most known

J

for recovering from a career-ending elbow injury that was repaired by a revolutionary tendon transplant. He earned the Comeback Player of the Year Award in 1976 after a year and a half of rehabilitation from the injury. The four-time All-Star player started 700 games, which places him among career pitching leaders.

John started his baseball career in Little League. He was a pitcher from the beginning because he liked being the center of attention. His father, a semi-pro player, was the coach of his team. The younger John advanced to Babe Ruth and American Legion ball, where he threw two no-hitters for Post 346.

In high school John lettered in basketball and baseball. His basketball skills earned him many scholarship offers, but he was an even better baseball pitcher. Several major league teams made him offers, and he finally signed with the Cleveland Indians in 1961 for $40,000. He was sent to Class D Dubuque, Iowa. He won his first minor league game and went 10-4 on the year with a 3.17 ERA.

John's performance earned him a promotion to Class A Charleston, W. Va., in 1962. By July he was 6-5 and the Indians moved him up to Triple A Jacksonville, Fla. John began 1963 in Jacksonville, but was sent down to Charleston. He responded by going 9-2 with a 1.61 ERA. He was brought back to Jacksonville in mid-season.

After the season was over, the Indians called him up to finish out the year. John's first appearance in the majors came on Sept. 6. He came into the game against the Washington Senators in the seventh inning. The Indians were down 6-2. He pitched an inning and gave up an unearned run. He was 0-2 in Cleveland.

1964 saw John on the opening-day roster for the Tribe. He recorded his first Major League win on May 3 against Baltimore. In late July he was sent down to Class AAA Portland, Ore. Then he was called up again in September when rosters were expanded. His record was 2-9 with the Indians on the year.

In the off-season the Indians dealt the left-hander to the Chicago White Sox with Tommie Agee and John Romano for Camilo Carreon and Rocky Colavito. John joined a much better team. He helped the Sox finish second in 1965 with his 14-7 performance.

1966 was similar; John went 14-11. The following year his ERA continued to improve to 2.47. The Southsiders couldn't give him much run support and he ended up with a 10-13 record. Six of his victories were shutouts!

For the next three season with the Sox, John recorded losing records on a team that couldn't help him much. His ERA hovered around 3.40. In 1970 he married Sally Simmons in Plainfield during the All-Star break.

In December 1971, the Sox dealt him to the Dodgers for Richie Allen and minor leaguer Steve Huntz. John pitched well in his first year for Los Angeles, but he had elbow problems near the end of the season. Dr. Frank Jobe performed elbow surgery on him to remove bone chips.

John bounced back from surgery with his best season yet in the majors. His 16-7 record led the league in winning percentage (.696). The Dodgers finished second.

The Hoosier hurled six straight victories to begin the 1974 campaign. By the All-Star break he was 13-3, but Mets manager Yogi Berra didn't select him for the All-Star team.

Then tragedy struck. On July 17 he was pitching against Montreal when he hurt his arm. His season was over and his career hung on a thread. At the end of the season, Jobe performed his now famous tendon transplant surgery on the pitcher. He took tendons from John's right forearm to repair the left elbow. John was on the shelf for all of 1975 and rehabed the elbow. He bounced back to the starting rotation in 1976 and finished 10-10 to earn the comeback award.

By 1977 he was fully recovered from the effects of his injury and led the Dodgers march to a pennant with a 20-7 record. Then he aided the Dodgers to the World Series by beating the Phillies in the League Championship Series. He didn't have the same success in the World Series, losing to the Yankees in Game Three.

John continued his masterful pitching in 1978. He was tabbed for the All-Star squad, but he didn't pitch in the game. After compiling a 17-10 record, he shut out the Phillies in the LCS. Again the Dodgers faced the Yankees in the series. John pitched the first game and won easily. He also started Game Four, but didn't get a decision in the loss.

After the season, he became a free agent and signed with the Yankees. He couldn't beat'em, so he joined'em. John pitched well for the pinstripes in 1979 (21-9) and was again named to the All-Star team.

1980 featured the pitcher on the All-Star team for the fourth time. He won twenty-two games on the year and started Game Three of the LCS against Kansas City. He got no decision in the loss that ended the hopes of the Yankees.

During the strike-shortened season of 1981, John had a superb 2.64 ERA and 9-8 record. He won the first game of the LCS against Oakland which helped in the sweep. In the World Series, he shut out his old Dodger teammates in Game Two. He also started Game Six and ended with no decision, as the Yankees lost the game and the series.

After going 10-10 in 1982, the Yankees traded him to California near the end of season. Thanks to John's 4-2 record in September, the Angels made the playoffs. However, he couldn't get the team to the World Series, even though he won and lost a game to the Milwaukee Brewers.

John's pitching performance began to slide in 1983. He had a losing record the next three seasons. After a 2-4 start in

Tommy John pitched for twenty-six years in the majors.

1985, the Angels waived him. Oakland picked him up and he finished out the season there. He again became a free agent and signed with the Yankees. After a 2-7 start in 1989, John was released and he decided to retire.

John now lives in Fort Lauderdale. In 1993 he coached a high school baseball team. During the summer he had hip replacement surgery. He and his wife have four children: Tami, Tommy III, Travis, and Taylor.

Bob Johnson (Robert Dale)
Born: April 25, 1943, Aurora
6'4", 220, Pitcher
New York, NL, 1969
Kansas City, AL, 1970
Pittsburgh, NL, 1971-73
Cleveland, AL, 1974
Atlanta, NL, 1977
TR, 28-34, 3.48 ERA, 183 G, 2 SHO
BL, .096, 157 AB, 15 H

Johnson was a much more effective working from the bullpen than as a starter. His best season was in 1973, when he was 4-2 with a 3.62 ERA in forty-eight relief appearances.

Elmer "Hickory" Johnson
(Elmer Ellsworth)
Born: June 12, 1884, Beard
Died: Oct. 31, 1966, Hollywood, Fla.
5'9", 185, Catcher
New York, NL, 1914
TR, TR, .167, 11 G, 12 AB

Wallace Johnson (Wallace Darnell)
Born: Dec. 25, 1956, Gary
6', 185, First and second baseman
Montreal, NL, 1981-83

San Francisco, NL, 1983
Montreal, NL, 1984, 86-90
BB, TR, .255, 428 G, 569 AB, 5 HR

Johnson was used as a utility infielder at first and second with the Expos and Giants during his nine years in the majors.

At Indiana State University, Johnson set several records, hit a whopping .507, and swiped thirty-six bases in his senior year. After being drafted by Montreal in the sixth round of the 1979 free-agent draft, he played well in the minors — hitting .338 at West Palm Beach in 1980 — which led him to a September callup in 1981 with the Expos.

When Johnson first came up to the majors, Indianapolis' Rodney Scott was planted solidly at second base. In 1983 Johnson was traded to the Giants for Mike Vail. The following year he came back to Montreal.

In 1990 he won his salary arbitration case against Montreal for $295,000. His .163 average apparently didn't live up to his salary, so he was released.

Barry "Bearcat" Jones
(Barry Louis)
Born: Feb. 15, 1963, Centerville
6'4", 225, Relief Pitcher
Pittsburgh, NL, 1986-88
Chicago, AL, 1988-90
Montreal, NL, 1991
Philadelphia, NL, 1992
New York, NL, 1992
Chicago, AL, 1993
TR, 33-33, 23 SV, 3.66 ERA, 348 G, 433 IP, 250 SO
BR, .071, 14 AB, 1 H

Jones was released in May

1993 by the Chicago White Sox, but he hasn't retired yet and plans to be at spring training in 1994 with some team. He is best known for being the best set-up man for Bobby Thigpen's major-league record fifty-seven saves in 1990.

Like many major leaguers, Jones began playing baseball at age five in a Pee Wee League. While he was in Little League, he would sometimes replay the game at night in his sleep. "I walked out on the porch a couple of times," he recalled. "My mom threatened to take me out of baseball."

He started pitching in Little League, but didn't get serious about the position until his junior year at Centerville High School. His coach, Dale Hatcher, encouraged him. "He thought I had the potential to play in the big leagues," Jones said.

Several no-hitters earned him some reputation, and scouts from every major league team started showing up at the small town located near Richmond. "I had good speed with my fast ball," he admitted. He also lettered in football and basketball. In his senior year he didn't play football because the team voted him out. He tried to join the team two weeks into the season and his teammates didn't agree with the move.

While playing with American Legion Post 65 of Richmond in the national tournament, Jones was seen by Larry Smith, the head coach of Indiana University, who offered him a scholarship. The Texas Rangers had drafted him in the sixth round.

He opted for college and went to IU for the next three years. After his junior year in 1984, Pittsburgh drafted him in the third round and signed him to a contract for $28,000. He was assigned to Class A Watertown, where he was used as a starter and went 6-3 with a 3.43 ERA.

The Hoosier became a relief pitcher in 1985 and climbed up the minor-league ladder quickly. After ten saves and a 1.21 at Prince William, he stepped up to Class AA Nashua, where he was just as good with twelve saves and a 1.55 ERA. He landed in Triple A Hawaii at the end of the season.

After he had saved seven games for Hawaii in 1986, the Pirates called up him up in mid-season. His major league debut came on July 18 against San Diego. A month later he was called upon to relieve in a suspensed game. "I pitched four innings and got my first win. That may be my longest stint in the majors," he explained.

Jones was on the opening-day roster for the Pirates in 1987. He made five appearances before being sent down to Vancouver on April 24. He was recalled to the Pirates on June 18 and finished the year with a 2-4 record.

1988 was a much better year for the hurler. He went all the way until May 14 and thirteen innings pitched before he allowed a run. The Pirates decided to deal the hurler to Chicago for Dave LaPoint on Aug. 13.

He was pitching well for the White Sox the following season when he suffered an elbow

"I walked out on the porch a couple of times. My mom threatened to take me out of baseball."
Barry Jones

Walt Justis

J

injury. He went on the disabled list on May 4 to have bone chips removed from his right elbow. He rehabilitated the elbow in the minors and made his way back to Chicago on Sept. 2.

Jones rebounded from the year he would like to forget to have the best season of his career in 1990. He became the main set-up man for Thigpen, who was unstoppable that year. Jones preserved thirty leads — by far the most in the majors —when he set-up thirty-two of Thigpen's fifty-seven saves. Even in Thigpen's shadow, he shone with an 11-4 record and 2.31 ERA.

In the off-season, the White Sox dealt the big reliever to Montreal with Ivan Calderon for Tim Raines, Jeff Carter, and Mario Brito. The Expos had a bullpen by committee, and Jones was used as a setup man as well as the stopper on occasion. He recorded thirteen saves and had a 4-9 record in pitching his most innings in the majors.

The Expos traded him in the winter to Philadelphia for Darrin Fletcher. He was 5-6 when the Phillies released him in July only to have the New York Mets sign him the following month. He was ineffective in New York, so he was cut loose by the Mets.

The White Sox gave him another try by signing him as a minor league free agent in January 1993. After spring training he was assigned to Triple A Nashville. Chicago called him up on April 26. A month later he was released after an 8.59 ERA. "It was just a numbers game in Chicago, and it was better for me to come

home," he said. "I enjoyed having the summer off."

The Hoosier picked up the nickname "Bearcat" from his fellow players because he was "quick as a cat" during pitcher fielding practice.

He's now living in Murrysville, Pa., with his wife, Anita Burris of Chalfant, Pa., and their two sons, Preston and Spencer. He plans on finishing his degree after baseball and is interested in coaching baseball.

Walt "Smoke" Justis (Walter Newton)
Born: Aug. 17, 1883, Moores Hill
Died: Oct. 4, 1941, Lawrenceburg
5'11", 195, Pitcher
Detroit, AL, 1905
TR, 0-0, 8.10 ERA, 2 G
BR, .000, 1 AB

Bob Kahle (Robert Wayne)
Born: Nov. 23, 1915, New Castle
Died: Dec, 16, 1988, Inglewood, Calif.
6', 170, Pinch hitter
Boston, NL, 1938
BR, TR, .333, 8 G, 3 AB

Kahle was with the Indianapolis Indians in 1937, the year before he got a call from the Boston Braves for a brief stint.

Ron Keller (Ronald Lee)
Born: June, 3, 1943, Indianapolis
6'2", 200, Relief Pitcher
Minnesota, AL, 1966, 68
TR, 0-1, 3.43 ERA, 9 G
BR, .000, 2 AB

John Kerins (John)
Born: July 15, 1858, Indianapolis
Died: Sept. 8, 1919, Louisville, Ky.
5'10", 177, First baseman, catcher, outfielder
Indianapolis, AA, 1884
Louisville, AA, 1885-89
Baltimore, AA, 1889
St. Louis, AA, 1889-90
BR, TR, .252, 556 G, 2224 AB, 20 HR

Jeff King (Jeffrey Wayne)
Born: Dec. 26, 1964, Marion
6'1", 180, Infielder
Pittsburgh, NL, 1989-93
BR, TR, .252, 523 G, 1786 AB, 46 HR
2 LCS, .205, 12 G, 39 AB

A first-round selection of the Pittsburgh Pirates in 1986 draft, King has shown his versatility by being able to play any infield position. At the University of Arkansas he set school records in home runs (42) and RBI (204), as well as the single-season record for RBI (82) and a share of the home run record (17) with Kevin McReynolds. He was the starting third baseman for the Pirates in 1993.

King remembered throwing a baseball around when he was three years old, while still living in Indiana. "My dad played professional ball a little bit," he said. "I had two brothers that played, too. It [baseball] was part of the family." His father, Jack King, played in the Philadelphia Phillies' organization in 1953-54.

His family moved to California when he was four years old. He began playing Little League baseball at age nine. At first he was a pitcher and a catcher. His family moved to Colorado when he was in seventh grade. In the summers he played on a Babe Ruth team that went to the World Series three years in a row. In high school he lettered in basketball and baseball.

When he graduated from Rampart High School in 1982, the Chicago Cubs drafted him in the twenty-third round. "I never signed with them," he said. He decided to attend the University of Arkansas on a baseball scholarship instead. King set many batting records at Arkansas. In 1985 he helped lead the team to a third-place finish in the College World Series with his .369 average and seventeen homers. He was named an All-American, All-Southwest Conference, and All-World Series in 1985. The Sporting News named him College Player of the Year.

K

Jeff King

K

His performance at Arkansas earned him a first-round selection by the Pirates in the 1986 draft. He declined to reveal what the Pirates gave him to sign. Because of his experience in college, the Pirates assigned him to their Class A Prince William, team where he went 2-for-3 with a triple and two RBI in his professional debut. The following year King started in Salem, where he clobbered twenty-six round trippers in ninety games. His success there elevated him to Class AA Harrisburg, Pa. The former Hoosier also spent 1988 in Harrisburg and hit .255 with fourteen homers. He had an eleven-game hitting streak in August going 18-for-40 (.450).

After spring training in 1989, he started the season in Triple A at Buffalo, N.Y. When Sid Bream was placed on the disabled list on May 30, King was called up. He made his major league debut on June 2 as a pinch hitter and promptly stroked a double off Rick Aguilera. In fact, the rookie's first major league home run came off Aguilera on July 25 that year. He had another key homer that season. It came off Scott Sanderson in the bottom of the 18th inning to give the Pirates a 5-4 victory over Chicago in the Pirates longest game in Three Rivers Stadium history — five hours, forty-two minutes.

1990 became King's first full year in the majors. He started eighty-five games at third base and was also used as a pinch hitter when he wasn't starting. His first career pinch-hit home run came on May 25 against San Francisco, a two-run shot off of Atlee Hammaker. Then in July

The Pirates have signed Jeff King through the 1994 season.

he hit his first career grand slam off of Giants' Ed Vosberg at Three Rivers. King knocked five dingers in August and September, including a two-homer game against the Mets. His productivity helped the Pirates win the National League East. However, his power didn't stretch into the League Championship Series, when he went just 1-for-10. The Pirates lost the series in six games to the Reds.

Opening Day 1991 found King at third again. After twenty-three games and hitting .250, he suffered a lower back strain and was put on the disabled list on May 15. He returned on May 30 and appeared in ten games before the injury reoccurred. He was able to knock out three homers in his last six at bats before hurting his back again. The Pirates put him back on the DL, and he missed the rest of the season. He did return to Buffalo on a rehab assignment on August 28 for nine games with the Bisons. He had surgery in November to repair the back problem — a ruptured disc in his lower back.

King's comeback from the injury was slow at first in 1992. After batting just .187 with six home runs in sixty-two games, the Pirates optioned him to Buffalo. With the Bisons he got back his batting stroke and hit .345 in seven games. The Pirates had traded third baseman Steve Buechele to the Cubs, so King was needed to fill the void at third. He responded with a .268 average, eight homers, and forty-five RBI in sixty-nine games to aid the Pirates to its third straight first-place finish. King showed his versatility as he played at least one game in each infield position. On Sept. 9 he launched his second grand slam of his career.

In the LCS he played in all seven games and hit .241, as he was 7-for-29. Four of his hits were doubles. Unfortunately, the Pirates lost to the Atlanta Braves and failed to get to the World Series for the third year in a row.

With the loss of Barry Bonds, the Pirates looked to King to provide more power in 1993, but he couldn't fill that void. However, the Pirates still more than tripled his salary when they signed him for $2.4 million in December 1993 to a one-year contract. He could be a free agent after that.

King now resides in Wexford, Pa., with his wife, Laura, and three children: Audrey, Jeffrey, and Cody.

Matt Kinzer (Matthew Roy)
Born: June 17, 1963, Indian-
apolis
6'3", 210, Pitcher
St. Louis, NL, 1987
Detroit, AL, 1990
TR, 0-2, 13.10 ERA, 9 G
BR, .000, 1 AB

Ron Kittle (Ronald Dale)
Born: Jan. 5, 1958, Gary
6'4", 215, Outfielder, first
baseman, designated
hitter
Chicago, AL, 1982-86
New York, AL, 1986-87
Cleveland, AL, 1988
Chicago, AL, 1989-90
Baltimore, AL, 1990
Chicago, AL, 1991

Outfielder, designated hitter
BR, TR, 843 G, .239, 2708 AB, 176 HR
1 LCS, 3 G, .286

Kittle was a prolific home run hitter, but injuries hampered his professional career. The minor-league MVP clobbered ninety home runs in two seasons before coming to the majors. In his first full year in the majors, he was named to the All-Star Team and was named Rookie of the Year. The iron worker was a very popular player in Chicago and played for the White Sox on four different occasions.

Kittle's baseball career started the way it ended — with a bang! At age five he threw a baseball through the front door window. He grew up across the street from a baseball diamond. "We played almost every single night," he said.

At eight he began playing with the Aetna Little League. Since Brooks Robinson was his idol, he chose third base as his position. "I was number five until I grew up. Then I was number fourteen or thirteen because I was the biggest player on the team," he explained.

Even as a youngster, Kittle hit the ball over the fence. And he had an extra incentive. "My dad gave me a dollar per homer in Little League," he said. His father later cut that to a quarter after his son hit so many.

In his freshman year, Kittle attended Andrean High School, a Catholic school. He wanted to play on the baseball team, but he wasn't allowed to try out because he was a freshman. His father offered to buy uniforms for the team, but school officials wouldn't budge. Kittle promptly transferred to public school so he could play baseball. He went to Gary Wirt High School and later got some revenge by hitting a home run against Andrean. He hit fourteen homers during his high school career and batted around .500, but scouts didn't take any notice. He also lettered in football and basketball. During the summers he played for a Senior Little League until he was fifteen.

After he was graduated from high school in 1976, he immediately went to work in a steel plant, toiling up to fourteen hours a day as an iron worker. "I was cleaning my boots one day and I saw this paper below my feet that said the Dodgers were holding a tryout camp in La Porte," he said. "My dad said I had to go. He took me to the tryout. That's where I put on a hitting display." The barrage of home runs earned him a $5,000 contact from Los Angeles.

After spring training the next year he was assigned to Class A Clinton, Iowa. Not long after his professional career started, it nearly ended. "I slid across home plate and the catcher landed on me," he explained. He suffered crushed vertabrae in his neck. He played sporadically the rest of the season. After the season he had a spinal fusion operation and the Dodgers released him. "I was told I would never play baseball again."

He tried to come back to baseball in 1978 from the operation, but his neck was too stiff.

Ron Kittle had a big home run swing.

The following year he hooked on with a semipro team in Chicago. In his first game he hit for the cycle! Kittle was back. The Chicago White Sox got wind of Kittle's power and gave him a personal tryout at Comiskey Park.

"I hit ball after ball in the seats at Sox Park. On my last swing, I hit one on the roof and the lenses on my glasses popped out," he recalled. The Sox signed him and assigned him to Double A Knoxville, Tenn. He still suffered a stiff neck and felt like "Frankenstein."

In 1980 he was dropped to Class A Appleton, Wisc., as a catcher. After making the All-Star team halfway through the year, he was promoted to Class AA again at Glen Falls, N.Y. He was there two weeks when he tore ligaments in his thumb from sliding into tree roots at second base. He was out for the season.

The thumb was healed and the neck was getting better the next year when he returned to the Glen Falls team. He hammered out forty homers and 102 RBI in 100 games to win MVP honors. He also hit .324, but missed the triple crown by .001 of a point.

Kittle's superb performance earned him a promotion to Triple A in 1982. At Edmonton he outdid his performance from the year before. He hit fifty homers and 144 RBI. He was named Minor League Player of the Year. At the end of the season, the Sox brought him up. He gained his first hit — a double — off of Frank Tananna of the California Angels. His first home run came against Frank Viola of the Minnesota Twins on the last day of the season.

Kittle became an instant hero in 1983 for the Southsiders. His power hitting earned him a spot on the All-Star Game held at Comiskey Park. "I was leading both leagues in home runs with twenty-one at the All-Star break," he said. The power hitter didn't hit a homer in the game, but he did knock out a single to help the American League win 13-5.

During the season, Kittle and Greg Luzinski made for a formidable home-run duo and helped lead Chicago to a Western Division crown. Kittle had thirty-five homers on the year and 100 RBI to earn the Rookie of the Year Award. He also led the league in strikeouts with 150. He said the strikeouts came because of "rookie-year abuse from umpires." In the playoffs Kittle had just two hits and missed a game after being hit in the knee. The Sox lost the series to Baltimore.

In the opening series of 1984, Kittle hurt his shoulder when he ran into the wall in right field. The Sox moved him to the designated hitter spot for awhile. "I shouldn't have played. I was playing hurt every day. I always played hurt," he said. Kittle still managed thirty-two home runs, but only seventy-four RBI as his average dropped to .215.

1985 was a mirror of the 1984 season for the Hoosier. Kittle ran into the outfield wall again to aggravate the shoulder injury. But he didn't dare complain about it. "If I had a belly-

"I shouldn't have played. I was playing hurt every day. I always played hurt." Ron Kittle

K

"I should have quit, but I just wanted to play." Ron Kittle

ache, I would get it from everybody," he said about his fellow players. He split the season between outfield and DH and hit twenty-six dingers with fifty-eight RBI. His average increased to .230, as the Sox finished third.

Midway through the 1986 season Manager Tony LaRussa got fired after the Sox got off to a 26-38 start. "I stood up for him in the newspaper and got traded for voicing my opinion," Kittle said. The Sox traded him to the Yankees for catcher Ron Hassey.

He wasn't in New York long before he began making waves. In a game against the Milwaukee Brewers, Kittle got the only hit in a loss. That led owner George Steinbrenner to call Kittle a "savior." Kittle remarked to the press that if Steinbrenner wanted a savior, "he should have signed Jesus Christ."

Kittle got off to a hot start in 1987 and was hitting over .300 when the assistant trainer kiddingly twisted his neck on the training table. The neck popped and pinched a nerve. "The neck killed me," he said. After hitting twelve homers in 159 at bats and forty days on the DL, Kittle was released by the Yankees.

The Cleveland Indians picked him up in 1988. "I was their insurance policy," Kittle claimed. The Indians used him strictly as a designated hitter. He knocked out eighteen homers in seventy-five games for the sixth-place Indians.

After the season Kittle became a free agent and signed with the White Sox again. He hardly played in spring training and at the beginning of the season, but then Dan Pasqua was injured. While playing first base, Kittle collided with Rob Deer and suffered a back injury. He was put on the DL for much of the season and had surgery on two lower discs in his back.

In 1990 he was leading the Sox in home runs and RBI when he was traded to the Baltimore Orioles for Phil Bradley. He appeared in just twenty-two games the second half of the season. "I was abused over there. I wasn't liked there," he explained. At the end of the season the Orioles exercised the buyout clause of his contract and let him go after paying him $100,000.

The Indians invited him to spring training in 1991, where he had a real good spring. However, the Indians decided they would have to pay him too much and let him go. He finished the spring with the Sox, who assigned him to Triple A Vancouver. After knocking in twenty-three RBI in seventeen games the Sox brought up him. "I was Bo Jackson's insurance policy," he said. The Sox released him after a month. In his last at bat, he hit a homer.

"I should have quit, but I just wanted to play," he said.

Kittle now lives in Valpariso, with his wife, the former Laura Cooke of Miller, and his daughter, Hayley, and son, Dylan. During the summer he does a TV baseball show. He raises money for charities through Ron Kittle's Indiana Sport Charities.

Chuck Klein (Charles Herbert)
Born: Oct. 7, 1904,

Indianapolis
Died: March 28, 1958, Indianapolis
6', 195, Outfielder
Philadelphia, NL, 1928-33
Chicago, NL, 1934-36
Philadelphia, NL, 1936-39
Pittsburgh, NL, 1939
Philadelphia, NL, 1940-41
BL, TR, .321, 1753 G, 6486 AB, 300 HR
1 WS, .333, 5 G, 12 AB, 4 H

Klein set several National League records during his fourteen-year career in the majors. He was inducted into the National Baseball Hall of Fame in 1980 and the Indiana Baseball Hall of Fame in 1981.

Klein's professional career began in 1927 with Evansville of the Three-I League. The following year he went to Fort Wayne of the Central League. He showed he could hit the long ball with twenty-six home runs.

1928 became his rookie year in the majors with Philadelphia. He hit .360 and knocked out eleven home runs in sixty-four games. That earned him a regular job in the outfield for the Phillies the following year, and he hit forty-three home runs. In one four-game stretch from July 13-16, he hit six home runs in the friendly confines of the Baker Bowl, which had a short porch (280 feet) in right field.

The following season Klein scored 158 runs in 1930 to break the NL record. He also broke the NL mark for extra base hits (107) in a season, hitting fifty-nine doubles, eight triples, and forty home runs.

The power hitter continued to terrorize pitchers and was named MVP in 1932, when he led the league in steals, total bases, and runs scored.

The following year he was named to the first All-Star Game in Chicago. He also won the triple crown as he hit twenty-eight homers, 120 RBI, and a .368 batting average. After the season, the Phillies traded him to Chicago for three players and $65,000.

At Wrigley Field, many of his flyballs became long outs, but he still hit twenty home runs on the year. The Hoosier was named to the 1934 All-Star Game and helped lead the Cubs to the World Series in 1935.

The Cubs traded him back to Philadelphia in 1936. The best game of his career came on July 10, when he clotted four dingers in a ten-inning game. He married Mary Torpey that year.

Klein's performance began to trail off in 1937. The Phillies released him in 1939, and he was picked up by the Pirates in mid-season. When he was released by Pittsburgh the next spring, the Phillies again picked him up. He played with the Phillies until 1941 and coached the following year with them.

His name is still in the record books. He holds the modern NL record in outfield assists with forty-four, because he knew how to field the caroms off the corrugated tin wall in the Baker Bowl.

Charlie Knepper (Charles)
Born: Feb. 18, 1871, Anderson
Died: Feb. 6, 1946, Muncie
6'4", 190, Pitcher

K   Charlie Knepper

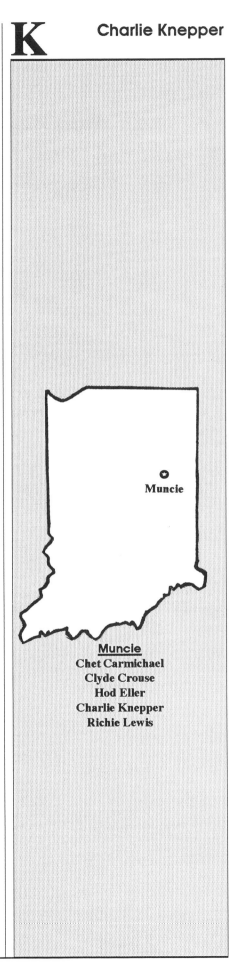

Muncie

Muncie
Chet Carmichael
Clyde Crouse
Hod Eller
Charlie Knepper
Richie Lewis

K

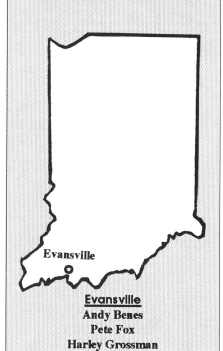

Evansville

Cleveland, NL, 1899
TR, 4-22, 5.78 ERA, 27 G
BR, .135, 89 AB, 12 H

Punch Knoll (Charles Elmer)
Born: Oct. 7, 1881, Evansville
Died: Feb. 8, 1960, Evan-
sville
5'7", 170, Outfielder,
catcher, first baseman
Washington, AL, 1905
TR, BR, .213, 79 G, 244 AB

Hub Knolls (Oscar Edward)
Born: Dec. 18, 1883, Val-
paraiso
Died: July 1, 1946, Pitcher
6'2", 190
Brooklyn, NL, 1906
TR, 0-0, 3.86 ERA, 2 G
BR, 1.000, 1 AB, 1 H

**Bruce Konopka (Bruno
Bruce)**
Born: Sept. 16, 1919, Hammond
6'2", 190, First baseman,
outfielder
Philadelphia, AL, 1942-43,
46
BL, TL, .238, 45 G, 105 AB

Konopka spent parts of three
seasons with the Athletics before
signing with the Atlanta Crack-
ers in January 1947. Atlanta
returned him to Philadelphia in
May 1947 and the Athletics
released him.

**Clarence "Big Boy" Kraft
(Clarence Otto)**
Born: June 9, 1887,
Evansville
Died: March 26, 1958, Fort
Worth, Texas
6', 190, First baseman
Boston, NL, 1914

TR, BR, .333, 3 G, 3 AB

**Steve "Lefty" Kraly (Steve
Charles)**
Born: April 18, 1929, Whiting
5'10", 152, Pitcher
New York, AL, 1953
TL, 0-2, 3.24 ERA, 5 G
BL, 7 AB, .000

Kraly had only half a season
in the majors, but he walked
away with one of the most prized
possessions in baseball — a
World Series ring. He was a
member of the 1953 Yankees,
which won its record fifth
straight World Series. He also
has a perfect game to his credit.

When Kraly was eight he
carried the glove and spikes for a
left-handed pitcher on a local
semipro team. "I just wanted to
become a baseball player and a
pitcher," he explained.

He played sandlot ball as a
child. Then the twelve-year-old
Hoosier joined a community
league and was picked for an
All-Star Team that went to play
a game at Comiskey Park for the
Chicago Tribune.

At age fourteen Kraly began
playing for Crows Athletic Club,
the semipro team he had admired
as a youngster. That summer he
hurled a perfect game! Many of
the players were much older than
he.

In his four years at Whiting
High School, Kraly lettered in
baseball, basketball, and track.
Although he disliked track, he
now admits it was the best sport
for building up his legs and
endurance.

Kraly was given a baseball
and basketball scholarship to
Indiana University. When it

came time for tryouts, he and nine other freshmen were told by the coach that the squad was already picked. Even though the team had a dismal record the year before, Kraly wasn't considered for the pitching staff. The players challenged the coach to a game, but the coach refused. "We went to the athletic director and he said, 'Why not!' We had our bags packed. We were going to leave anyway," he explained. He ended up striking out seventeen batters to lead the freshmen over the varsity squad 10-0.

Kraly left IU and signed a contract with the New York Yankees. He received a $4,000 signing bonus in 1948 and $90 a month to pitch for Class D Independence, Mo. Mickey Mantle was one of his teammates.

The following year he went to Class C Joplin. Then the U.S. Army drafted him for the Korean Conflict. The soldier returned to baseball in 1953 to play Class A ball at Binghamton, N.Y. He got off to a hot start and by the end of July was 19-2 with a league-leading 2.08 ERA. The Yankees decided to call him up. "I really didn't want to go, in essence, because I wanted to win thirty games in the minors. I was shocked when I was told where I was going," he explained. He was named Most Valuable Player for the Eastern League.

One day when Kraly was loosening up his arm in the Yankee bullpen, he unexpectedly got called into the game. "I was scheduled to start a few days later in Washington. I was just tossing the ball around," he

recalled. "Lefty" responded by shutting down the White Sox and getting credited with the save.

The Hoosier hurler started three games and relieved in one for the Yankees, who cruised to their fifth straight pennant. In the series Kraly was scheduled to start the fifth game, but his home back in Indiana caught fire and the Yankees took him out of the lineup. The Yanks still won the series and Kraly was given a ring.

During a spring training game in 1954, Kraly was pitching against St. Louis when he hurt his arm throwing a curveball. The damaged tendon cost him his job on the Yankees and he ended up going to Kansas City, a Class AAA team.

The following year the minor league franchise moved to Denver and Kraly had a winning record. "I was being recalled by the Yankees and pitched a game against Minneapolis. I went out in the top of the ninth and couldn't get the ball to the plate," he said. His arm puffed up like a balloon. He was sent to New Orleans where doctors discovered a blood clot to the bone. He was given nine shots to relieve the problem.

The Yankees never called upon Kraly and he spent the rest of his baseball days in the minors. In 1959 he went to play for Nashville for $1 just so he could play. "I made more money there than I ever did with the Yankees," he admitted. He had a 13-2 record.

In 1961 the expansion New York Mets bought his contract,

K

Steve Kraly

"I was being recalled by the Yankees and pitched a game in Minneapolis. I went out in the top of the ninth and couldn't get the ball to the plate." Steve Kraly

93

Jaynie Krick

Abbreviations

AA — American Association
AAGPBL — All-American Girls Professional Baseball League
AB — at-bats
BB — bats both
BL — bats left
BR — bats right
ERA — earned-run average
FL — Federal League
G — games
IP — innings pitched
K — strikeout
LCS — League Championship Series
NA — National Association
NL — National League
NNL — Negro National League
PL — Player's League
SHO — shutouts
TL — throws left
TR — throws right
UA — Union Association
WS — World Series

but he decided to retire. "Baseball was changing. I had to put my family first," he said.

Kraly had a "live fastball" and also threw a curveball, changeup, and screwball. "The secret is to throw the curve on 3-2," he said.

He went to work for IBM and had a twenty-nine-year career with the company. Now retired, he is the scorekeeper for the Binghamton Mets, a Class AA team of the New York ballclub.

He is married to Irene Horton of Harpersville, N.Y. They have four children: Kathleen, Steven, Thomas, and Robert. Thomas is a varsity high school baseball coach and Steven gave baseball a shot until his junior year in college.

Jaynie Krick
Born: Auburn
Pitcher
AAGPBL, 1949-52
Grand Rapids, AAGPBL, 1952

Bob "Red" Larmore (Robert McCahan)
Born: Dec. 6, 1896, Anderson
Died: Jan. 15, 1964, St. Louis, Mo.
5'10", 185, Shortstop
St. Louis, NL, 1918
TR, BR, .286, 4 G, 7 AB

Wayne LaMaster (Wayne Lee)
Born: Feb. 13, 1907, Speed
Died: Aug. 4, 1989
5'8", 170, Pitcher
Philadelphia, NL, 1937-38
Brooklyn, NL, 1938
TL, 19-27, 4 SV, 5.83 ERA, 71 G, 2 SHO
BL, .234, 107 AB, 25 H

Don Larsen (Don James)
Born: Aug. 7, 1929, Michigan City
6'4", 225, Pitcher
St. Louis, AL, 1953
Baltimore, AL, 1954
New York, AL, 1955-59
Kansas City, AL, 1960-61
Chicago, AL, 1961
San Francisco, NL, 1962-64
Houston, NL, 1964-65
Baltimore, AL, 1965
Chicago, NL, 1967
TR, 81-91, 3.78 ERA, 412 G
BR, .242, 596 AB, 144 H, 14 HR
5 WS, 4-2, 2.75 ERA

Larsen's perfect game in the 1956 World Series may have been the greatest World Series performance ever. It was a bright spot in a roller-coaster career.

Though Don was born in Indiana, Larsen's family moved to California during his youth and he finished high school there. He began his professional baseball career in 1947 in Aberdeen, S.D. He spent six years in the minors, then broke into the majors with the St. Louis Browns in 1953. He went 7-12 in his first season. A good hitter, Larsen set a Major League record for consecutive hits (7) by a pitcher.

In 1954 the franchise moved to Baltimore. Larsen didn't get much run support from the lowly Orioles and ended up with a 3-21 record to lead the league in losses. During the off-season, he was part of an eighteen-player trade with New York. His performance improved dramatically there though, and he was 9-2 with a 3.06 ERA in 1955.

During spring training in 1956, Larsen smashed up a car at 5:30 one morning. "Man [Larsen] was either out too late or up too early," manager Casey Stengel told reporters. Larsen had broke curfew. During the 1956 campaign, he worked on a no windup deliver to improve his effectiveness and control and ended the season with a 11-5 record.

Larsen started the second game of the World Series against Brooklyn with a wild performance. After walking four batters, he was pulled in the second inning.

In Game Five the Yankees called upon the right-hander again. It was a pivotal game as the series was tied at two games apiece. A crowd of 64,519 crammed into Yankee Stadium on a chilly Monday afternoon to watch the contest between the two New York teams. A hitters' breeze blew out to left field.

Using the abbreviated

L

Don Larsen was perfect at the right time.

L

windup to hide the ball better, Larsen struck out Junior Gilliam to open the game. Then he nearly walked Pee Wee Reese before gunning him down.

The perfect game nearly ended in the second inning. Jackie Robinson smashed a liner down to third base which Andy Carey couldn't handle. It went off Carey's glove to Gil McDougald, who threw out Robinson by a half step at first.

In the third inning, Larsen continued his pinpoint control and struck out Roy Campanella. Then opposing pitcher Sal Maglie hit a little liner that Mickey Mantle had to hustle to get.

Larsen got behind in the count to Duke Snider in the fourth inning, and Snider almost made him pay for it by hitting a home run — foul. After he retired Snider, thoughts of a perfect game started entering the minds of announcers and fans alike.

The Yankees took a little pressure off Larsen in the bottom of the fourth when Mantle hit a homer to put the Yankees ahead 1-0. It was the first hit for New York.

Hodges took Larsen deep in the fifth inning, but Mantle backhanded the fly in left center. Larsen breezed through the sixth. The Yankees added another run in the bottom half of the inning. The pressure of a perfect game began to effect Larsen, who ducked into the runway between innings to catch a quick smoke.

"You can just feel the tension in Yankee Stadium," said announcer Bob Wolff of WINS radio at the beginning of the eighth inning. "The drama rises as this game progresses."

By the ninth inning the fans were on the edge of their seats and cheered at every strike thrown. The last batter to face Larsen in the game was pinch-hitter Dale Mitchell, a left-hander. "He really scared me," Larsen said later. "I knew how much pressure he was under. He must have been paralyzed. That made two of us."

Mitchell was called out on strikes by umpire Babe Pinelli, calling his last game, to put the icing on the perfect cake. Catcher Yogi Berra leaped on Larsen and the rest of the Yankees mobbed the pitcher.

After the former Hoosier retired from the game, he said: "I still find it hard to believe I really pitched the perfect game. It's almost like a dream, like something happened to somebody else."

Larsen's success on the mound continued for a couple of years before going south in 1959 as his ERA dipped to 4.33 and his record to 6-7. The Yankees traded him Kansas City after the 1959 season. His career hit bottom in 1960 as he was 1-10. In 1961 the Athletics dealt him to the White Sox, where he was 7-2 the rest of the season.

Larsen went over to the National League with San Francisco in 1962 and had stops in Houston and Baltimore before his up-and-down career ended with the Chicago Cubs in 1967.

During his career, Larsen was used sixty-six times as a

"I still find it hard to believe I really pitched the perfect game. It's almost like a dream, like something happened to somebody else." Don Larsen

pinch hitter and knocked out fourteen home runs. He distinguished himself better at the plate than in front of it. Had it not been for the perfect game, Larsen would likely be remembered as an average pitcher.

Danny Lazar (John Dan)
Born: Nov. 14, 1943, East Chicago
6'1", 190, Pitcher
Chicago, AL, 1968-69
TL, 0-1, 5.56 ERA, 17 G
BL, .000, 6 AB, 0 H

Don Leppert (Donald George)
Born: Oct. 19, 1931, Indianapolis
6'2", 220, Second baseman
Pittsburgh, NL, 1961-62
Washington, AL, 1963-64
BR, TR, .229, 190 G, 532 AB, 15 HR

Leppert didn't hit many home runs in his short career, but he made them count. He was a member of the 1963 All-Star Team.

At Wabash College, he was known more in track than in baseball. He threw the shotput and discus. Leppert signed in 1955 with the Milwaukee Braves and was assigned to Evansville.

After six years in the minors, Leppert broke into the majors in 1961. He became the twentieth player to hit a home run in his first at-bat on June 20.

He was traded to the Washington Senators in 1963. On April 11 he hit three consecutive homers in Robert Kennedy Stadium.

After baseball, the Indianapolis native went into the insurance business in Greenwood.

Richie Lewis (Richie Todd)
Born: Jan. 25, 1966, Muncie
5'10", 175, Pitcher
Baltimore, AL, 1992
Florida, NL, 1993
TR, 7-4, 3.86 ERA, 59 G

After years of suffering from a mysterious elbow problem, Lewis finally broke into the majors in 1992 and was drafted by the expansion-franchise Florida Marlins. He had many pitching and stealing records while in high school.

Lewis was four when he began playing T-Ball. At seven he was in Little League playing the infield and pitching. "I had a gun! I didn't know where it was going though," the right-hander admitted. Lewis' baseball skills were always ahead of those boys his age, so he lied about his age in order to play with the older boys.

After Little League, he played Babe Ruth and American Legion ball. At Muncie South High School, where his father was the baseball coach, Lewis lettered in football, basketball, and baseball. As a junior, he played wide receiver on the football team and was named All-State. On the baseball diamond, he hurled three no-hitters as a junior and a total of five during his high school career to rank him in the top five in the state record book in both categories. Even more remarkable was his record of striking out twenty batters in a seven-inning game. The fleet-footed player was a prolific base stealer and recorded 107 swipes, third best in state

Indiana High School Record Book

BASES ON BALLS IN A CAREER
1. 111 — Mike Shelburne
2. 110 — *Richie Lewis*

STOLEN BASES IN A CAREER
1. 154 — Brian Hicks
2. 145 — Greg Yeend
3. 107 — *Richie Lewis*

STRIKEOUTS IN A GAME (7 innings)
1. 22 — Danny Gunn
2. 21 — Rich Spanton
3. 20 — *Richie Lewis*

NO-HITTERS IN A SEASON
1. 4 — Dave Highmark
2. 4 — Marvin Julien
3. 4 — Jon Boothe
4. 3 — *Richie Lewis*

NO-HITTERS IN A CAREER
1. 8 — Marvin Julien
2. 7 — Dave Highmark
3. 6 — Steve Snyder
4. 6 — Ben Kraszyk
5. 6 — Pat Underwood
6. 5 — *Richie Lewis*

PUTOUTS & ASSISTS IN A CAREER
1. 391 — Steve Hartly
2. 385 — Ron Smith
3. 385 — Jon Hershburger
4. 367 — Doug Schreiber
5. 359 — Shane Kemerly
6. 350 — *Richie Lewis*

Glenn Liebhardt

L

Richie Lewis has overcome his injuries to make it to the majors.

history.

After he graduated in 1984, he decided to attend Florida State University on a scholarship. Off the field, Lewis majored in telecommunications for a possible career in broadcasting after baseball. On the field he was progressing fine and mowing down college players. In a game against UNC-Charlotte, he struck out twenty-two. "The Little Man," as he was called in college, helped FSU reach the College World Series in 1986 with his fifteen wins. But he threw too much. "I threw myself out," he added. He started experiencing elbow problems, which lowered him to a second-round pick by the Montreal Expos in June 1987 for a $100,000 bonus.

The Hoosier went to Class AA Jacksonville in 1988, where he started in twelve games and pitched well (5-3, 3.38 ERA) before his elbow problems cropped up again.

In 1989 he was still with Jacksonville and started seventeen games, earning a 5-4 mark and 2.58 ERA. His elbow was still giving him problems.

Lewis went down to Class A West Palm Beach to start the 1990 season before he was sent back to Jacksonville later. The elbow still bothered him. In 1991 he was shipped to Double A ball at Harrisburg, Pa., where he appeared mainly in relief. After a 6-5 record in twenty-four appearances, he was sent to the Indianapolis Indians. After five games in Indianapolis, Montreal dealt him to the Baltimore Orioles for Chris Meyers, a first-round pick. Baltimore assigned

him to Rochester, N.Y.

Through the 1990 and 1991 season, his elbow problems persisted. During this period he never thought about quitting, but he was getting tired of the persistent problem. Tests confirmed that Lewis had a break in the middle of the bone! A "scope" was performed and a three-inch screw was put in the bone.

Lewis felt much better about the arm and was 10-9 with Rochester in 1992. In late July Baltmore called him up to the majors. His first game was on July 31 at Fenway Park. Wade Boggs was his first batter. He threw him an inside fastball that sawed off Boggs' bat, resulting in a infield blopper. The new pitcher held firmly in the rain-shortened game for his first major league victory.

When expansion draft time came in November, Baltimore didn't protect Lewis and the Marlins picked him in the second round. Lewis did some drafting of his own and acquired free agent Andrea Tette of Rochester, N.Y., to be his wife.

Lewis was used mainly in middle relief and was the set-up man for stopper Bryan Harvey in 1993. He compiled a 6-3 record with a 3.26 ERA.

Glenn "Sandy" Liebhardt (Glenn John)
Born: March 10, 1883, Milton
Died: July 13, 1956, Cleveland, Ohio
5'10", 175, Pitcher
Cleveland, AL, 1906-09
TR, 37-34, 2.18 ERA, 91 G
BR, .147, 190 AB, 28 H

Liebhardt was 18-14 for Cleveland in 1907. His son, who was born in Cleveland, pitched in the 1930s for the Philadelphia Athletics and St. Louis Browns.

Nemo Leibold (Harry Loran)
Born: Feb. 17, 1892, Butler
Died: Feb. 4, 1977, Detroit, Mich.
5'6", 157, Outfielder
Cleveland, AL, 1913-15
Chicago, AL, 1915-20
Boston, AL, 1921-23
Washington, AL, 1923-25
TL, BR, .266, 1258 G, 4167 AB, 1109 H
4 WS, .161, 13 G

One of the smallest Hoosier players to ever make the majors, Liebold earned his nickname from the comic strip character Little Nemo. He was an excellent fielder.

Marshall Locke (Marshall)
Born: Unknown, Indianapolis
Died: Unknown
Outfielder
Indianapolis, AA, 1884
.241, 7 G, 29 AB, 7 H

Kenny Lofton (Kenneth)
Born: May 31, 1967, East Chicago
6', 180, Outfielder
Houston, NL, 1991
Cleveland, AL, 1992-3
BL, TL, .299, 316 G, 1219 AB

Lofton was the runner-up Rookie of the Year in 1992 after a solid season with the Cleveland Indians. He set an American League rookie record by stealing sixty-six bases, and also led the league in steals in 1992 and 1993. He received one the richest contracts ever given to a young player before the 1993 season, a four-year deal worth $6.3 million.

Lofton was a four-year starter in baseball at Washington High School in East Chicago, where he was born and raised. After graduating, he attended the University of Arizona. He didn't play varsity baseball until his junior year, then played just five games. Still, he was drafted by Houston and went to Class A Auburn of the New York-Pennsylvania League during the summer, where he played in forty-eight games and hit .214.

L

Kenny Lofton

Kenny Lofton has put a lot of speed into the Cleveland lineup.

The following season he returned to Auburn for thirty-four games before being promoted to Asheville of the South Atlantic League.

In his first full year in the minor leagues in 1990, he played at Class A Osceola of the Florida State League. After hitting .355 in May, he was named to the league's All-Star Team.

He started the 1991 season at Triple A Tucson and led the Toros in at-bats, runs, hits, triples, and stolen bases.

The Hoosier's excellent performance earned him a callup to the Astros on Sept. 14 and he was put in the lineup that same day against the Cincinnati Reds. His first big-league hit was a single off Randy Myers. He went 3-for-4 and scored three runs in the game. In twenty games with Houston the rest of the year he hit .203.

In December Houston traded him to Cleveland. After spring training in 1992, the Indians brought him up to play centerfield. Enjoying an outstanding rookie season, he led the American League in stolen bases with sixty-six. His swipes shattered the former league record of fifty stolen bases by John Cangelosi in 1986. Lofton was the first rookie to lead the league in steals since Luis Aparicio in 1956 and set a team record in stolen bases.

Lofton played most of the second half of the season with a broken hamate bone in his left hand. Following post-season surgery to repair the injury, Lofton was one of several young players the Indians decided to sign to long-term contracts.

Grover Lowdermilk (Grover Cleveland)
Born: Jan. 15, 1885, Sanborn
Died: March 31, 1968, Sanborn
6'4", 190, Pitcher
St. Louis, NL, 1909, 1911
Chicago, NL, 1912
St. Louis, AL, 1915
Detroit, AL, 1915-16
Cleveland, AL, 1918
St. Louis, AL, 1917-19
Chicago, AL, 1919-1920
TR, 23-40, 3.81 ERA, 122 G
BR, .131, 191 AB, 25 H

Grover was the older of the Lowdermilk brothers. He had a good fastball, but he couldn't control it. He walked 296 batters in 590 innings. Although a member of the 1919 Black Sox, Lowdermilk wasn't involved in the scandal.

Lou Lowdermilk (Louis Bailey)
Born: Feb. 23, 1887, Sanborn
Died: Dec. 27, 1975, Centralia, Ill.
6'1", 180, Pitcher
St. Louis, NL, 1911-12
TR, 4-5, 3.38 ERA, 1 SV, 20 G
BL, .136, 22 AB, 3 H

The younger of the Lowdermilks joined his brother on the 1911 St. Louis team. His brother was much more successful in the majors.

Harl Maggert (Harl Vestin)
Born: Feb. 13, 1883,
Cromwell
Died: Feb. 7, 1963, Fresno,
Calif.
5'8", 155, Outfielder
Pittsburgh, NL, 1907
Philadelphia, AL, 1912
TL, BR, .250, 75 G, 248 AB,
1 HR

Johnny Mann (John Leo)
Born: Feb. 4, 1898, Fontanet
Died: March 31, 1977, Terre
Haute
5'11", 160, Third baseman
Chicago, AL, 1928
BR, TR, .333, 6 G, 6 AB

Doris Marsh
Born: Elkhart
Pitcher
Fort Wayne, AAGPBL, 1945
0-2, 3 G, 17 IP

**Don Mattingly (Donald
Arthur)**
Born: April 20, 1961, Evans-
ville
6', 192, First baseman, des-
ignated hitter
New York, 1982-93
BL, TL, .309, 1560 G, 6173
AB, 209 HR, 999 RBI

Mattingly's train is steaming
toward the Hall of Fame unless
his career derails. The Most
Valuable Player of 1985 has
been named to the American
League All-Star team six times
and has won eight Gold Gloves
through the 1993 season.

Mattingly started racking up
records at an early age. The
Evansville Memorial player was
an all-star defensive back in
football and an all-conference
basketball player. But he shone

even brighter on the baseball
diamond. As a junior he led his
high school team to a state
baseball championship in 1978.
He hit two triples and drove in
two RBI to lead Evansville
against Blackford, 7-1, in the
championship game.

In his senior year he once
again took Memorial back to the
championship game. The young
ace from the Crescent City
started the game, but was relieved after giving up three runs
in four innings. He came back to
pitch again in the tenth inning,
but Evansville went on to lose.
He was honored with the L.V.
Phillips Mental Attitude Award.
Mattingly's considered the best
hitter ever in the Final Four
tournament and his name still
dots the Indiana High School
Record Book for triples and RBI.

The New York Yankees
drafted Mattingly in the June
1979 amateur draft. He was the
19th pick overall and went
straight to the Oneonta of the
Rookie League, where he hit
.349.

In 1980 he was sent to Class
A Greensboro and hit .358. That
earned him a trip to Double A
Nashville, where he hit over
.300. His steady performance at
Class AAA Columbus the
following year earned him a call
from the Yankees, and he played
in seven games and went 2-for-
12.

Mattingly split the 1983
season between Columbus and
New York, belting his first major
league homer on June 24. His
career minor league average was
a lofty .332.

1984 became his first full

M

Indiana High School Record Book

RBI IN A CAREER
1. 159 — Rob Coffel
2. 142 — Joe Luce
3. 141 — Guy Finch
4. 140 — *Don Mattingly*

TRIPLES IN A SEASON
1. 12 — Mike Deck
2. 10 — *Don Mattingly*

TRIPLES IN A CAREER
1. 25 — *Don Mattingly*

**Don Mattingly would like to
lead the Yankees to post-
season play.**

Don Mattingly

Myear in the majors and he made the most of it. The rookie was picked for the All-Star Team! Going into the final game of the season, he was two percentage points behind teammate Dave Winfield for the batting title. He went 4-for-5 and edged out Winfield on the last at bat to win the title with a .343 average. It made him the first Yankee lefty to hit over .340 since Hall of Famer Lou Gehrig hit .351 in 1937.

The Hoosier hit for power in 1985, connecting for thirty-five home runs and 145 RBI. He had a twenty-game hitting streak during the season, the longest of his career. Again he was named to the All-Star Team. He also picked up his first Gold Glove Award and he was named American League MVP.

In 1986 Mattingly continued to pound the ball. He set new club records for doubles (53) and hits (238) in a season. He also became the first Yankee since Gehrig to garner three consecutive 200-hit seasons. Again he picked up a Gold Glove and a spot on the All-Star team.

During the 1987 campaign, Mattingly got into a home-run binge in July. In an eight-game stretch from July 8-18, he hammered out ten homers to tie Dale Long's record streak in 1956. But he did have more homers than Long, so he set a record for the most dingers in an eight-game stretch. Mattingly continued the hitting streak of extra base hits to tie former Yankee great Babe Ruth. Ironically, on the night the streak ended, he tied the major league record of twenty-two putouts by a first baseman in a nine-inning game. During that phenomenal season he also hit six grand slam home runs! This gave him another Major League record.

For the next two seasons Mattingly continued to hit over .300 and collected thirty-seven doubles each season. He went to two more All-Star games and picked up two more Gold Gloves. He also tied a fielding record by leading American League first basemen in fielding percentage for four consecutive years.

Then back problems arose in 1990. It slowed the Yankee captain so much that he played in just 102 games. His batting average dropped off to a career low .256. His power numbers also dropped off to a mere five homers on the season. In fact, the following year he didn't hit his first homer of the season

Don Mattingly has invested some of his baseball money in this restaurant in his hometown of Evansville.

until April 23 after a 312 at-bat drought. He recovered to a .288 average and thirty-five doubles, but only nine homers. His numbers were similar in 1992. He picked up his seventh Gold Glove after the season.

Mattingly's injury woes appeared in the 1993 campaign again. He was put on the fifteen-day disabled list because of a muscle strain in his lower left rib cage. He recovered from that injury and, after the All-Star break, he returned to form. In a four-game stretch, he drove in nine runs and hit .579 to be named the AL Player of the Week for the first time in five years. He also went on a thirteen-game hitting streak to raise his average to .312. More importantly, the Yankee captain was helping his team fight for a pennant. Unfortunately, the Yankees fell short of a pennant, something the Yankee captain wants dearly.

Mattingly had surgery in November 1993 to reduce tendinitis in his right wrist. He earned yet another Gold Glove for 1993.

The Hoosier lives in his hometown of Evansville in the off-season and owns a restaurant, "Mattingly's 23." He has a wife, Kim, and three children, Taylor, Preston and Jordan.

While Mattingly's train is headed to Cooperstown, he'd first like to stop at the World Series.

Hal Mauck (Alfred Maris)
Born: March 6, 1869, Princeton
Died: April 27, 1921, Princeton

5'11", 185, Pitcher
Chicago, NL, 1893
TR, 8-10, 4.41 ERA, 23 G
BR, .148, 61 AB, 9 H

Rob Maurer (Robert John)
Born: Jan. 7, 1967, Evansville
6'3", 210, First baseman
Texas Rangers, AL, 1991-92
BL, TL, .120, 21 G, 25 AB

Maurer has been called up to the majors twice in September, but knee problems have hampered his progress in baseball. He began the 1993 season on the disabled list. In high school he was All-State in baseball and football.

Maurer began his baseball career by playing in Little League. He attended Evansville's Mater Dei High School and lettered three times in baseball and football and twice in wrestling. In his senior year he was all-conference in three sports, and during the summer he played American Legion baseball.

After he was graduated in 1985, he stayed in his hometown by attending the University of Evansville. His excellent play earned him All-Midwestern Cities Conference honors in 1987 and 1988 and a sixth-round selection by the Rangers in the draft. He went to Butte, Mont., and was the Pioneer League's top hitter with a .391 average — the highest average ever for a Ranger minor leaguer in a short-season league. That earned him a promotion to Charlotte in the Florida State League in 1989, where he hit .276. In the off-season, he coached the freshman

Rob Maurer's baseball future seems uncertain due to injuries.

wrestling team at his alma mater, where he wrestled once.

In 1990 he was with Class AA Tulsa and led the Texas League in slugging percentage (.578) and was second in home runs with twenty-one. The Evansville native played first base in the Texas League All-Star Game. During the season he suffered two injuries: a sprained ankle and tendinitis in his achilles heel.

1991 became a banner year for the Hoosier. As a first baseman for the Class AAA Oklahoma City 89ers, he was selected as the Rangers' Minor League Player of the Year and as the American Association's Rookie of the Year. He led the league in total bases (245), extra base hits (64), doubles (41), walks (96), slugging (.534), and on-base percentage (.420). Maurer also hit twenty home runs. He was named to the association's post-season All-Star Team and played in the AAA All-Star Game. The Rangers called him up on Sept. 6 and he appeared in thirteen games, starting twice as the designated hitter.

In 1992 he had another good year playing at Triple A with Oklahoma City. He finished third in the league in at-bats (493), doubles (34) and walks (75). He also led first basemen with a .994 fielding percentage with just seven errors on the year. Texas again called him up at the end of the season. He went 2-for-9 in eight games. In the off-season he underwent arthroscopic surgery to remove damaged cartilage from his right knee.

He hurt the knee again during spring training and went on the DL on March 27. He never played during the year and his future is in question.

He lives in Evansville and is married to the former Erika Inman.

Milt May (Milton Scott)
Born: Aug. 1, 1950, Gary
6', 190, Catcher
Pittsburgh, NL, 1970-73
Houston, NL, 1974-75
Detroit, AL, 1976-79
Chicago, 1980-83
San Francisco, NL, 1980-83
Pittsburgh, NL, 1983-84
TR, BL, .263, 1192 G, 3693 AB, 77 HR
2 LCS, 1 WS, .400, 5 AB, 2 H

May followed in the footsteps of his father, Merrill "Pinky" May, who played in the majors in the 1940s. He was a steady performer behind the plate for several teams in the fifteen years he played in the majors.

May was raised on a 140-acre farm and learned how to play from his father. "He really didn't push me. He was very supportive of it," said May. At age nine he joined the local Little League and played there for a year before his dad decided to sell the farm and manage a minor league team.

The family wound up in St. Petersburg, Fla., where May played the remainder of his Little League years. He pitched and played third, as his father had. In the summers the family would follow the father around the minor leagues. "We'd go every summer to where he was and I'd be a bat boy," May recalled.

May went on to play in a senior league, then American Legion ball in the summers. At St. Petersburg High School he played for the baseball team, but the facilities were poor and the school didn't have a field. "We didn't have a very good team," he added.

In his senior year he became a catcher for one game. That game was scouted by Pittsburgh scout Max Mackin, who liked May's performance so well he offered him a contract. May had a couple of college scholarship offers, too. His dad helped him with negotiations and May signed for $13,000, enough in 1968 to pay for his college tuition for four years.

After signing he went to the Rookie League in Bradenton, Fla. In the fall he attended Manatee Junior College. In 1969 the receiver moved up the Class A League at Gastonia, N.C. In 1970 he jumped up to Triple A at Columbus, Ohio. Pittsburgh called for him in September that year. His first hit was a pinch-hit single off of Reggie Cleveland of St. Louis.

1971 became his rookie year, as he made the club after spring training. The twenty year old was a back-up catcher to Manny Sanguillen. May caught thirty-one games and hit .278, as the Pirates won the National League East. He got to pinch hit once in the League Championships Series against San Francisco. In the World Series he made two pinch-hit appearances and collected a hit in the losing effort.

May's performance in 1972 was an instant replay of the year before, as was the Pirates. He had one of the best days of his career in a doubleheader in Atlanta, as he went 6-for-8. In the LCS against the Cincinnati Reds, he collected one hit in two at bats in a game he caught. The Pirates lost the LCS in five games to the Big Red Machine.

In 1973 May's role expanded and he caught nearly half of the Pirates games and hitting .269. But the Pirates decided to swap him to Houston for pitcher Jerry Reuss, who became Pittsburgh's most winning pitcher in 1974. May became the starting catcher for the Astros, hitting at a .289 clip. Although he got a starting role, he missed the success of the Pirates, who finished first in both 1974 and 1975. Houston finished last in 1975 and May's average dropped to .241.

The Astros traded May along with Dave Roberts and Jim Crawford to Detroit for Terry Humphrey, Gene Pentz and Mark Lemongello. May, suffering a broken ankle early in the season, played very little during the year. He rebounded the next year to become the Tigers' starting catcher. He found some power that year and hit twelve home runs. He had a similar year in 1978, as Detroit finished in the middle of the pack.

A younger Lance Parrish beat out May for the starting spot in 1979, so the Tigers decided to deal him to the Chicago White Sox for cash. May was the starting catcher before hurting his shoulder. At the end of the

M

season he became a free agent and signed with the San Francisco Giants, who were in need of a starting catcher.

During the strike of 1981, May had the best average of his career, hitting .310. Seventeen of his hits were doubles. His average dropped off in 1982, but he stroked nine homers on the year. He had to share the limelight with Bob Brenly in 1983 and in the middle of August the Giants traded him to Pittsburgh for Steve Nicosia. The Pirates had Tony Pena behind the plate, so May knew he would be a backup catcher the rest of his career at Pittsburgh.

The transplanted Floridian decided to retire after the 1984 season because his body was telling him so. "Everything bothered me," he admitted. "I wasn't having fun anymore."

The catcher took a year off from baseball before getting back on the horse again as a hitting and catching coach in the minor leagues.

In 1987 he returned to the Pirates as the hitting coach, where he has remained through the 1993 season. Ironically, he wishes he would have worked more on his hitting when he was in the majors. "I think a catcher at times neglects his hitting," he said.

He owes his success in the major leagues to his father. "In general, my dad helped me the most with my game. A lot of players said he was the best fundamental coach around," May explained.

May now resides in Bradenton, where the Pirates have their

Milt May is now a batting coach with the Pittsburgh Pirates.

spring training camp. He is married to the former Brenda Boyd of Palmetto, Fla. They have a daughter, Merrily, and son, Milton. His son is a catcher and third baseman at Manatee Community College and is interested in following in his father's footsteps. "That's what he wants to do. He's a pretty good little player," May said.

Perhaps there will be a third-generation May in the majors some day, as Pittsburgh has drafted Milton.

Merrill "Pinky" May (Merrill Glend)
Born: Jan. 18, 1911, Laconia
5'11", 169, Third baseman
Philadelphia, NL, 1939-43
BR, TR, 665 G, .275, 2215 AB, 4 HR

May led the National League in fielding at third base for three of the five seasons he played in the major leagues. His playing career was virtually ended by the war, but he went on to manage in the minor leagues for many more years. His son also became a major leaguer.

Growing up on a farm in Lake Oney near Corydon, May first got interested in baseball when he was six. At Center Elementary School he played town ball. The game involved a pitcher and catcher and several fielders. There were only two bases — home and a base in center field, about 150 feet away. "You hit a ball and you had to run from home plate to that base before the defense could get the ball and throw it in front of you," he explained. "If they threw it in front of you before you got to the base that was an out. You continued hitting until you made an out."

When he went into high school, he played baseball until the program was cut, which left him running track and shooting hoops. After he graduated in 1928, his brother paid Merril's way to Indiana University. In his freshman year he wasn't eligible to play varsity. But Everett Dean, who coached basketball and baseball, recognized his talents and had May playing varsity the next year.

During one college game in his sophomore year, New York Yankee scout Paul Krichell took an interest in May, who went 3-for-4. The only thing Krichell didn't like was his running ability. But May was quick to get a jump on the ball at short-stop or in the outfield. A couple of players gave him his nick-name, "Pinky."

At the close of the season, Krichell called for May. "I think I ran most of the way. I was out of breath when I got there," he said. May's coach helped him get a $1,300 contact. He now admits that he illegally received $350 during each of his last two years at IU. He received the remainder after college.

May reported to the Yankees' Class D team in West Virginia and was paid $350 a month. The following year he was promoted to Class C in Durham, but his salary dropped to $250. The players agreed to cut their salary in half in order for the league not to fold. Manager Bill Skift turned him into a third baseman.

Krichell was one of the coaches at spring training in 1935 and told him he would never make it past Class C because he was trying to pull everything. "That made me a little red ass," he said. "He woke me up. I said to myself, 'I'll show that guy I can hit the ball to right field.'" The move to third and ability to hit to right acceler-ated his career.

"My bulldog attitude helped me a little, too," Pinky admits.

He moved up to Class A ball in 1934 and Triple A the next year at Newark. He stayed at Newark for two years and went to Oakland in 1937. He was brought back to Newark in 1938. "You could only draft one player off a minor league club. After the third year, the Phillies took me," he said.

May pulled a muscle in spring training in 1939 and missed the first few games of the season before he broke into the majors. He doesn't remember his first hit. On the year he hit .287 with twenty-seven doubles and sixty-two RBI for the last-place Phillies.

In 1940 he bettered his average to .293, fielded flawlessly and was picked for the 1940 National League All-Star team. He struck out only thirty-three times on the year in 501 at bats.

1941 wasn't any better for the Phillies; they won only forty-three games. Pinky's average dropped off a bit to .267, but his fielding was excellent.

The world was at war in 1942 and Philadelphia was

"That made me a little red ass. He woke me up. In my mind I'll show that guy I can hit the ball to right field." Pinky May

107

Mfighting for its life as well. Pinky's batting average (.238) continued to drop for the second year in a row. He remembers one nightmare game in which he made three errors in one game. The game was played in St. Louis. "There was a ball hit down to me and I threw it low to first base for an error. And it wasn't too long later that another ball was hit to me and I fielded it and threw it to first base and it was low. That made me mad. So, I said that the next one wasn't going to be low. And about that time they hit another one down to me, and I threw the hell out of it over the first baseman's head into the right-field bleachers," he explained.

At the close of the 1943 season, May was drafted into the Navy. He played for the service all-star team in Hawaii. "The fields were very good. The playing conditions weren't very good, but we felt all right about it," he said. He was later stationed on the island of Tinian where B-29s were launched to bomb Japan.

After the war was over, he tried to mount a comeback to the majors, although by now his arm was dead and he was thirty-five years old. He was cut during spring training in 1946 by the Phillies. He decided to stay out of baseball the rest of the year.

The following year, fellow Hoosier Billy Herman was managing Pittsburgh and gave him a shot at making the team. "He agreed to take me to spring training with the Pirates and if I didn't make the club he'd try to place me as high as they could."

The Pirates offered him a managing job with the Class A Albany team. Instead of trying to make the team, May took the managing position.

May went on to manage minor league teams for the Cleveland Indians, New York Yankees, and Cincinnati Reds until the early 1970s. Now looking back on his career, he wishes he had tried to make the Pirates in 1947, because he would have been eligible for retirement pay had he made the team and played another game in the majors.

He moved to Bradenton, Fla., in 1959 where his son, Milt, grew up to become a player in the major leagues for fifteen years. His son is now the hitting coach for the Pittsburgh Pirates.

Pinky now resides in San Antonio with his wife, Jane Weaver, from Elizabeth. Their other son, Merrill Jr., and daughter, Mira Jane LaBeau, also reside in San Antonio. Pinky still gets requests for autographs and signs all of them.

Joe McCabe (Joseph Robert)
Born: Aug. 27, 1938, Indianapolis
6', 190, Catcher
Minnesota, AL, 1964
Washington, AL, 1965
TR, BR, 28 G, .174, 46 AB, 1 HR

McCabe was a most valuable player at Purdue University and was the second best hitter in the Big 10 Conference in 1960. A separated shoulder limited his effectiveness in the major leagues, so he became a pilot.

Raised on a farm in Advance, McCabe played catch with the other boys soon after he started school. "When I was a little kid I wanted to play baseball. I wanted to be on a bubblegum card," he remembers.

He began playing organized baseball when he was ten in the nearby Lebanon Little League. "I became a catcher, because nobody else wanted to be. I had a pretty good arm," he said. He became an All-Star in Little League before moving on to Babe Ruth and American Legion ball.

In his junior year of high school, his family moved to Lebanon. At Lebanon High School, he lettered in football, basketball, and baseball. When he graduated in 1956, he was offered a football scholarship by some small colleges, but the larger universities wanted the good hitting catcher. Also, the Detroit Tigers and Chicago White Sox showed interest in him, but neither would offer him any bonus to sign a major league contract. He decided to go to college not far down the road at Purdue.

In college he played freshman basketball before deciding to concentrate only on baseball. He started as an engineering student, switched to science, and graduated with a degree in education. In baseball he remained as a catcher and excelled. In his senior year he led the team in batting and finished second in the conference with a .425 average. He was named as the team's MVP and received All-American mention. "We had

six guys that signed major league contracts. Bernie Allen and I were the only players to make it to the majors," he explained.

The Hoosier receiver signed a contract with the Senators and received a bonus of $25,000, a large sum in 1960. McCabe was assigned to the Class D Erie, Penn., which won the New York-Pennsylvania League that year. "We had two guys out of prison. One was a Cuban and the other a Puerto Rican. We had some veterans, too," he said.

In 1961 McCabe was initially sent to Double A Nashville, Tenn., before dropping down to Class B Wilson, N.C. He hit over .300 and was named to the All-Star team in the Carolina League. He spent 1962 at Vancouver, where he once had a twenty-one-game hitting streak, a record that he thinks still stands today.

After spring training in 1963, McCabe was elevated to Triple A at Dallas-Ft. Worth. In July he suffered an injury. "I slid head first into second and my left arm went under the bag," he explained. He separated his shoulder, but he stayed in the lineup the rest of the game. He never went on the disabled list, either. Manager Jack McKeon didn't think much of the injury. "I got on the bad side of him, because I was dogging it. I couldn't even lift the arm hardly," he said. The injury severely affected his abilities.

1964 became his rookie season in the majors, as he went up to the Minnesota Twins (formerly the Senators) right

Joe McCabe got his wish and got his face on a baseball card.

Joe McCabe

Mafter spring training. He was a backup receiver to Earl Battey, an All-Star catcher. His first game came against the new Washington Senators. He started the second game of a double-header and got his first major league hit off Buster Narum. In one game, he was involved in a triple play and didn't realize it until he read about it the next day in the newspaper. To this day he can't remember how it happened. "I remember more about my days at Purdue than I do about the majors," he admitted.

The move to the big leagues also meant more air travel for McCabe, who had a fear of flying — aerophobia. "I was a white-knuckled flyer!"

At the end of June the Twins were mired in sixth place and not playing well. McCabe was hitting a measly .158. He heard rumors that he and Allen, his Purdue buddy, were going to be traded, but Allen got injured to squelch the deal. "They were going to shake up the team. They took the guys from the bench and sent us all to the minors," he explained. He went to Class AAA Charlotte, N.C., and didn't play much the rest of the season.

The Twins dealt him in October to the Senators for Ken Retzer. "I read it in the paper when I was at home," he recalled. "I felt like a modern-day slave." The trade spurred him to think seriously about an alternative career.

The Senators brought him up to the majors after spring training and he backed up Mike Brumley. He hit his only home run of his major league career at Cleveland off Jack Kralick. After playing in just fourteen games and hitting .185, he was sent down to Hawaii of the Pacific Coast League. Indianapolis also was in the league at the time. When Hawaii came to Indianapolis to play a series, the Indians declared Aug. 13 as Joe McCabe Night. The city of Lebanon gave him a key to the city, too. The game was played on Friday the 13th. "I took a foul tip and broke my finger," he said. The broken finger ended his season.

"I thought I was unlucky, but it turned out to be my luckiest," he explained. He decided it was time to change careers. He wanted to become a pilot, although he was "scared to death" of flying. "I said to myself that if I learned how to fly that I'd get over the fear."

He obtained his pilot's license in the off-season and decided to leave baseball in his exhaust. "I was more concerned with my whole life rather than what was going on at the time," he commented.

When he first became a pilot, he hung on to baseball by teaching the game at the Ft. Lauderdale Baseball School for seven years. Currently a pilot for United Airlines, he thinks he's the only pro baseball player ever to become an airline pilot.

In 1990 he married Anita Moore of Anderson. He has two children by a previous marriage, Robbie and Lisa, and two children with his present wife, Sheri and Todd Embry. He also has two grandchildren. "I've had two careers that most kids would give their right arm to do."

Tom McCarthy (Thomas Patrick)
Born: May 22, 1884, Fort Wayne
Died: March 28, 1933, Mishawaka
5'7", 170, Pitcher
Cincinnati, NL, 1908
Pittsburgh, NL, 1908
Boston, NL, 1908-09
TR, 7-8, 2.34 ERA, 25 G
BR, .140, 57 AB, 8 H

Al McCauley (Allen)
Born: March 4, 1863, Indianapolis
Died: Aug. 24, 1917, Wayne Township
6', 180, Pitcher, first baseman
Indiananpolis, AA, 1884
Philadelphia, NL, 1890
Washington, AA, 1891
TL, 2-7, 5.09 ERA, 10 G
BL, .251, 188 G, 677 AB, 2 HR

McCauley was a pitcher for Indianapolis in 1884. He left the mound to become a fielder for Philadelphia and Washington.

Lloyd McClendon (Lloyd Glenn)
Born: January 11, 1959, Gary
6', 212, Catcher, first basman, outfielder
Cincinnati, NL, 1987-88
Chicago, NL, 1989-90
Pittsburgh, NL, 1990-93
BR, TR, .245, 519 G, 1112 AB, 31 HR
3 LCS, .625, 16 AB

McClendon has become one of the highest paid platoon players currently in Major League Baseball. He tied a League Championship Series record in 1992 for consecutive hits. His ability to play several positions has proven valuable to the teams he's played with in his seven seasons in the majors.

As early as seven, McClendon wanted dearly to play in Little League. "I remember my disappointment in not being able to play because I was too young," he recalled. He finally got his chance to play at age nine and by the time he was ten he was beginning to excel at the game. He started displaying home run power and became an all-star pitcher and catcher the final two years of Little League in Gary.

At age twelve his Little League All-Star team made it to the Little League World Series in Williamsport, Pa. Although his team lost to Taiwan in the final game, McClendon went 5-for-5 in the series. All were home runs! He drove in ten RBI in two games. Taiwan pitchers were smart to intentionally walk him three times in the final game.

At Gary Roosevelt High School, McClendon lettered in football, basketball, and baseball. In the summers he played in the Senior League for the Anderson Company. "My pitching days were pretty much over by those days," he explained. He caught and played third base.

By the time he was sixteen he joined the Steel City Giants, a semipro team in a league filled with ex-major leaguers much older than he. His play there got

M   Lloyd McClendon

Lloyd McClendon

Lloyd McClendon has proven to be a versatile player.

Mthe attention of big league scouts. In his senior year he led his high school team into the state regionals and was named to the All-State team.

His performance on the field earned the 1977 graduate a baseball scholarship to nearby Valpariso University. Coach Emery Bauer told him it was important to learn to play other positions to enhance his chances at playing in the major leagues. McClendon learned to play anywhere on the field.

After his junior year, he was drafted by the New York Mets and signed for $12,500. He was assigned to Kingsport, Tenn., in the Rookie League. After fourteen games there, he was sent to Little Falls, Minn., for the rest of 1980. In 1981-82 he played for Class A Lynchburg, Va., where he clobbered eighteen home runs in 1982. In 1983, he was promoted to Waterbury. He spent the first half of 1984 with Vermont before going to Wichita, Kansas. After spring training with the Reds in 1985, he was assigned to Class AAA Denver, Colo. He played the next two seasons there and hit sixteen and twenty-four home runs, respectively. One of his best minor league games came against the Indianapolis Indians in the Western Division Championship. The Gary native collected four hits and scored four runs to lead Denver to a 9-5 victory.

He found himself on the opening-day roster for the Reds in 1987. The Reds traditionally play the first game of the season for the National League at Riverfront Stadium, and

McClendon got a chance to pinch hit in the game. "I'll never forget. I hit the ball and my legs felt like they were glued to the ground," he recalled A couple of days later in his first start, McClendon picked up his first major league hit off of David Palmer of the Atlanta Braves, a two-RBI double. After hitting only .208 in forty-five games, McClendon was sent by the Reds to Nashville, Tenn., for more work. But the following year he was back on the Reds filling in where he was needed. The Reds were competitive both years and fought for the West crown before settling for second place.

After the 1988 season, McClendon was traded to the Chicago Cubs, who assigned him to Triple A Iowa. He hit .321 in Iowa before the Cubs bought him up in mid-season. In his first at bat in a Cub uniform, he hit a three-run homer to win the game. He filled in at catcher and first base in helping the Cubs to a Eastern Division title with his twelve homers forty RBI, his most productive year in the majors. "That was a team that wasn't suppose to win. We went out and played with a lot of heart and a lot of soul. That was very gratifying," he explained.

He hit only one home run for the Cubs the following year, but what a clout — his first grand slam on April 17. Near the end of the 1990 season the Cubs dealt him to Pittsburgh, which won the division title that year. The Pirates continued their winning ways in 1991, as McClendon played in eighty-five games and contributed with a .288 average.

This Hoosier has had his share of injuries over the years, but nothing major enough to keep him out of the lineup for long. His worst injury came during spring training in 1992 when he dislocated his shoulder. But by the time the season started he was ready. The injury may have been the reason his numbers were down in 1992, but he still hit .253 and aided the Pirates to their third divisional crown in a row. He hit .727 in the LCS against Atlanta pitching. He had eight straight hits for an LCS record.

Before spring training in 1993, the Pirates signed him to a two-year contract for $750,000 a year. "As far as utility players are concerned, I feel I'm getting paid right at the top of the list and that's an asset to my character and the belief the Pirates have in my character," he commented.

1993 looked like a rebuilding year for the Pirates during spring training in Bradenton, Fla., with a lot of new faces. McClendon thought his role may be expanding with the club in 1993. "I've been fortunate to play for a guy like Jim Leyland, who's a class act. I might add that his staff is at the top of the class. They truly care about the players and the families," he said. In 1993, he saw action in 88 games and had eleven doubles.

McClendon attributes his success in baseball to his late father, Grant McClendon. "It wasn't so much what he taught me on the field but the things he taught me off the field—about

learning how to win and how to lose," he explained. "There's too much emphasis on winning, not enough emphasis on what the game can teach you about life."

The Hoosier player now resides in Merrillville in the off season with his wife, Ingrid Scott of Gary, and his two children, Schenell and Bo. His five-year-old son is just now getting into the game, but Dad is not going to push him. "I think a lot of parents put too much pressure on their kids and expect too much out of them," he said.

About his future, the McClendon said: "Maybe I'll manage some day. I really haven't made up my mind. I've had a lot of offers to stay in the game." The African-American is also concerned about racial problems in the area where he grew up. "It's kind of distressing to see all the problems that they're having in the Black community in Northwest Indiana. I'd like to have a hand in doing something about that."

Billy McCool (William John)
Born: June 14, 1944,
Batesville
6'2", 200, Relief pitcher
Cincinnati, NL, 1964-68
San Diego, NL, 1969
St. Louis, NL, 1970
TL, 32-42, 58 SV, 3.60 ERA
BR, 101 AB, 7 H, .069

McCool was the 1964 National Rookie Pitcher of the Year. The following two years he became the second-best relief pitcher in the league with twenty-one and eighteen saves, respectively. A knee injury in the 1966 All-Star Game altered his

M

"It's kind of distressing to see all the problems that they're having in the Black community in Northwest Indiana. I'd like to have a hand in doing something about that."
Lloyd McClendon

M

Billy McCool was the Cincinnati Reds stopper for a season.

pitching delivery and eventually ruined his pitching arm.

An uncle introduced him to the game when he was six. He started playing in the Lawrenceburg Little League as a pitcher when he was nine. "As a little leaguer, I was terrible," McCool remembered. "My only saving grace when I was young is that I had the same coach from Little League through high school."

After Little League, he played in the Kiwanis League for two years. During his teen years he was nearly untouchable, while playing in high school and an American Legion League. He pitched several no-hitters and began to make a name for himself.

McCool started trying out for the majors when he was fourteen. The Cincinnati Reds held a tryout camp every year at nearby Greendale. At the first camp, he struck out the three batters he faced. When asked about his age, he said he was fifteen — too young. The next year he did just about as well and said he was sixteen — still too young. When he was sixteen, he finally told the truth about his age and the scout accused him of lying! The Reds began following his progress.

His Legion team finished in the state finals every year he played with it. "That's were I started attracting scouts," he said. And the scouts were impressed with his fastball.

Nearly every major league team contacted him. The Philadelphia Phillies treated him to a 1961 World Series game in Cincinnati and offered him a $75,000 contract. Yet McCool wanted to finish his last year of Legion ball because he felt he owed it to his coach. He used the extra time to decide on what team he wanted to sign with. He narrowed the field down to the Phillies, Reds, and California Angels. "I asked for rosters to look at the left handers they had. I saw a lot of opportunity with the Reds," he said.

The Reds offerd him a signing bonus of only $7,500, but with a lot of incentives. The money didn't mean that much to him at the time. He just wanted to choose the team with the quickest route to the majors.

He chose the Reds and he went to spring training in 1962. Afterwards, he was assigned to the Class A Tampa, Fla. Although he had a low ERA in the league, his record was 5-13, because the team wasn't giving him any run production. "I walked into the manager and said, 'I quit!'" Instead of accepting his resignation, the Reds promoted him to San Diego, a Triple A team. He pitched better there, going 4-0. The Reds came to town for an exhibition game, and McCool got a chance to strut his stuff. He mowed down six Reds in three innings, and made an impression on the Reds staff.

The Reds wanted to bring him up to the majors at the end of the season, but McCool felt he had pitched enough innings during the summer. He wanted to give his arm a rest before going to Winter Ball. The coaches invited him to a hotel room in Cincinnati to try and convince him to pitch for the Reds in two days in Chicago, but McCool was firm on his decision. Manager Fred Hutchinson finally agreed with the eighteen-year-old youngster.

After spring training in 1964, the Reds bought McCool up to the majors as a relief pitcher. He sat on the bench for about two months before Hutchinson finally put him in a game. He gave up his first major league hit to Johnny Callison, but he gave up no runs.

More and more he got the call as the new left-handed stopper for the Reds, who were making a run at the pennant. They fell just short. McCool appeared in forty games, averaging a strikeout a game and 2.43 ERA. His record was 6-5 with seven saves. His performance earned him the rookie pitching award. He traveled to New York to receive the award in a special ceremony after the season ended.

McCool became the stopper the next year. The Hoosier recorded twenty-one saves in all, the second best total in the league behind Ted Abernathy of Chicago. His ERA went up to 4.29 and his record was 9-10.

In 1966 McCool was breezing along with an excellent ERA and was picked for the All-Star Game. While pitching in the All-Star game, he injured his knee. "I caught my spikes in the rubber and tore a cartilage in my knee," he explained. This was in the days before arthroscopic surgery, so the doctors fitted him with a fiberglass knee brace. The brace changed his delivery because the left leg would kick out quicker.

He decided to get rid of the brace, but this resulted in giving him arm problems. He still finished the year with eighteen saves, second in the league. His ERA improved to 2.49.

In the off-season the Reds obtained Abernathy from the Cubs and made him their stopper. Abernathy had a brilliant year, compiling twenty-eight saves with a 1.27 ERA. McCool's save total for the year was two! He made only thirty-one appearances and finished with a 3-7 mark and 3.43 ERA.

The next year McCool was injured again. A grounder was hit to him that he fielded cleanly, but his wrist locked up when he threw the ball to first and it sailed into the box seats. He was put on the disabled list for thirty days. He was never the same after that and picked up only two saves again. His ERA jumped to 4.94.

In 1969 McCool went to the expansion San Diego Padres. He led the team in saves with seven in fifty-four appearances. The Padres traded him during spring training the next year to St. Louis for Steve Huntz. He appeared in just eighteen games during the year and his ERA (6.14) reflected his wildness. The Cardinals sent him to the Kansas City Royals after the season ended.

The Royals, also an expansion club, assigned him to Omaha, Neb., their Triple A affiliate. McCool didn't like the manager, Jack McKeon. "We weren't the best of friends," is how he described the relationship. So he didn't stay long and

"I caught my spikes in the rubber and tore a cartilage in my knee."
Billy McCool

115

was dealt to the Minnesota Twins and was assigned to Class AAA Portland, Ore. After spring training in 1972, the Twins wanted him to go to Tacoma. He had just built a home and decided to retire.

After he retired from baseball, McCool became the sports director at WKDF in Dayton, Ohio. He now lives in Centerville, Ohio, with is wife, Carol, and three children: Angie, Megan, and Andy. "When I got out of baseball, I was done with baseball," he said. However, he still signs a lot of autographs.

Dave McDonald (David Bruce)
Born: May 20, 1943, New Albany
6'3", 215, Catcher, first baseman
New York , AL, 1969
Montreal, NL, 1971
BL, 33 G, .145, 62 AB, 1 HR

McDonald spent most of his professional career in the minors as a player and player/coach. His rookie baseball card is worth a lot of money, because he is teamed with New York Yankees catcher Thurman Munson.

When he was born, his father worked at a munitions plant in New Albany. Then the family moved to Grand Island, Neb., where McDonald grew up. At age four he picked up a bat and started swinging from the left side. "I was always a left-handed batter and a right-handed thrower," he explained.

Since his father had started the Little League program in the town, he fit right in. During his four years in the league, the young McDonald's team won the city championship several times with him behind the plate catching and hitting.

His high school didn't have a baseball team — it was too cold in Nebraska in the spring — so he played football and ran track. During the summers he played in a Senior League and later with the American Legion. After his senior year, he was given a football scholarship by the University of Nebraska, which would also let him play baseball in the spring. His father had been a professional football player with the Chicago Bears and Philadelphia Eagles, so everyone thought he was going to follow in his dad's footsteps. However, his Legion team did so well and went to the regionals where some scouts saw him. They were impressed and the New York Yankees offered him a bonus of $25,000, a lot of money in 1961. His dad encouraged him to sign because it was an easier route than playing football. He did sign, which ended his college playing days. "Back then if you were a pro, you couldn't compete in college athletics," he said. He disappointed a lot of townspeople.

After spring training in 1962, the Yankees sent him on a sixty-six-hour bus ride to Idaho Falls, Idaho for Class C ball. When the Rookie League season opened, he was shipped to Harlan, Ky. Then he went to the Class B League in Greensburg, N.C. His roommate happened to be a promising pitcher named Denny McClain. Being a catcher, McDonald sometimes went on

Dave McDonald got his day in the sun with the Yankees.

road trips with other clubs. Upon return from one trip, he found his car missing. "McClain missed his girlfriend, so he took my car and drove it to Chicago to see his girlfriend," he said chuckling about the incident.

McDonald rose slowly in the minors. "It was so hard to advance in that organization back then because they had so many good ballplayers," he explained.

In 1965 he switched from catching to first base because his glasses kept fogging up. Then in 1966 he began going to the major league spring training camp each year. "I was always the twenty-sixth man on a twenty-five-man roster," he said.

Finally in 1969 he got his chance at the majors. He had been on the Class AAA Syracuse team that had won the Governor's Cup. The Yankees called him up after the playoffs, along with Munson. His first major league hit came off John Hiller of the Detroit Tigers. He went 5-for-23 with the Yankees.

After spring training in 1970 he was again assigned to Class AAA. On May 15 the Yankees traded him to the Montreal Expos for Gary Waslewski. In his first at bat with the Expo's Class AAA Buffalo team, he homered off Rick Wise. The expansion Expos were still a growing organization at this time. "We were on a road trip and all of a sudden they said, 'Well, we moved the franchise. You aren't going home.' It was ugly!" The franchise moved from Tidewater, Va., to Winnipeg, Canada.

To make matters worse, the Expos traded him to San Francisco for Ron Hunt in December. Just before the end of spring training, the Giants shipped him back to Montreal.

1971 was a yo-yo season for McDonald. He began at Triple A, but the Expos decided to call him up after he got four hits off Expo pitching in an exhibition game against Winnipeg. He stayed a month and a half with the Expos before he was sent back to Winnipeg. At the end of the season he was again called back to Montreal. During the season he hit his only major league home run in Montreal.

At the end of the 1971 season he was traded to the New York Mets. He went to the Class AAA team at Tidewater as a player/coach for the next three seasons. The Mets offered him a managing job in Modesto, Calif., but he decided he wanted to settle down and raise his family of four daughters: Dawn, Deidre, Dara, and Danielle. He's married to the former Brenda Willis of Shelby, N.C.

McDonald finished a college degree and plans to retire from his truck driving job in a couple of years. He lives in Pompano Beach, Fla.

Jouette Meekin (Jouette)
Born: Feb. 21, 1867, New Albany
Died: Dec. 14, 1944, New Albany
6'1", 180, Pitcher
Louisville, AA, 1891-2
Washington, NL, 1892-3
New York, NL, 1894-99
Boston, NL, 1899

Dave McDonald plans to retire soon and will stay in sunny Florida.

M

Pittsburgh, NL, 1900
TR, 153-133, 2 SV, 4.07 ERA, 324 G, 9 SHO
BR, .243, 1098 AB, 267 H

Meekin's best year was in 1894 when he went 33-9 for New York. He also won more than twenty games in 1896 (26-14) and 1897 (20-11).

**Naomi "Sally" Meier
Born: Nov. 17, 1926, Fort Wayne
5'9", 148, Outfielder
Rockford, AAGPBL, 1946-47
Fort Wayne, AAGPBL, 1947-48
Chicago, AAGPBL, 1948
Racine, AAGPBL, 1949
Kalamazoo, AAGPBL, 1949
Fort Wayne, AAGPBL, 1950-51
BR, TR, .212, 450 AB, 240 H
(1946-48 stats)**

A top rookie in 1946, Meier's career ended because of a compound fracture of her right ankle during the 1951 season.

Meier manned left field for the Rockford Peaches in 1946 and hit .249, one of the best averages in the league. Her average dropped off to .153 the next season as she played sixty-eight games with Rockford and twenty-four with the Fort Wayne Daisies.

In 1948 Meier led the Chicago Colleens in batting average (.222), total hits, runs scored, and RBI. Then she went to the Racine Belles and Kalamazoo Lassies. The graduate of Central High School returned to her hometown in 1950 to play with the Daisies again.

In the twenty-first game of 1951 season, Meier slid into second and broke her ankle. She didn't play the rest of the season. She was shipped to the Muskegon Belles in 1952, but never played a pro game again.

**Butch Metzger (Clarence Edward)
Born: May 23, 1952, Lafayette
6'1", 185, Relief Pitcher
San Francisco, NL, 1974
San Diego , NL, 1975-77
St. Louis, NL, 1977
New York, NL, 1978
TR, 18-9, 3.75 ERA, 191 G
BR, 15 AB, .000**

Metzger won Rookie of the Year and set a major league rookie record of seventy-seven appearances in 1976. He tied another major league pitching mark and set another during his career. However, his bright future ended promptly two years later after he suffered shoulder tendinitis.

When Metzger was four, his family moved from Indiana to California. He remembered throwing a baseball around when he was six and he really wanted to play baseball when he was eight, but he was too young for Little League. "I was really heart-broken when I was told I couldn't play," he recalled.

The next year he began his baseball career in the Flora Little League, near Sacramento. He played just about every position. "I might have missed my calling as a catcher," he said. Metzger admitted he wasn't the best of Little Leaguers and didn't make the all-star squad until he was twelve. He advanced to Babe Ruth League and recalled being

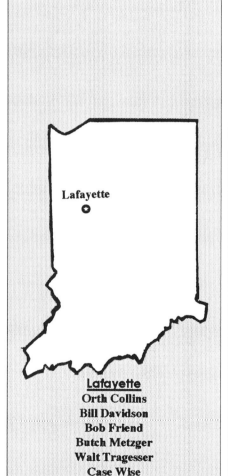

Lafayette
Orth Collins
Bill Davidson
Bob Friend
Butch Metzger
Walt Tragesser
Case Wise

overpowered by the older players in his first year.

At John F. Kennedy High School, he finally became serious about pitching in his junior year, but wanted to play football, too. "A few scouts called my father and put a bug in his ear about me becoming a baseball star, but not good enough to become a NFL player," he said. So, he quit football to concentrate on baseball.

The 1970 graduate was selected in the second round of the amateur draft by the San Francisco Giants. He had some scholarship offers, but he took the $27,000 signing bonus and went directly to the Rookie League in Great Falls, Montana. "I did terrible," he remembered. "I was 2-9. That was a humbling experience. In one game I didn't get past the second inning." However, Metzger was young and had a live arm with a fastball in the low 90s, so the Giants weren't about to give up on their investment so quickly.

The following year he began at Class A Decatur, Ill., in the Midwest League. Again he did poorly and went sent back down to the Rookie League when it opened in June. "That was a real heartbreaker for me, but it turned out to be a Godsend," he added.

He learned a valuable lesson about baseball in the Rookie League. "Nobody gives you a job. You have to take a job away from somebody," he said. He began to fight back and earned his way back to Decatur to begin the 1972 season. Two-thirds of the way through the season he earned a promotion to Double A Amarillo, Texas. He was put in the starting rotation right away and went 3-2 with a shutout.

Metzger started 1973 at Amarillo and moved up to Class AAA Phoenix, again about two-thirds the way through the season. It was a big step for the hurler and he stumbled to a losing mark. "You had to know more about pitching techniques," he explained. The hurler learned the techniques and recorded a 12-10 mark the next year. It earned him a September callup to the Giants.

He remembers his first game af if it were yesterday. "Ron Bryant didn't get out of the second inning in Atlanta. The call came down to the bullpen. I was so nervous. Charlie Fox waved for me to come in," he said. Men were on first and second with Dusty Baker at the plate and Hank Aaron on deck. Behind the plate there was the biggest TV camera I ever saw. The red light was on. I felt kind of numb," he said. He got Baker to pop out and walked Aaron before getting the next man out and escaping without giving up a run. Later in the month he picked up his first win.

During the winter of 1974, he was traded to the San Diego Padres. At spring training he was a casuality in the first cut and was sent to Hawaii of the Pacific Coast League. After compiling a 15-7 record, he again was called up in September. He again won a game.

In 1976 he went to spring training "on a mission to make the team." He not only made the

M

team, but he became the stopper. He mystified hitters and chalked up ten straight wins with an ERA under 1.00 before he picked up his first loss. The streak set of ten straight wins tied a major league mark for a relief pitcher. And his twelve straight wins at the beginning of a career set another record.

Batters finally began to get to the rookie hurler by the end of the season. "I realized nobody was that good. I didn't even know the hitters that well," he said. Still, he ended the year with a 11-4 record and sixteen saves.

During the winter the Padres acquired Rollie Fingers and Metzger was relegated to a set-up man for the future Hall of Famer. Soon he was dealt to St. Louis for John D'Acquisto and Pat Scanlon. "It was a blessing in disguise. I went from a fifth-place team to a first-place team," he said. He ended the season with a 4-2 record and seven saves.

At spring training in 1978 he butted heads with manager Vern Rapp. He called it a "personality conflict." Because of the conflict, training didn't go well and the Cardinals sold him to the New York Mets.

With New York he was ineffective and his ERA fell off to 6.57." I tried to do too much too soon. I had tendinitis in my shoulder. I should have told the manager. I tried to be the tough guy," he explained.

The Mets sold him to Philadelphia, who sent him to Triple A Oklahoma City. Even though he demonstrated he could still pitch, he wasn't called up the rest of the year.

In 1979 the Phillies wouldn't give him a contract and he went to spring training as a non-roster player. After getting ripped by Pittsburgh in a spring game, he got his release. He joined a new league called the Inter-American League, which had teams in the Caribbean. After a month, the league went bankrupt. He is still owed $5,000!

Metzger didn't have an agent, so he wrote about twenty teams to try and comeback to the majors. The Milwaukee Brewers and Atlanta Braves offered him a contract and he signed with the Braves, who assigned him to Triple A Richmond. He led the team in saves. Near the end of the season he didn't make the Braves, so he asked Aaron, a minor league official for the club, if he was in Atlanta's plans. A couple of days later Aaron told him he wasn't in the Braves' crystal ball, so Metzger asked for his release. It was the end of his career.

Now the forty-one-year-old firefighter plays semipro ball with actor Kevin Costner for the Sacramento Smokies. He's also a scout for the California Angels. He is married to the former Cynthia Henninger of Omaha and they have two children, Martin and McKenzie. He hopes some day that his son will be fortunate enough to make it to the majors.

**Jim "Rifle Jim" Middleton
(James Blaine)
Born: May, 28, 1889, Argos
Died: Jan. 12, 1974, Argos
5'11", 165, Pitcher**

"I realized nobody was that good. I didn't even know the hitters that well." Butch Metzger

New York, NL, 1917
Detroit, AL, 1921
TR, 7-12, 8 SV, 4.50 ERA, 51 G
BR, .119, 41 AB, 5 H

Don Miles (Donald Ray)
Born: March 13, 1936, Indi-
anapolis
6'1", 210, Outfielder
Los Angeles, NL, 1958
BL, TL, .182, 8 G, 22 AB

Not many players would ever think about returning to baseball after a four-year hiatus, but Miles tried.

The Ben Davis High School graduate played football and baseball at Indiana Central before being signed with no bonus by Brooklyn Dodgers' scout Stanley Feezle in 1956. After a couple of years in the minors with Kokomo, Victoria, and St. Paul, he was brought up to the majors in 1958. A leg injury sidelined the speedster and he was sent back to the minors.

After two more years in the minors, Miles retired from the game to become the overseer of a million-dollar ranch. Four years later he decided to return to baseball. He shed ninety pounds to get back into shape and signed with the Chicago Cubs for no bonus. The Cubs assigned him to Dallas-Ft. Worth. After hitting just .224, he was released in June 1965 to end his bid at returning to baseball.

Bruce Miller (Charles Bruce)
Born: March 4, 1947, Fort Wayne
6'1", 185, Infielder

San Francisco, NL, 1973-76
BR, TR, .246, 196 G, 553 AB, 136 H

Miller was a utility infielder with the Giants for four seasons.

At Columbia City High School, Miller lettered in baseball and basketball. During the summers he played Connie Mack and Stan Musial League ball. He helped W&W Gravel to the Indiana state and regional Connie Mack championships.

After high school, he went to play baseball at Indiana University. In 1969, his junior year, he hit .354 and was named All-Big Ten Conference shortstop and was voted the team's Most Valuable Player. During the summer of 1969, he played semipro ball with Sturgis, S.D., and batted .367.

He was first signed with the Chicago White Sox in 1970 and led the Northern League in defense at shortstop. Then in 1971, he went to the Southern League and made the Class AA All-Star Team. He became an All-Star in the Pacific Coast League in 1972 when he moved up to Triple A. The White Sox traded him to the California Angels for pitcher Eddie Fisher.

The following season he was sent to San Francisco, which assigned him to Phoenix. He didn't strike out until his 103rd official time at bat! The Giants finally called for the Hoosier on Aug. 4 that year.

The Giants sent him back down to Phoenix in 1974 and recalled him on June 3. He was put in the lineup immediately and went 4-for-4, his best game in the majors.

Abbreviations

AA — American Association
AAGPBL — All-American Girls Professional Baseball League
AB — at-bats
BB — bats both
BL — bats left
BR — bats right
ERA — earned-run average
FL — Federal League
G — games
IP — innings pitched
K — strikeout
LCS — League Championship Series
NA — National Association
NL — National League
NNL — Negro National League
PL — Player's League
SHO — shutouts
TL — throws left
TR — throws right
UA — Union Association
WS — World Series

M

Dyar Miller hopes to make it back to the majors as a pitching coach.

Miller had the defensive skills needed in the majors, but he had no power behind the plate. It took him 403 at-bats in the majors before he hit his first home run. "Now that got me believing I can hit Number Two," he said after the feat. He never did his second homer in his short stay in the majors.

Dyar Miller (Dyar K.)
Born: May 29, 1946,
Batesville
6'1", 210, Pitcher
Baltimore, AL, 1975-77
California, AL, 1977-79
Toronto, AL, 1979
New York, NL, 1980-81
TR, 23-17, 22 SV, 3.23 ERA,
251 G
BR, .250, 4 AB, 1 H

Miller began baseball as a catcher, but ended up on the other end as a pitcher. He was used primarily as a relief pitcher in the majors and is now a pitching coach in the Cleveland Indians organization.

The farm boy began building his arm at age five throwing a ball against the steps. Then his family moved to Missouri. "I was seven and listened to the St. Louis Cardinals on the radio. I wanted to be a baseball player," he said.

His family moved back to Indiana and he began playing organized baseball when he was twelve with the Knothole League in Napoleon. He started off playing shortstop and outfield. At New Point High School he lettered in basketball and baseball. He started pitching in high school and once struck out all but one batter in a game. The

high school played only seven games in a season, but he played more with the American Legion Post in Osgood.

He graduated from his class of fourteen students in 1966 and went to Utah State on a partial baseball scholarship. "They wanted me to play football, too," he said. He was a catcher in college and attended Utah State until the university dropped the baseball program in 1968.

Miller returned to Indiana to play for a semipro team in his old hometown of Batesville. The Philadelphia Phillies spotted him and signed him as a catcher for $1,500 on July 7. He went to Huron, S.D., and played in the Rookie League for three weeks before the Phillies decided they had seen enough and released him.

The Vietnam War was in full swing and he was 1A, so he joined the Air Force Reserves to avoid being drafted. Miller still wanted to play in the pros, so he turned to a distant family member in Cincinnati — Jim Frye. Frye was scouting for the Baltimore Orioles at the time. The Orioles signed Miller and he was assigned to Class A Stockton, Calif., after spring training in 1969. "I was the tenth pitcher — just barely made the team," he said.

He remembers a game during the year that probably launched his career. The Orioles came to play Stockton in an exhibition game. "I was well rested. I pitched the last four innings and struck out six batters to get the win," he said.

The following year he was

assigned to Class AA Dallas-Ft. Worth. In one game during the season, he pitched a no-hitter for seven innings in a game. He finished the season with a 12-10 record. But he was not so lucky the next year, as he ended up with a 3-8 mark. "It's tough going back to the same league," he explained.

In 1972 he stayed in the same league again, but Baltimore moved the franchise to Nashville, N.C. He was 4-2 on the year. However, he got his big break in the winter and went to pitch in the Mexican League. In one game he fanned eighteen batters on the way to a no-hitter. "That helped me get more recognition," he admitted.

The Mexican performance helped Miller make the move to Triple A. He went to Rochester, N.Y. He hurt his lower back during the season, an obvious setback. The hurler did go to winter ball again though. He rebounded the following year with a 14-8 record and the team won the Governor's Cup. "I pitched the final game and beat Scott McGregor," he said. In the winter Miller went to Puerto Rico to play Winter Ball again. Manager Frank Robinson started using him as a relief pitcher, which led him to a major league contract and assignment to the forty-man roster.

After spring training in 1975 he was pitching well at Rochester with a 5-0 record and seven saves in short relief when the Orioles called him up. Miller came into his first game on June 12 against the Oakland A's. The game was in the twelfth inning

and the score was still tied. He struck out Billy Williams to get out of the inning. The thirteenth inning wasn't so lucky for him: he gave up the winning run to Joe Rudi for his first loss in the majors. He rebounded for his first win against the Texas Rangers a short time later. Miller says now he enjoyed the season because Baltimore was "in the hunt." The Orioles finished second and he ended with a 6-3 record and eight saves with a 2.74 ERA. Hitters were baffled by his variety of pitches: slider, screwball, forkball, curve, and ninety-mph fastball.

Baltimore was in the hunt again the next year and Miller helped the team by saving seven games. In a game against the Boston Red Sox he gave up a single to Carl Yastrzemski before retiring twenty-one in a row for the win.

The following year the Hoosier got off to a bad start with the Orioles and had a 5.73 ERA when he was sold to the California Angels in mid-season. He became the set-up man to stopper Dave LaRoche. His ERA improved to a respectable 3.03 and he compiled a 4-4 record and four saves for the Angels.

Miller improved to a 6-2 record and 2.65 ERA in forty-one appearances in 1978. He'll never forget one game that Nolan Ryan pitched. Since Ryan was going to pitch on Sunday, Miller decided to stay out all night, since he figured he wasn't going to be needed. Ryan wasn't having a good day and losing 6-2, so Miller was brought in early. "They just about had to carry me

M

off the mound in the eighth inning," he said. The Angels won the game.

Not too far into the 1979 season, Miller was sold to the Toronto Blue Jays. The mid-season move didn't sit well with him and his ERA jumped to 10.80 in Toronto. "I was there about a month when they optioned me to Denver with the idea that Montreal would buy me. I went to Montreal spring training, but was released the last day and hooked on with the Mets," he said, explaining his travels.

The Mets made him a player/coach. He had a fine year for the fifth place Mets, 1.93 ERA in thirty-one appearances. The following year he started getting sick and didn't pitch as well, so the Mets released him at the end of the season. He called other teams, but couldn't land a major league contract, so he settled for a minor league contract with Class AAA Louisville, Ky. Then in 1983 he found out he had colon cancer and had surgery.

After that he wasn't effective on the mound, so he began a coaching career in the minors and instructional leagues. He's been with the St. Louis Cardinals, Chicago White Sox, Detroit Tigers, and now with the Cleveland Indians at their Triple A Charlotte club. "I threw an hour batting practice every day last year," Miller said.

During his coaching career in the minors he has seen about fifty players advance to the major leagues, including Joe McGrane and Mike Dunne. He helped Bobby Thigpen develop a

good slider. "That's the thing about coaching, it's real rewarding," he explained. "I naturally would like to return to the major leagues as a pitching coach. Then front office work later."

He is married to the former Bertha Jo Williams of Batesville, which he still calls home today. They have four children: Scott, Matthew, Christopher, and Sara Mae. Matthew is a pitcher at the University of Evansville.

Fred "Speedy" Miller (Frederick Holman)
Born: June 28, 1886, Fairfield
Died: May 2, 1953, Brookville
6'2", 190, Pitcher
Brooklyn, NL, 1910
TL, 1-1, 4.71 ERA, 6 G
BL, .250, 8 AB, 2 H

Ralph Miller (Ralph Joseph)
Born: Feb. 29, 1896, Fort Wayne
Died: March 18, 1939, Fort Wayne
6', 190, Infielder, outfielder
Phliadelphia, NL, 1920-21
Washington, AL, 1924
BR, TR, .248, 163 G, 557 AB, 3 HR

Roscoe "Roxy" "Rubber-legs" Miller (Roscoe Clyde)
Born: Dec. 2, 1876, Greenville
Died: April 18, 1913, Corydon
6'2", 190, Pitcher
Detroit, AL, 1901-02
New York, NL, 1902-03
Pittsburgh, NL, 1904
TR, 39-45, 5 SV, 3.45 ERA, 102 G

BR, .160, 288 AB, 46 H

After an excellent rookie season, Miller's career went south and he was traded.

Walt Miller (Walter W.)
Born: Oct, 19, 1884, Gas City
Died: March 1, 1956, Marion
5'11", 180, Pitcher
Brooklyn, NL, 1911
TR, 0-1, 6.55 ERA, 3 G
TR, .000, 4 AB, 0 H

Roy "Deedle" Moran (Roy Ellis)
Born: Sept. 17, 1884, Vincennes
Died: July 18, 1966, Atlanta, Ga.
5'8", 155, Outfielder
Washington, AL, 1912
BR, TR, .154, 7 G, 13 AB

Forrest More (Forrest)
Born: Sept. 30, 1883, Hayden
Died: Aug, 17, 1968, Columbus
6', 180, Pitcher
St. Louis, NL, 1909
Boston, NL, 1909
TR, 2-10, 4.73 ERA, 25 G
BR, .107, 28 AB, 3 H

Phil Morrison (Philip Melvin)
Born: Oct. 18, 1894, Rockport
Died: Jan. 18, 1955, Lexington, Ky.
6', 175, Pitcher
Pittsburgh, NL, 1921
TR, BB, 0-0, 0.00 ERA, 1 G

Mal Moss (Charles Malcolm)
Born: April 18, 1905, Sullivan

Died: Feb. 5, 1983, Savannah, Ga.
6', 175, Relief Pitcher
Chicago, NL, 1930
TL, 0-0, 1 SV, 6.16 ERA, 12 G
BR, .273, 11 AB, 3 H

Ray Mowe (Raymond Benjamin)
Born: July 12, 1889, Rochester
Died: Aug. 14, 1968, Sarasota, Fla.
5'7", 160, Shortstop
Brooklyn, NL, 1913
TL, BR, .111, 5 G, 9 AB

Billy "Muff" Muffett (Billy Arnold)
Born: Sept. 21, 1930, Hammond
6'1", 198, Pitcher
St. Louis, NL, 1957-58
San Francisco, NL, 1959
Boston, AL, 1960-62
TR, 16-23, 15 SV, 4.32 ERA, 125 G

Muffet had brief success as a stopper for St. Louis one season. He had more success as a pitching coach for several teams.

"I guess I held a bat in my hand as soon as I was able to walk," Muffet reportedly said about his baseball beginnings. Named in honor of Indianapolis 500 driver Billy Arnold, he signed with Cubs in 1949 with no bonus.
The following year he married.

After six years in the minors — he spent two years in the Korean War — Muffet finally was called upon by the Cardinals on Aug. 3, 1957, during a pennant race. He picked up eight saves in twenty-three appearances.

In 1960 he was dealt to Boston, where he was 6-4 with a 3.24 ERA. He record dropped to 3-11 the next year with Boston before dropping out in 1962 altogther. He became a pitching coach for several teams after his playing career ended.

Leo "Red" Murphy (Leo Joseph)
Born: Jan. 7, 1889, Terre Haute
Died: Aug. 12, 1960, Racine, Wisc.
6'1", 180, Catcher
Pittsburgh, NL, 1915
TR, BR, .098, 34 G, 41 AB

Dennis Musgraves (Dennis Eugene)
Born: Dec. 25, 1943, Indian-apolis
6'4", 188, Pitcher
New York, NL, 1965
TR, 0-0, 0.56 ERA, 5 G
BR, .000, 2 AB, 0 H

Art Nehf (Arthur Neukom)
Born: July 31, 1892, Terre Haute
Died: Dec. 18, 1960, Phoenix, Ariz.
5'9", 176, Pitcher
Boston, NL, 1915-19
New York, NL, 1919-26
Cincinnati, NL, 1926-27
Chicago, NL, 1927-29
TL, 184-120, 13 SV, 3.20 ERA, 451 G
BL, .210, 915 AB, 192 H, 8 HR
5 WS, 12 G, 4-4, 2.16 ERA

Inducted into the Indiana Baseball Hall of Fame in 1989, Nehf is remembered best for his World Series peformances. He is among the leaders in several series pitching categories.

Nehf began his professional career in 1913 with Kansas City. He also played with Sioux City and Terre Haute in the minors. After leading the Central League with 218 strikeouts and a 1.38 ERA, he joined the Boston Braves late in 1915.

The lefty went 17-8 in 1917 and topped National League pitchers in complete games (28) the next season. On Aug. 18, 1918 he pitched a twenty-one-inning game only to lose 2-0 to Pittsburgh.

After posting an 8-9 record in 1919, the Braves traded the winning pitcher in mid-August to the New York Giants for four players and cash. Nehf helped the Giants in the pennant race by going 9-2 the rest of the season, but Cincinnati still won out.

The following season Nehf won a career high twenty-one games, while losing a dozen. He helped the Giants to the pennant the next season with a 20-10 mark. He lost two World Series games to the Yankees in the series, but his team only scored one run in eighteen innings. However, he shutout the crosstown rivals in the seventh game to give the Giants the series. Nehf helped the Giants to a series victory again the next year when he won Game Five, the final game of the series.

In 1923, Nehf shut out the Yankees in Game Three of the World Series, but he lost Game Six. The following season he was 14-4 for the Giants and hit five homers, including two in one game!

The Giants sold Nehf to Cincinnati in 1926, where he pitched infrequently. The Reds released him the following season and Chicago picked him up. He rebounded for thirteen wins with the Cubs in 1928. His last major league appearance came in Game Four of the 1929 World Series.

Nehf is a career leader in World Series marks in walks (32), shutouts (2), complete games (6), games (12), losses (4), and innings pitched (79). He had thirty shutouts during his career. He also equaled the National League record for double plays (20) in 1920.

Bill Nelson (William F.)
Born: Sept. 28, 1863, Terre Haute
Died: June 23, 1941, Terre Haute
Pittsburgh, AA, 1884
Pitcher
TR, 1-2, 4.50 ERA, 3 G
BR, .167, 12 AB, 2 H

N

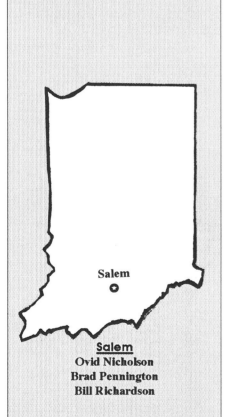

Salem

Salem
Ovid Nicholson
Brad Pennington
Bill Richardson

Joel "Sailor" Newkirk (Joel Inez)
Born: May 1, 1896, Kyana
Died: Nov. 22, 1966, Eldorado, Ill.
6', 180, Pitcher
Chicago, NL, 1919-20
TR, 0-1, 7.00 ERA, 3 G
BR, .000, 4 AB, 0 H

Ray Newman (Raymond Francis)
Born: June 20, 1945, Evansville
6'5", 205, Relief pitcher
Chicago, NL, 1971
Minnesota, AL, 1972-73
TL, 3-3, 4 SV, 2.97 ERA, 45 G
BL, .143, 7 AB, 1 H

Maury "Newt" Newlin (Maurice Milton)
Born: June 11, 1914, Bloomingdale
Died: Aug. 14, 1978, Houston, Texas
6', 176, Pitcher
St. Louis, AL, 1940-41
TR, 1-2, 1 SV, 6.35 ERA, 15 G
BR, .125, 8 AB, 1 H

Doc Newton (Eustace James)
Born: Oct. 26, 1877, Mount Carmel
Died: May 14, 1931, Memphis, Tenn.
6', 185, Pitcher
Cincinnati, NL, 1900-01
Brooklyn, NL, 1901-02
New York, AL, 1905-09
TL, 53-72, 3 SV, 3.22 ERA, 177 G
BL, .172, 436 AB

Newton has the dubious distinction of being one of the worst fielding pitchers in the game.

After attending Morris Hall College, Newton began playing professional baseball in 1897 with Norfolk. He also played for Indianapolis in 1899 before breaking into the majors with Cincinnati.

In 1900 he set the modern single season National League record for errors by a pitcher with seventeen for Cincinnati and Brooklyn.

His best season came in 1902 when he was 15-14 with a 2.42 ERA for the Dodgers. In 1906 he was in ill health, but the Highlanders (now the Yankees) felt he was not staying in shape and suspended him.

In 1909 he was sent down to Newark. He spent the rest of his professional career in the bush leagues, playing in Louisville, Memphis, Galveston and Chattanooga. He retired from baseball in 1916.

He had eight shutouts during his eight years in the majors.

Ovid Nicholson (Ovid Edward)
Born: Dec. 30, 1888, Salem
Died: March 24, 1968, Salem
5'9", 155, Outfielder
Pittsburgh, NL, 1912
BL, TR, .455, 6 G, 11 AB, 5 H

Rabbit Nill (George Charles)
Born: July 14, 1881, Fort Wayne
Died: May 24, 1962, Fort Wayne
5'7", 160, Infielder
Washington, AL, 1904-07
Cleveland, AL, 1907-08
BR, TR, .212, 295 G, 963 AB, 204 H

Nill began his professional career with Davenport of the Three-I League and was with Colorado Springs of the Western League before the Senators acquired him in 1904. He operated a garage in Fort Wayne after baseball.

Peaches O'Neill (Philip Bernard)
Born: Aug. 30, 1879, Anderson
Died: Aug. 2, 1955, Anderson
5'11", 165, Catcher
Cincinnati, NL, 1904
BR, TR, .267, 8 G, 15 AB, 4 H

George Orme (George William)
Born: Sept. 16, 1891, Lebanon
Died: March 16, 1962, Indianapolis
5'10", 160, Outfielder
Boston, AL, 1920
BR, TR, .333, 4 G, 6 AB, 2 H

Orme was with Brantford in the Michigan-Ontario league before signing with Boston.

Al "The Curveless Wonder" Orth (Albert Lewis)
Born: Sept. 5, 1872, Tipton
Died: Oct. 8, 1948, Lynchburg, Va.
6', 200, Pitcher, outfielder
Philadelphia, NL, 1895-01
Washington, AL, 1902-04
New York, AL, 1904-09
TR, 203-183, 8 SV, 3.37 ERA, 440 G
BL, .274, 603 G, 1683 AB, 12 HR

Orth was a versatile player and sometimes played in the outfield or pinch hit when he wasn't on the mound.

The Tipton native broke into the majors in 1895 with Philadelphia and was 8-1 in eleven games. His 2.49 ERA in 1899 was the best in the league and he walked only nineteen men on the season. In 1901 he led the league in shutouts (6).

Orth won fourteen or more games every season until he went 10-22 in 1903 after being traded to Washington. The Senators sent him to the New York Highlanders the following season.

He earned his nickname because he couldn't throw a curveball. But after learning to throw the spitball, he had his best season in 1906 (27-17) and led the league in innings pitched and complete games (36). However, the following year Orth fell on hard times and his record dropped to 14-21. A 2-13 mark in 1908 spelled the end of his career in the majors.

His 389 career hits is among the all-time best for pitchers. He had twelve career homers and pinch hit seventy-eight times.

Bill Owens
Born: 1901, Indianapolis
Shortstop
Washington, NNL, 1924
Chicago, NNL, 1925
Indianapolis, NNL, 1926
Memphis, NNL, 1929

Owens played professional baseball for eleven years, several of which were in the Negro Leagues. He is a long-time resident of Indianapolis.

While in his teens, Owens practiced with the Indianapolis ABCs. Then in 1922 he began

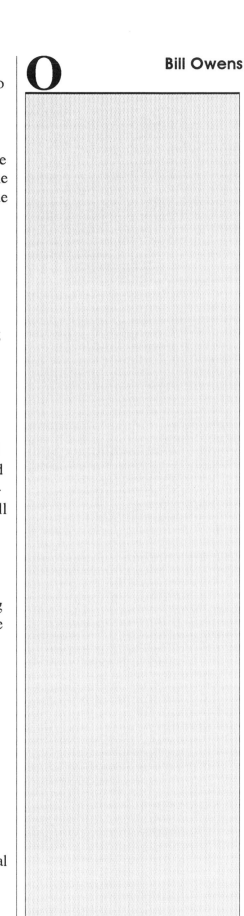

O

barnstorming with several teams.

In 1924 he hooked on with the Washington DC Potomacs of the Negro American League. He was paid $1.50 a day to play. Then he got a raise to $37.50 a week.

The following year the shortstop with the rifle arm played for the Chicago American Giants. Once he jumped up and grabbed a line drive bare handed. He was a singles hitter and rarely clouted a home run.

He returned to his hometown in 1926 to play a year for the ABCs. During the off-season he was stabbed in Indianapolis and was out of baseball for a year as a result of the injury.

In 1928 he began managing a semipro team in Indianapolis. Then the following year he played a season for Memphis of the Negro Western League.

He played for a few more seasons before quitting baseball altogether during the Great Depression. He became a carpenter and settled down in Indianapolis.

Biography courtesy of Hoosier Sports Heroes, by Dale Ogden, Guild Press of Indiana, 1990.

Ray Oyler (Raymond Francis)
Born: Aug. 4, 1938, Indianapolis
Died: Jan 26, 1981, Redmond, Wash.
5'11", 170, Utility infielder
Detroit, AL, 1965-68
Seattle, AL, 1969
California, AL, 1970

BR, TR, .175, 542 G, 1265 AB, 15 HR

Oyler owns the dubious distinction of having the lowest career batting average (.175) of a player other than a pitcher or catcher.

The graduate of Cathedral High School broke into the majors in 1965 with Detroit. He was an excellent fielder and hit five homers in his first season. His average was a dismal .186 though.

He was drafted by the expansion Seattle Pilots. The fans organized the "Ray Oyler Fan Club" in spring training. He responded by hitting a homer in the Pilots first home game. After a .165 average he was traded to Oakland, who sent him to California four months later for cash.

Oyler hit a paltry .083 in 1970, his last in the majors.

Joe "Packy" Pactwa (Joseph Martin)
Born: June 2, 1948, Hammond
5'10", 185, Pitcher
California, AL, 1975
TL, BL, 1-0, 3.94 ERA, 4 G

Jeff Parrett (Jeffrey Dale)
Born: Aug. 26, 1961, Indianapolis
6'3", 195, Relief Pitcher
Montreal, NL, 1986-88
Philadelphia, NL, 1989-90
Atlanta, NL, 1990-91
Oakland, AL, 1992
Colorado, NL, 1993
TR, 49-33, 22 SV, 3.87 ERA, 381 G
3 LCS, 0-0, 11.59 ERA, 2 IP
BR, .087, 23 AB, 2 H

Parrett signed as a free agent with the expansion-franchise Colorado Rockies in January 1993. He was the setup man for American League MVP and Cy Young winner Dennis Eckersley in 1992. He led all relievers in the National League in 1989 with twelve wins.

Parrett was born in Indianapolis and six months later his family moved to Lexington, Ky., where he now lives with his wife, Debbie. He was graduated from Lafayette High School in 1979 and attended the University of Kentucky.

In June 1983 he was drafted in the ninth round by the Milwaukee Brewers and was assigned to Paintsville. After fanning twenty-one hitters in seventeen innings and winning two games, the fireballer was quickly promoted to Beloit, Wisc. He began the following season at Beloit and was con-verted to a reliever halfway through the season. He finished the season with a 4-3 mark and 4.52 ERA.

Parrett was promoted to Class AA Stockton in the California League in 1985 and led the league with a 2.75 ERA. The right hander also recorded eleven saves in 127 innings worked. On Dec. 10 he was selected by Montreal in the special Rule V draft.

In 1986 he found himself on the twenty-five-man opening-day roster of the Expos. However, he was hit hard in his twelve appearances and was shipped back to his birthplace with the Class AAA Indianapolis Indians. He spent the rest of the season with the Indians.

Parrett began 1987 with the Expos, but saw no action and was sent back to Indianapolis again. But his 2.01 ERA with the Indians earned him a return to Montreal on June 15. He recorded his first big league victory five days later at St. Louis. Three days after that he earned his first save at Pittsburgh. During a hot stretch in August, he retired twenty-four consecutive batters. He finished the year with six saves and a 7-6 record.

1988 became Parrett's first full year in the majors. His season was interrupted with a stint on the disabled list after lacerating his right index finger on an attempted bunt in batting practice. Otherwise, he became only the Expo's third reliever to record ten or more victories and he led NL relievers with twelve wins on the season. He also had

P-Q

Jeff Parrett is one of the mainstays of the Colorado Rockies bullpen.

131

P

six saves on the year to go along with his 2.65 ERA.

The Expos dealt Parrett to Philadephia on Dec. 1 in a three-man deal for starter Kevin Gross. Parrett shared the stopper role with Roger McDowell until July 3, when he made his first major league start. A month later he was traded to the Braves with two players to be named later in exchange for Dale Murphy and a player to be named.

Parrett began the season with a save, but he struggled in May, which precipitated a demotion to Triple A Richmond, Va., on June 9. He returned to the Braves in late July for a week, earning his only big league win on July 30 against the Pirates. The Hoosier was sent back to Richmond on Aug. 2 for the remainder of the season.

The Braves let Parrett go his own way and the Oakland A's invited him to spring training in 1992 as a non-roster invitee. He fought his way back and became one of the best relief pitchers on the Oakland staff during the year and helped the A's to a pennant, allowing just two earned runs in sixteen innings for a 1.10 ERA through eight appearances. Parrett was 7-0 on the year before suffering his only setback on the year at Kansas City. He completed the year with 3.02 ERA. His performance undoubtedly raised his stock on the free-agent market and he signed with the Rockies on Jan. 22, 1993.

Parrett was 3-3 for the expansion club with a 5.38 ERA. He appeared in forty games and started six of them, because the Rockies were having trouble with their starting pitching staff.

Ken Penner (Kenneth William)
Born: April 24, 1896, Booneville
Died: May 28, 1959, Sacramento, Calif.
5'11", 170, Pitcher
Cleveland, AL, 1916
Chicago, NL, 1929
TR, 1-1, 3.55 ERA, 9 G
BL, .167, 6 AB, 1 H

Brad Pennington (Brad Lee)
Born: April 14, 1969, Salem
6'5", 205, Relief Pitcher
Baltimore Orioles, AL, 1993
TL, BL, 3-2, 4 SV, 6.55 ERA, 34 G

Pennington is being billed as the Orioles' closer of the future. He was named as one of the Top 10 prospects in the International League in 1992 and broke into the majors early in 1993.

Pennington first played baseball in Little League and Babe Ruth League in Pekin. At Eastern High School he was a standout athlete, lettering in baseball, basketball, and track. After he was graduated in 1987, he attended Bellarmine College and Vincennes Junior College, studying business administration.

The Baltimore Orioles had been watching the big lefthander and grabbed him up in the twelfth round of the June 1989 free agent draft. He was assigned to Bluefield, a Rookie League team. He struggled with a 6.58 ERA and 2-7 record on the year. However, on two occasions he carried two no-hitters into the eighth inning. The next year wasn't much better, as Pennington racked up a 4-9 mark with a 5.18 ERA at Wausau. But in mid-season he was shifted to the bullpen, where he began to show that he was more valuable in relief than as a starter. The Orioles were high on him because of his ability to strikeout batters. He also was gaining more control of his pitches — a fastball, curveball, and slider.

In 1991 Pennington was still mired in the Rookie League at Kane County, but he began to prove himself and allowed just one run in nine appearance at one stretch. He was soon moved up to Class A Frederick, Md. While he still lost games at Frederick, his ERA improved to 3.92 and he was made the team's stopper, chalking up thirteen saves on the season. Over nine straight games he didn't allow an earned run and ended the season with five saves in six games.

Pennington's stock rose like a bull market in 1992, as he started in Single A and ended up at Triple A. After an ERA of 2.00 in eight games at Frederick, Baltimore promoted him to Class AA Hagerstown, Md. In nineteen games there he came across with seven saves and a 2.54 ERA. That was enough to convince Baltimore that he was good enough to move up to Class AAA Rochester. Again the fiery lefty proved himself in a short time. His ERA was an excellent 2.08 and he fanned fifty-six batters in thirty-nine innings. He held Triple A batters to a .101 average. His combined statistics for 1992 were 3-5, 2.24 ERA with fourteen saves, fifty-

four walks, and 104 strikeouts in seventy-six innings.

In spring training in 1993 Baltimore put Pennington to work against major leaguers right away, as he threw against the Pittsburgh Pirates in the first exhibition game of the year. He was again assigned to Rochester, but he was called up in mid-April when lefthander Fernando Valenzuela was sent back to Triple A for more work. Pennington made his debut April 17 in a 7-5 loss to California. When he came into the game, there were runners at the corners and the score was tied 5-5. He retired pinch-hitter Louis Polonia to escape that jam, but he gave up a RBI triple to J.T. Snow the next inning to gain the loss. He finished the season with a 3-2 record for Baltimore; however, the rookie gave up seven homers and compiled a 6.55 ERA. The Orioles will look to him in 1994.

Brad Pennington broke into the majors in 1993 with Baltimore.

June Peppas (June A.)
Born: June 16, 1929, Fort Wayne
First baseman, Pitcher
Fort Wayne, AAGPBL, 1948-49
Racine, AAGPBL, 1949-50
Battle Creek, AAGPBL, 1951
Kalamazoo, AAGPBL, 1951-54
TL, 6-4, 3.32 ERA, 13 G
BL, .300, 783 AB, 235 H
(1953-54 stats)

Peppas was one of the best hitters the last two years of the girl's baseball league.

Before she joined the pro league in 1948, Peppas played fast-pitch softball with Bob's Inn in Fort Wayne. She received the

P

Sportsmanship Award one season. She reports that she joined the pros "because of the skirts." The league instituted skirts to make the pros more feminine than the softball leagues, where players wore pants. However, skirts led to painful "strawberry" scars when the girls slid into bases.

Primarily a first baseman, Peppas pitched in the last season of the league. She led the Kalamazoo Lassies over the Fort Wayne Daisies in the last game of the league.

In 1980 she began writing and publishing the AAGPBL Newsletter, which provides news to the women of the league.

Stan Perzanowski (Stanley)
Born: Aug. 25, 1950, East Chicago
6'3", 190, Pitcher
Chicago, AL, 1971, 74
Texas, AL, 1975-76
Minnesota, AL, 1978
TR, 5-11, 2 SV, 5.10 ERA, 37 G
BB, .000, 2 AB, 0 H

Born in Indiana, Perzanowski grew up in Chicago and came up with the White Sox. His best year was in 1975 with the Texas Rangers, as he went 3-3 with a 3.00 ERA. He is the cousin of former Dodger pitcher Ron Perranoski.

Jeff Peterek (Jeffrey Allen)
Born: Sept. 22, 1963, Michigan City
6'2", 200, Pitcher
Milwaukee, AL, 1989
BL, TL, 0-2, 5.25 ERA, 7 G

Anna Petrovic
Born: Aurora
AAGPBL, 1944

Al Pilarcik (Alfred James)
Born: July 3, 1930, Whiting
5'10", 180, Outfielder
Kansas City, AL, 1956
Baltimore, AL, 1957-1960
Kansas City, AL, 1961
Chicago, AL, 1961
BL, TL, 668 G, 1614 AB, .256, 22 HR

Pilarcik was an excellent defensive outfielder and used as a pinch hitter 115 times during his seven years in the majors. He was inducted into the Indiana Baseball Hall of Fame in Jaspar in 1987.

When Pilarcik began playing baseball at age five, there were no organized baseball leagues in Whiting. There were no uniforms or pressure. "We just played. It was sanctioned by the Whiting Community Center," he said.

He received his first baseball uniform when he went to Whiting High School in 1944. In 1948, the year Pilarcik was graduated, he was spotted by St. Louis Browns scout Lou Maglo and invited to a tryout in Branson, Missouri. Out of 350 players, he and two others were offered contracts with Kansas City, an American Association team. He signed a New York contract and went to Independence to play Class D ball. He was seventeen. In his first year he played with another seventeen year old — Mickey Mantle.

The outfielder climbed the minor leagues like a ladder, going to Class C ball in Joplin,

Class B in Quincy and Class A in Muskegeon. "In those days if you had a good year, you moved up a notch," he explained. He soon moved up to Beaumont, Texas, and played for manager Rogers Hornsby. Then he went to Class AAA Syracuse.

Just about the time the majors were about to call, the U.S. Army called instead. The country was involved in the Korean Conflict. Pilarcik spent the next two years in the Army as an infantryman, but he never saw action. That doesn't mean he wasn't in any danger. "We had four guys killed in basic training when a guy pulled a grenade," he said.

When his stint was over, he came back to Birmingham, Ala., where Ralph Houk was managing. The following year he landed in Columbus, Ohio. By mid-June he had eighteen home runs and seventy-five RBI. "I had one of those miracle years," he explained. The Kansas City Athletics bought his contract from the Yankees and he was called up to the majors. His first major league game came against the Baltimore Orioles. He played in sixty-nine games for the last-place A's and hit .251.

The Orioles traded for him after the season was over. Pilarcik and Art Ceccarelli went to the O's for Ryne Duren and Jim Pisoni. He responded to the trade by playing the best year of his career as a starting centerfielder for the Orioles. He hit .278 with nine homers and forty-nine RBI. His defensive statistics were even better as he committed just one error and had fifteen assists,

second in the league.

Pilarcik's average dropped to .243 the following year and he managed only one homer on the year. He rebounded in 1959 to hit .282. The Orioles platooned him in the outfield, so he started only 106 games. However, he was used frequently as a left-handed pinch hitter.

Pilarcik's role as a starter on the team further subsided in 1960 as he began seventy-five games in the outfield, but he was called on many times to pinch hit. His average dropped off to .247. Baltimore was in the hunt for the pennant and finished second behind the Yankees.

He remembered a game late in the season against the Red Sox in which he robbed Ted Williams of a homer in the fourth inning in Fenway Park. "I was playing 420. I was halfway out of the ballpark. He hit it like a golf ball," Pilarcik said. Later in the game Williams hit another ball his way, but it hit the right field facade and was called a home run. Pilarcik caught it and the umpire called for the ball, since Williams' career was coming to an end. As it turned out, it was the last homer for the Hall of Famer.

The Orioles dealt Pilarcik back to the A's in January 1961 in a multi-player trade involving Whitey Herzog. He lasted until June with Kansas City. Then he was involved in another multi-player trade that sent him to Chicago White Sox along with another Hoosier, Don Larsen. In one game with the Sox he played all three outfield positions.

Pilarcik is a Hall of Famer

"We had four guys killed in basic training when a guy pulled a grenade." Al Pilarcik

135

Dan Plesac

P himself. The Indiana Baseball Hall of Fame in Jasper inducted him in 1987 to recognize him for his major league career and high school coaching accomplishments. He coached the Lake Central High School team for twenty-four years before calling it quits in 1987. He still teaches high school and lives in Schererville with his wife, the former Theresa Grzych of St. John. They have a daughter, Kathy, and two grandchildren, Elizabeth and James.

In looking back at his career, he reflected, "I just enjoyed baseball. I also enjoyed hustling."

Dan Plesac (Daniel Thomas)
Born: Feb. 4, 1962, Gary
6'5", 215, Relief Pitcher
Milwaukee, AL, 1986-92
Chicago, NL, 1993
TL, 31-38, 133 SV, 422 G
BL, .000, 1 AB

A three-time All-Star, Plesac set several franchise marks in saves at Milwaukee early in his career. Arm problems hampered his career in 1991. He signed with the Cubs as a free agent before the 1993 campaign.

Plesac grew up in Gary and played Little League as a youngster. When he was eight, his father took him to a Chicago Cubs-St. Louis Cardinals game in Wrigley Field. He also attended several White Sox games at Comiskey Park.

In his junior year of high school his family moved to Crown Point. The tall schoolboy found basketball and baseball to his liking and he earned All-

State honors in both sports at Crown Point High School. He also earned All-American honors in basketball. He was graduated in 1980 and was selected by the St. Louis Cardinals in the second round of the June draft. But the teen decided to attend North Carolina State instead of signing a professional contract. While Dan was at NC State, his brother Joe was the first player chosen in the 1982 draft, but arm injuries would end Joe's career at Triple A a few years later.

Plesac followed in his brother's footsteps the next year — being selected in the first round by the Milwaukee Brewers. The crafty lefty was assigned to Paintsville of the Appalachian Rookie League. He went 9-1 in fourteen starts. He led the league in winning percentage and strikeouts.

In 1984 Plesac split the season between Stockton of the California League and Class AA El Paso, Texas. The following year he stayed at El Paso and went 12-5. He was named to the Texas League All-Star team.

After spring training in 1986, the Brewers kept him on the opening-day roster as a reliever. He earned his first major league win on April 18 against the New York Yankees when he pitched four shutout innings. Plesac picked up his first save on May 2 against the California Angels. In all, he appeared in fifty-one games and recorded fourteen saves during the year.

Plesac became the best stopper on the team in 1987 and one of the best lefthanded relievers in the league. For this he was

Dan Plesac joined the club he used to watch as a youngster.

chosen for the All-Star Game, pitching a perfect inning. He went on to record twenty-three saves on the year with a 2.61 ERA.

1988 saw Plesac in the All-Star Game once again. He was unstoppable in one nine-game stretch in July, recording nine saves in a row. Perhaps all the work tired him and he developed tendinitis in his left shoulder in August. Still he ended the season with thirty saves, fourth highest in the league.

For the third year in a row he was picked for the All-Star Game in 1989. He had a career-low 2.35 ERA in setting a Brewers' record with thirty-three saves. He also became the first Brewer to record 100 saves. Plesac baffled batters with his slider and held them to a .213 average. At one point in the season he recorded saves in fourteen consecutive chances. He signed a lucrative three-year contract at the end of the year.

His effectiveness dimmed in 1990 as his ERA rose to 4.43. However, he appeared in career-high sixty-six games and re-corded twenty-four saves on the year. The following year he was moved from the lefthanded-stopper role to middle relief with the rise of Doug Henry. Then he moved from the bullpen to the starting rotation in early August. In his first start he beat Texas. In all, he made ten starts on the season and recorded eight saves on the year. The change in roles helped him lick the tendinitis problem he was still having.

He started a couple more games in 1992, but he was used mainly in middle relief again. On the next to last day of the season he became the Brewers all-time leader in appearances with 365. He posted a 5-4 record on the year with a 2.96 ERA.

Plesac became a free agent after the 1992 campaign and signed a two-year contract with the Cubs, the team he loved as a child. The Cubs used him as a middle reliever during the 1993 season. He contributed with a 2-1 record in fifty-seven games for the Northsiders. He complained about his role, but his ERA was an unimpressive 4.74 and he gave up ten home runs in sixty-three innings of work.

He now lives in St. Charles, Ill., with his wife, Leslie, and daughter, Madeline.

Odie Porter (Odie Oscar)
Born: May 24, 1877, Borden
Died: May 2, 1903, Borden
Pitcher
Philadelphia, AL, 1902
0-1, 3.38 ERA, 1 G
.000, 3 AB, 0 H

LaVerne Price
Born: Terre Haute
AAGPBL, 1944

Bill "Clint" Prough (Herschel Clinton)
Born: Nov. 28, 1887, Markle
Died: Dec. 29, 1936, Richmond
6'3', 185, Pitcher
Cincinnati, NL, 1912
TR, 0-0, 6.00 ERA, 1 G
BR, .000, 1 AB, 0 H

Tex Pruiett (Charles LeRoy)
Born: April 10, 1883, Osgood

Troy Puckett

P

Died: March 6, 1953, Ventura, Calif.
Pitcher
Boston, AL, 1907-08
5-18, 4 SV, 2.82 ERA, 48 G
.134, 67 AB, 9 H

Troy Puckett (Troy Levi)
Born: Dec. 10, 1889, Winchester
Died: April 13, 1971, Winchester
6'2", 185, Pitcher
Philadelphia, NL, 1911
TR, BL, 0-0, 13.50 ERA, 1 G

Don Rader (Donald Russell)
Born: Sept. 5, 1893, Wolcott
Died: June 26, 1983, Walla Walla, Wash.
5'10", 164, Shortstop, outfielder
Chicago, AL, 1913
Philadelphia, NL, 1921
BL, TR, .286, 13 G, 35 AB

Toad Ramsey (Thomas A.)
Born: Aug. 8, 1864, Indianapolis
Died: March 27, 1906, Indianapolis
Pitcher
Louisville, AA, 1885-89
St. Louis, AA, 1889-90
TL, 114-124, 3.29 ERA, 248 G
BR, .204, 858 AB, 175 H

Ramsey was baseball's first knuckleball pitcher. He had an excellent career going until he drank himself into trouble and out of baseball.

The knuckleballer led the American Association in complete games in 1886 when he won thirty-eight games. He had two straight one-hitters during the season. He gunned down 499 men that year.

The following season he had thirty-seven wins and led the league in strikeouts (355). He pitched a no-hitter against Baltimore. The lefty ace would have probably won forty games on the season, but he was suspended in May and August because of drinking. He reportedly pitched one game drunk. And he was arrested for hitting a woman in a bar.

His drinking problem finally caught up with him in 1888 and Ramsey's record dived to 8-30. During the season he wound up in jail for drinking and not paying his debts. His career was never the same after that.

He died of pneumonia in his hometown of Indianapolis.

Bill "Bedford Bill" Rariden (William Angel)
Born: Feb. 4, 1888, Bedford
Died: Aug. 28, 1942, Bedford
5'10", 168, Catcher
Boston, NL, 1909-13
Indianapolis, FL, 1914
Newark, FL, 1915
New York, NL, 1916-18
BR, TR, .237, 982 G, 2877 AB, 7 HR

Nicknamed for his hometown, Bedford Bill played in two World Series during his decade in the majors.

He came up with the Boston Braves in 1909. When the Federal League formed in 1914, Rariden jumped to the Indianapolis Hoosiers and helped the team to a pennant, while leading the league in putouts and assists. The following season he had a career best .270 batting average.

After the Federal League folded, he was purchased by the New York Giants. During the 1917 World Series, the receiver failed to cover home in a rundown and allowed a run, which led to a White Sox victory.

Rariden was traded to Cincinnati for Hal Chase in 1919 and was a back-up receiver.

Larry Ray (Larry Dale)
Born: March 11, 1958, Madison
6', 190, Outfielder
Houston, NL, 1982
BL, TR, .167, 5 G, 6 AB, 2 H

R

Ron Reed (Ronald Lee)
Born: Nov. 2, 1942, La Porte
6'6", 215
Atlanta, NL, 1965-74
St. Louis, NL, 1975
Philadelphia, NL, 1976-83
Chicago, AL, 1984
TR, 146-140, 103 SV, 3.46
ERA, 751 G
BR, .158, 620 AB, 98 H
2 WS, 0-0, 1.69 ERA

Reed is one of few major league baseball players to play pro basketball. He was named to the Indiana Baseball Hall of Fame in 1990.

Reed lettered in football, basketball, and baseball at La Porte High School. After he graduated, he went to Notre Dame and became an All-American basketball player, setting the college's rebound record. His rebounding prowess led him to the National Basketball League. He joined the Detroit Pistons in 1965 as a sixth man for the team.

During the summers he played minor league ball. He made it to the majors in 1966 with Atlanta. After he had played both sports for the next two years, the Braves signed him to a two-year contract that made him leave the NBA. He scored 951 points and had 762 rebounds in 119 games with the Pistons.

In 1969 he helped Atlanta to the LCS after a 18-10 season. He lost to the Mets in Game Two of the LCS.

Reed was traded to St. Louis in May 1975. Then he went to Philadelphia in December of the same year for Mike Anderson. The Phillies turned him into a short reliever. He had a career best seventeen saves in 1978 and

led the majors with thirteen relief wins the following season. One of his career 103 saves came in Game Two of the 1980 World Series.

A baseball field in La Porte is named after the pitcher who now lives in Milburn, Ga.

Rita Rehrer
Born: Fort Wayne
Peoria, AAGPBL, 1946
.000, 1 G, 3 AB

Charlie "Pop" Reising (Charles)
Born: Aug. 28, 1861, Indiana
Died: July 16, 1915, Louisville, Ky.
Outfielder
Indianapolis, AA, 1884
.000, 2 G, 8 AB, 0 H

Andy Replogle (Andrew David)
Born: Oct. 7, 1953, South Bend
6'6", 205, Pitcher
Milwaukee, AL, 1978-79
BR, TR, 9-5, 4.01 ERA, 35 G

The South Bend Clay pitcher took his team to the state baseball championship crown with a 14-1 record in 1970. The number-one pick of the Baltimore Orioles in 1977 was waived the next year and picked up by the Milwaukee Brewers. He slipped back into the minors in 1979.

Charlie Reynolds (Charles Lawrence)
Born: May 1, 1865, Williamsburg
Died: July 3, 1944, Denver, Colo.
Catcher

Indiana High School Record Book

AT BATS IN A SEASON
1. 152 — Dan Gibson
2. 146 — Bill Adaschick
3. 144 — Mark Evenson
4. 140 — Brian Piotrowicz
5. 139 — *Andy Replogle*

R

Kansas City, AL, 1889
Brooklyn, AL, 1889
.217, 13 G, 46 AB, 10 H

Sam Rice (Edgar Charles)
Born: Feb. 20, 1890, Morocco
Died: Oct. 13, 1974, Rossmor, Md.
5'9", 150, Outfielder
Washington, AL, 1915-33
Cleveland, AL, 1934
BL, TR, .322, 2404 G, 9269 AB, 2987 H
1 WS, .364, 33 AB, 12 H

Rice overcame age and personal tragedy to become one of the greatest singles hitters in the game. He led the American League in several categories during his career. He was inducted into the Hall of Fame in 1963 and the Indiana Baseball Hall of Fame in 1979.

Rice's family moved to Illinois during his younger days. He played town team baseball as a teenager. After marrying Beulah Stam in 1908 and becoming the father of two children, he experienced tragedy. An April 1912 tornado killed his wife, children, and entire family. After the tragedy, he began his professional career with Muscatine, Ill., of the Central Association, but he wasn't successful. He drifted around for awhile and joined the Navy in 1913.

In 1914 he became a pitcher for Petersburg, Va., and posted a 9-2 record. The following year he compiled a 11-12 mark, but he was a better hitter and outfielder.

Rice was sold to Washington where he saw limited action on the mound. Because he was a good pinch hitter, the Senators took him off the mound and put him in right field. In 1917 the twenty-seven year old hit .302 and swiped thirty-five bases.

In 1920 Rice put together a twenty-nine-game hitting streak, leading the league in stolen bases (63) and putouts (454). He also recorded 211 hits, the first of his seven seasons with over 200 hits. In 1923 the fleet-footed outfielder led the league in triples (18). 1924 marked a thirty-one-game hitting streak on his way to leading the league in hits (216). On July 24, 1924, Rice had one of his best games when he hit three doubles and a triple.

Rice helped the Senators to the World Series three times during his career and hit .302 in the Fall Classic. His controversial catch in the 1925 World Series will long be remembered. He tumbled over the right-field barrier and emerged with the ball in his glove for the out.

In 1930 he hit .349 with 207 hits, becoming the only player to collect 200 hits at the age of forty. Two years later he hit .323 to become only one of dozen hitters to hit over .300 at his age. He saw limited action the next three seasons and finished out his career in 1934 at age 44.

Rice will be known as one was one of the hardest batters to strike out.

Duane Richards (Duane Lee)
Born: Dec. 16, 1936, Spartanburg
6'3", 200, Pitcher
Cincinnati, NL, 1960

Bill Richardson

R

"I used to steal bases when Bonnie Baker was manager of Kalamazoo. I stole quite a few."
Eilaine Roth

TR, BR, 0-0, 9.00 ERA, 2 G

Bill "Jumbo" Richardson (William Henry)
Born: Sept. 24, 1878, Salem
Died: Nov. 6, 1949, Sullivan
5'11", 200, First baseman
St. Louis, NL, 1901
BR, TR, .212, 15 G, 52 AB, 11 H

Ken Richardson (Kenneth Franklin)
Born: May 2, 1915, Orleans
Died: Dec. 7, 1987, Wood-land Hills, Calif.
5'11", 187, Outfielder, infielder
Philadelphia, AL, 1942
Philadelphia, NL, 1946
BR, TR, .114, 12 G, 35 AB, 4 H

Bruce "Marty" Robbins (Bruce Duane)
Born: Sept. 10, 1959, Port-land
6'2", 185, Pitcher
Detroit, AL, 1979-80
BL, TL, 7-5, 5.33 ERA, 25 G

Robbins was one of the best high school pitchers in Indiana history, but that success didn't carry over to the majors.

At Blackford High School he set school records and put his name in the Indiana high school record book. He had an excellent fastball, curve, and hard slider, which helped him mow down a remarkable 202 batters in his senior year — the second highest in Indiana history. He had a 12-2 record with a 0.93 ERA and took his team to the Final Four tour-nament.

The Detroit Tigers drafted him in the thirteen round, but he never succeeded in the majors as he had done in high school.

Mike Roesler (Michael Joseph)
Born: Sept. 12, 1963, Fort Wayne
6'5", 195, Pitcher
Cincinnati, NL, 1989
Pittsburgh, NL, 1990
Relief Pitcher
BR, TR, 1-1, 3.77 ERA, 22 G

Eilaine "I" Roth (Eilaine May)
Born: Jan. 17, 1929, Michi-gan City
Outfielder, utility infielder
Peoria, AAGPBL, 1948
Muskegon, AAGPBL, 1949-50
Kalamazoo, AAGPBL, 1950-51
BR, TR, .154, 39 G, 104 AB (1948 stats)

Roth joined the Peoria Redwings with her twin sister in 1948 and played for four seasons in the league.

Nicknamed "I" to distinguish her from her sister, she played basketball, field hockey, and soccer at Issac C. Elston High School in Michigan City. She began playing softball during the summers as a teen-ager.

The sisters were recruited at the same time by the pro league and put on the same team. Two years later the twins were sent to different teams. Eilaine went to the Kalamazoo Lassies. "I used to steal bases when Bonnie Baker was manager of Kalama-zoo. I stole quite a few," she said.

She admitted that she doesn't remember a lot of details about the games. "I remember throwing a ball over the backstop," said the outfielder.

The two girls aren't identical twins, but look a lot alike. They have been confused for each other at times.

Eilaine is glad she played in the league and enjoys some of the publicity the league is now getting. She was one of the girls to appear in the final scenes of the movie, "A League of Their Own," which described the league. She said the turning point in recognition for the league came about after the National Hall of Fame recognized the league in 1988.

1988 was the same year she retired from UpJohn in Kalamazoo. She now lives in Battle Creek. She is single and has never married, like many of the women who were in the league.

Elaine "E" Roth (Elaine Marjorie)
Born: Michigan City
Pitcher, Outfielder
Peoria, AAGPBL, 1948-49
South Bend, AAGPBL, 1950
Kalamazoo, AAGPBL, 1951-54
9-14, 2.85 ERA, 49 G
.222, 26 G, 54 AB, 12 H
(1953-54 stats)

Roth's best season came her rookie year when she was 18-15 on the mound for the Peoria Redwings. Sometimes she shared the outfield with her twin sister, who joined the league at the same time.

She was graduated from Issac C. Elston in Michigan City and played softball in an amateur softball league on the same team

as her sister.

She and her sister were recruited at the same time and played on the Peoria team for two years together.

The league split the two up in 1950, but they were joined together again the next season. Her sister dropped out after the 1951 season, but Elaine decided to continue.

"E," as she was nicknamed, was used only in relief in 1953. In 1954 she had the fifth-best ERA in the league, but didn't get the run support to post a 5-12 record.

As her sister did, she worked at UpJohn until retiring in 1989. She, too, appeared in the final scene of "A League of Their Own."

Edd Roush (Edd J.)
Born: May 8, 1893, Oakland City
Died: March 21, 1988, Bradenton, Fla.
5'11", 170, Outfielder
Chicago, AL, 1913
Indianapolis, FL, 1914
Newark, FL, 1915
New York, NL, 1916
Cincinnati, NL, 1916-26
New York, NL, 1927-29
Cincinnati, NL, 1931
BL, TR, .323, 1967 G, 7361 AB, 2377 H

Roush was one of the most feared hitters at the end of the dead-ball era. He led the National League in hitting twice and hit over .300 for eleven straight years. He was inducted into the Baseball Hall of Fame in 1962 and the Indiana Baseball Hall of Fame in 1979.

Roush began playing base-

Edd Roush was a great hitter of his time.

ball with his hometown semipro team, the Walk-Overs, as a teenager. He broke into professional ball in 1912 as a shortstop with Evansville of the Kitty League. He suffered a shoulder injury, which weakened his right arm, so he went to throwing and hitting left handed.

The Hoosier got a nine-game tryout with the Chicago White Sox in 1913, but he didn't prove himself and was sent to Lincoln, Neb. The following season he was lured to the new Federal League with a $225 monthly salary. The Hoosier also married Essie Mae Swallow of his hometown that year. Roush hit .333 for Indianapolis. The franchise moved to Newark in 1915 and he stayed with the league.

When the Federal League folded after 1915, he was sold to the New York Giants for $10,000. After he had hit .188 in thirty-nine games, the Giants traded him with Christy Mathewson and Bill McKenie for Buck Herzog and Wade Killefer.

The following season he began his run of eleven straight .300 seasons with a .341 average to win the NL batting title with a forty-eight-ounce bat, the heaviest in baseball. In 1919 he led the league again in average (.321) and helped lead the Reds to the pennant. He hit only .214 in the World Series, but the Reds won anyway when the Chicago White Sox players purposely threw the series in baseball's biggest scandal.

Roush became the only player ever ejected from a game for falling asleep. During a long

argument between his manager and umpires on June 8, 1920, Roush lay down in the outfield and fell fast asleep. Umpires had a hard time waking him, so he was ejected for delay of game.

Roush hit a career high .352 in 1921. He sat out most of the next season in a salary dispute. He held out frequently during his career in order to avoid spring training, while he felt was a waste of time.

He led the league in doubles (41) in 1923 and hit a league-leading twenty-one triples in 1924.

Cincinnati traded him to the Giants in 1927 for George Kelly. Roush was given a three-year contract for $22,500 a year, a hefty sum in those days. The following season he tore stomach muscles diving for a liner. The injury slowed the aging player, and the Giants moved to cut his salary in 1930 to $15,000. Roush refused to sign and sat out the season. The Giants released him the next year and he signed with the Reds again for one final season.

Roush coached the Reds in 1938 before retiring from baseball.

Patricia Roy
Born: Fort Wayne
Fort Wayne, AAGPBL, 1954
.079, 14 G, 38 AB, 3 H

Janet Rumsey
Born: Oct. 16, 1931,
Greensburg
Pitcher
Battle Creek, AAGPBL, 1951
South Bend, AAGPBL, 1951-54

**26-25, 2.32 ERA, 60 G
.202, 68 G, 158 AB (1953-54
stats)**

Rumsey was the best pitcher in the All American Girls Professional Baseball League in 1954, the last year of its existence.

The pitcher was very shy before joining the league. After being assigned to the Battle Creek Belles, she was reallocated to the South Bend Blue Sox during her first season. Her team won the championship in 1951 despite having only twelve players.

In 1953 Rumsey had a better than average ERA (2.42) but didn't get the run support and finished with an 11-19 record. She rebounded the next year to lead the league in ERA with 2.18. Her 15-6 record included a no-hitter on Aug. 24 vs. the Grand Rapids Chicks.

"For me playing baseball was a dream come true, as I enjoyed sports then and still enjoy sports," she has written.

**Amos "The Hoosier Thunderbolt" Rusie (Amos Wilson)
Born: May 30, 1871, Mooresville
Died: Dec. 6, 1942, Seattle, Wash.
6'1", 200, Pitcher
Indianapolis, NL, 1889
New York, NL, 1890-95, 97-98
Cincinnati, NL, 1901
TR, 248-170, 5 SV, 3.08 ERA, 462 G
BR, .250, 1721 AB, 430 H, 8 HR**

The Hoosier Thunderbolt was one of the best pitchers before the turn of the century. He was inducted into the Baseball Hall of Fame in 1977 and added to the Indiana Baseball Hall of Fame two years later. Rusie had a blazing fastball and led the league in strikeouts five times. He had eight seasons where he won twenty or more games and had one no-hitter.

Rusie quit school to work and play outfield for an Indianapolis semipro team. He began his major league career in Indianapolis in 1889. The Brotherhood Strike the next year put Indianapolis out of business and Rusie went to the New York Giants. He pitched New York's first no-hitter on July 31, 1891, against Brooklyn. The power pitcher gunned down more than 300 batters a year and won more than thirty games a year three seasons in a row for the Giants.

The likes of the Hoosier Thunderbolt and other power pitchers of the time led rule-makers to move the pitching distance from forty-five feet to sixty feet six inches in 1893. The move didn't hamper Rusie. During the 1893 season he set all-time single season records for games started (52), completed (50) and innings pitched (482). The following year he won thirty-six games.

In Rusie's first six seasons with the Giants, he led the league in strikeouts five times. He was, however, very wild and also led the league in walks from 1890-94. The fireballer once knocked out a batter for a day with an wild throw.

After the 1895 season, The

R

Hoosier Thunderbolt wanted more money. He was unhappy with his low pay — $6 an inning. The Giants wouldn't give him a raise and he sat out the 1896 season. Because of his absence, the Giants dropped to sixth place in the standings.

The Giants decided to meet Rusie's terms the following year and pay him $5,000 for the season. Ironically, opposing players talked about starting a "Rusie Fund" to pay him $5,000 not to pitch. He pitched the next two years for the Giants before holding out again in 1899. This time the Giants wouldn't buckle under his demands, so Rusie was out of baseball for two years during which time he drank heavily.

The Giants traded him to Cincinnati for Christy Mathewson, an action which is considered one of the worst trades ever in basesball. The Giants got a future Hall of Famer and the Red Stockings got a washed-up pitcher. Rusie pitched in only three games for Cincinnati in 1901, his last year in the majors.

After baseball he worked in Muncie and Vincennes before moving to Seattle. John McGraw hired him as a superintendent of the Polo Grounds in 1921.

Fritz "Dutch" Scheeren (Frederick)
Born: July 1, 1891, Kokomo
Died: June 17, 1973, Oil City, Pa.
6', 180, Outfielder
Pittsburgh, NL, 1914-15
BR, TR, .265, 15 G, 34 AB, 9 H

Al Schellhase (Albert Herman)
Born: Sept. 13, 1864, Evansville
Died: Jan. 3, 1919, Evansville
5'8", 148, Catcher, outfielder, shortstop
Boston, NL, 1890
Louisville, AA, 1891
.143, 16 G, 49 AB, 7 H

Dan Schneider (Daniel Louis)
Born: Aug. 29, 1942, Evansville
6'3", 170, Relief Pitcher
Milwaukee, NL, 1963-64
Atlanta, NL, 1966
Houston, NL, 1967, 69
TL, 2-5, 2 SV, 4.72 ERA, 117 G
BL, .172, 29 AB, 5 H

The $100,000 bonus baby in 1962 became only a mediocre middle-relief pitcher.

Jeff Schulz (Jeffrey Alan)
Born: June 2, 1961, Evansville
6'1", 185, Outfielder
Kansas City, AL, 1989-90
Pittsburgh, NL, 1991
BL, TR, .244, 40 G, 78 AB

Schulz played in Italy in 1993 and may be done with baseball. He teamed with Don Mattingly at Evansville Reitz Memorial and the two are still close friends.

His first experience with baseball came in the backyard as his father taught him the game. He was an All-Star outfielder in Little League and Babe Ruth League, where he first teamed with Mattingly. The two players went to high school together and provided a powerful offense.

Schulz helped his team to a state championship in 1978. The following year he went 9-for-10 in the Final Four and 4-for-5 in the championship game, both records. Unfortunately, Evansville lost the championship game to Logansport.

After Schulz graduated, he went to Western Kentucky for a year. Then he transferred to the University of Southern Indiana, where he was voted Great Lakes Valley MVP two years in a row.

The Kansas City Royals drafted him in the twenty-third round in 1983. After he received $10,000 for signing, he went to Butte, Mont., for rookie ball, continuing with stints at Charleston, W. Va.; and Ft. Meyers, Fla.; and Memphis, Tenn., before landing in Class AAA Omaha, where he played for five seasons.

The Royals brought him up at the end of the 1989 season. "I got my first hit off Nolan Ryan in my first at bat. The only other player to do that was Will Clark," he said.

Schulz received another September call-up in 1990. Then he decided to become a free agent and signed a contract with the Pittsburgh Pirates. After a year with the Pirates, he signed with

S

147

S

the Chicago Cubs. He played all of 1992 in Class AAA with the Cubs.

1993 saw the Hoosier in Italy with Bologna. He explained that baseball there was much like Triple A, but that he received more money.

Schulz is undecided about his future in baseball. "I'm not positive what I'm going to do next year," he said after the 1993 season. He's now into real estate sales and would like to finish his degree in special education. He still lives in Evansville with his wife, the former April Davis of Evansville, and two daughters: Lindsay and Molly.

Wayne Schurr (Wayne Allen)
Born: Aug. 6, 1937, Garrett
6'4", 185, Pitcher
Chicago, NL, 1964
TR, 0-0, 26 G, 3.75 ERA
BR, .000, 5 AB, 0 H

Schurr had half a season with the Cubs before elbow problems doomed his career.

Schurr's father was a semi-pro player, and he became involved with the team by shagging flyballs. At Salem Center High School, he was the co-captain of the basketball team and the pitcher for the baseball team. "I was terrible," he admitted. "We played eleven games and I was 2-9." He also played American Legion ball, where he pitched better and got the notice of the scouts.

Ray Lucas of the New York Giants signed Schurr to a contact in 1957 for $500. He went to Class D Michigan City. He was 6-2 with a 2.20 ERA. "I would

have won the pitching title if I would have had enough innings," he said.

The following year he went to Class B Eugene, Ore., and married Ann Foor of Kendalville. After the season he joined the National Guard.

In 1960, he threw a no-hitter in Victoria, Tex., before running into problems. "I ended up getting a real sore arm and nearly got released," he explained. Then he was called back to the Guard when the Berlin Crisis occurred.

He spent the next two seasons at Triple A, but the Giants didn't protect him and the Cubs drafted him in a special $25,000 draft during the winter.

1964 found Schurr on the opening-day roster of the Cubs. In the second game of the year in Pittsburgh, he got the call in the ninth inning against the heart of the order. He struck out Willie Stargell to end the inning and send the game into extra innings. He pitched another inning, but didn't get the decision.

Schurr threw mainly middle relief and was sent back down to Salt Lake City in mid-season. The next season he started some games for Salt Lake City, but didn't get a call back up to the majors.

In 1966 the California Angels traded for him, but he wouldn't sign a contract.

Schurr now lives in Hudson with his wife and won, Kelly, and works for Magnavox.

Art Schwind (Arthur Edwin)
Born: Nov. 4, 1889, Fort Wayne

Died: Jan. 13, 1968, Sullivan
5'8", 150, Third baseman
Boston, NL, 1912
BB, TR, .500, 1 G, 2 AB, 1 H

**Everett "Deacon" Scott
(Lewis Everett)
Born: Nov. 19, 1892, Bluffton
Died: Nov. 2, 1960, Fort
Wayne
5'8", 142, Shortstop
Boston, AL, 1914-21
New York, AL, 1922-25
Washington, AL, 1925
Chicago, AL, 1926
Cincinnati, NL, 1926
BR, TR, .249, 1654 G, 5837
AB, 1455 H**

Scott held the major league record for consecutive games played until Lou Gehrig came along. He was an excellent shortstop who led the league in fielding for his position for eight straight years. His best year behind the plate was in 1920, when he hit career highs in average (.269) and triples (12). He was inducted into the Indiana Baseball Hall of Fame in 1986.

**Rodney "Cool Breeze"
Scott (Rodney Darnell)
Born: Oct. 16, 1953, Indian-
apolis
6', 180, Infielder
Kansas City, AL, 1975
Montreal, NL, 1976
Oakland, AL, 1977
Chicago, NL, 1978
Montreal, NL, 1979-82
New York, AL, 1982
BB, TR, 690 G, .236, 2132 AB,
3 HR
1 LCS, 5 G, .167**

The speedy Scott swiped 205 bases during his eight-year major league career. He and Ron LeFlore teamed up to steal 160 bases in 1980 — he had sixty-three — to set a Major League record for a duo of base stealers on the same team. That same year he tied Omar Moreno for the most triples (13) in the National League.

Scott first started playing baseball at seven years of age when his grandfather, Charlie Woodruff, introduced him to the game. He learned to play every position in the Douglas Little League in Indianapolis. He ruled out playing catcher right away. When the batter swung, he'd blink and turn his head. This practice lasted until he got hit in the side of the face by a foul tip. At age ten he began playing basketball.

His first exposure on television came when he was twelve. A local television station aired his pitching performance in an All-Star game at Prentice Field at 38th and Emerson. He pitched a four-hit shutout and fanned seventeen batters from Franklin Little League at the District Championship.

After Little League, he played Junior Baseball for the WTLC Jets, a team sponsored by a local radio station. At age fifteen, Scott tried out for the Cincinnati Reds at a tryout camp held at Bush Stadium. "It was inspirational, because the scout picked me up at my house and took me to breakfast. I threw up all over the field 'cause I'd been drinking the night before and had a hangover," he admitted. "They said I was too young."

At Arlington High School, Scott was on the varsity baseball

Rodney Scott was a prolific base stealer and a good utility infielder.

S

team all four years, but he also did exceptionally well at basketball and scored forty-four points in one game. He was picked for both the state baseball and basketball all-star team, which played at the same time. Scott scored twenty-one points in the Indiana victory over Kentucky in Indianapolis. He chose the basketball team, because he had already decided on a baseball career after high school. Sunkist named him to their Prep All-American team and he was showered with scholarship offers, including an invitation from UCLA's John Wooden.

After graduation in 1972, he was drafted in the sixth round by the Kansas City Royals. He received a $2,500 bonus for signing and was sent to the Rookie League in Sarasota, Fla. He played infield and hit .376 in 35 games.

In 1973 Scott was promoted to the Class A League. He played at Billings, Mont., the first half of the season and then went to San Jose, Calif. The next year he stayed at Single A and played at Waterloo, Iowa, and San Jose. After a good spring in 1975, the Royals brought him up to the majors. The young speedy player was used sparingly as a pinch runner for designated hitter Harmon Killebrew or defensive replacement in late innings. As the only rookie on the team, he felt he wasn't getting any respect from Manager Whitey Herzog. "We were playing in Oakland and he pinch hit for me when we were losing 17-0," he explained. "I got mad and threw my bat." The incident

resulted in his shipment back to the minors. He landed at Jacksonville for twenty games and then to Omaha, both Triple A teams. In the winter he was traded for cash to Montreal. "I was sitting at home watching television when I found out I had been traded," he said.

The Expos sent him to Denver where he hit .307 in 114 games. In the off-season, the Expos traded him to the Texas Rangers for Jeff Terpko. His stay in Texas didn't last long enough for his luggage to catch up to him, as he was traded by Texas with Jim Umbarger and cash to the Oakland for Claudell Washington three days into spring training.

1977 became Scott's rookie year, as he appeared in 133 games for the A's. Late in the season, Scott butted heads with manager Bobby Winkles at a game in Milwaukee. After Scott failed to get a hit in his first at-bat, Winkles replaced him on the field. Later in the game, Scott decided to head to the showers, but Winkles told him to warm up a pitcher. He refused. His days at Oakland became numbered after that incident.

The A's traded him to the Chicago Cubs for Pete Broberg during the winter. He began the year at Wichita, Kansas, a Triple A team, before the Cubs called him up midway through the season. He was used primarily at third base, and he hit well at Wrigley Field. But his stint with the Cubs wouldn't last into the next year, as he lost his cool with Manager Herman Franks, who played a game of musical chairs with Scott in one game. Franks put Scott at third to begin the game. Then he moved him to second base and on to shortstop. "Then he wanted me to go back to second," he said. The two argued and Franks told him to go back to second or else. "I took the 'or else.'" The Cubs tried to fine him, but the way Franks told him resulted in Scott avoiding the fine. However, he couldn't avoid being traded at the end of the season to Montreal.

The good-hands fielder became the regular second baseman for the Expos in 1979 and found some power, as he hit all three of his only career home runs during the season. His first was the sweetest, as it came against the Cubs and pitcher Willie Hernandez.

1980 was Scott's most productive year in the majors, as he hit thirteen triples — the most in the league — and a career high forty-six RBI. It was his best year at stealing bases, too. He doesn't admit to being a fast runner, though. He said he stole most of the bases off the pitchers. "You might pickup something that they are doing and get a jump on them," he explained.

In the strike-shortened season of 1981, Scott suffered his only injury of his career. He jammed his shoulder and had to be put on the fourteen-day disabled list. He hit only .206 that year, but the Expos ended up winning the National League East. Scott played second in the LCS against Los Angeles and hit three singles in eighteen at bats. The Expos lost the series in five games.

Montreal wanted him to sign a three-year contact, but Scott wanted a million dollars. The Expos decided to release him. "Montreal could have sent me to Indianapolis. I would have been very popular there," he said, not understanding his release to this day.

Scott became a free agent and was signed by the New York Yankees, who sent him to Columbus, Ohio, a Triple A team. He went there for a spell before the Yankees called him up for ten games. Then New York decided to send him back down to Columbus. Scott elected not to accept the demotion and was released by the Yankees. Scott went off to play in the Mexican League to play for the next three years.

In 1990 he joined the Seniors League in Florida and played for West Palm Beach for two years. In 1992 he played for the New England Gray Sox, a team of retired major leaguers who play exhibition games against college and charity games. He also has played in some old-timers games for Upper Deck. In February 1993 he attended a Montreal Expos Fantasy Camp.

Scott feels that he was labeled as a "militant" and black-balled by the major league owners; otherwise, his career would have lasted longer in the majors. "There were some rumors that I used drugs. I had a lot of women in my room, but I never had drugs," he explained. Nowadays, he always carries some baseball cards of himself to show police officers when they stop him in his Mercedes.

S

"Because by this time the Black guys were big; the Black guys were fast; and the Black guys were mean." Mike Sember

The bachelor still lives in Indianapolis with his mother. He would someday like to coach or scout for the major leagues or a college.

Mike Sember (Michael David)
Born: Feb. 24, 1953, Hammond
6', 185, Shortstop
Chicago, NL, 1977-78
BR, TR, 12 G, .286, 7 AB

Sember was one of those players that was in the wrong place at the wrong time. He had enough talent to play in the major leagues, but was with the wrong team to break in. On top of that, he got into professional baseball more by chance than by choice.

While growing up in the Calumet Region, Sember first began playing baseball when he was nine years old. He had enough talent to make it to major Little League in his first year. At first he played second base and right field in spot duty, but later he became a shortstop and pitcher. He was invited to play Babe Ruth ball, but he decided to become a golf caddie instead.

When he attended Bishop Noll Institute, a Catholic high school, he played football and basketball, but no baseball. Then in his junior year he sprang up like a weed to six feet in height. He became the starting quarterback his senior year and wasn't tackled more than ten times the whole season. On the basketball team he was the starting point guard. He was on a roll. So, he decided to try out for the base-ball team and became the starting shortstop, although he hadn't played any baseball in four years. He did so well in his senior year that the school named him the most valuable athlete in the school. "I could have gone to any major college for a football scholarship," the 1971 graduate explained. He did receive a few baseball scholarships, but only to small schools.

"It was my intention to be a football player and play just enough to get a college scholarship with no intention of playing in the NFL," he reflected. "Because by this time the Black guys were big; the Black guys were fast; and the Black guys were mean. Sooner or later you were going to get a tough injury."

However, Sember was an "A" student and didn't really need a sports scholarship. He decided to attend Tulsa University on an academic scholarship. He liked the school because he could play more than one sport, too. "Back then it was tough to find a university that would let you play two sports," he explained.

In his freshman year he tried out for the baseball team and didn't make the cut. "I was demoralized because now I had to go to spring football. Then again, the football coach was expecting me because I was one of his prize recruits, as a freshman. Then the baseball coach called me up and said, 'I cut too many guys and I could use you,'" he remembered.

He made the team as a utility player. Tulsa had a great base-

152

ball team that year and went to the College World Series, finishing second. It was a great thrill for him, specially since he hadn't made the team at first. After his senior year, the Chicago Cubs picked him in the second round. . He signed for $40,000 and was assigned to Class AA Midland, Texas, for 1974.

By 1977 he had advanced to the major league spring training camp and was put on the Cubs forty-man roster. Sember got cut just before camp broke and was assigned to Witchita, Kansas, the Class AAA team.

When backup shortstop Mick Kelleher broke a finger in August that year, Sember was called up along with pitcher Dennis Lamp. The same day he got the call, his wife, a flight attendant, was reassigned from New York to Chicago. Good timing. He struck out in his first at bat with the Cubs, but he singled in a pinch-hit role some games later against San Francisco. He stayed with the Cubs the rest of the season, but appeared in only three games.

In 1978, Sember didn't get the call until the end of the season. He played in eight games for the Cubs that season. "What happened is that the Cubs whole starting infield, outfield, and catcher came from somewhere else. The only thing we had that was home grown was the pitching staff. All the guys that were having good minor league development had nowhere to go," he explained.

The following year he was again the odd man out after spring training. He asked the Cubs to trade him or release him. The Cubs put him on waivers and the Toronto Blue Jays picked him up. He was assigned to Syracuse, N.Y., the Class AAA affiliate. He wasn't used much there because he was a new player in the system, so he retired from baseball.

The communications major went into marketing and now lives in Boca Raton, Fla., with his wife, the former Diane Hill of Mount Vernon, Ill., and two sons, Michael and Ryan. He has a long commute, because he works in New York City.

Steve Senteney (Stephen Leonard)
Born: Aug. 7, 1955, Indianapolis
Died: June 19, 1989, Colusa, Calif.
6'2", 205, Relief Pitcher
Toronto, AL, 1982
BR, TR, 0-0, 4.91 ERA, 11 G

Bill "W.W." Shanner (Wilfred William)
Born: Nov. 4, 1894, Oakland City
Died: Dec. 18, 1986, Evansville
Pitcher
Philadelphia, AL, 1920
TR, 0-0, 6.75 ERA, 1 G
BL, .000, 1 AB

Bert Shepard (Robert Earl)
Born: June 18, 1920, Dana
5'11", 185, Pitcher
Washington, AL, 1945
TL, 0-0, 1.80 ERA, 1 G
BL, .000, 3 AB

Mike Simon (Michael Edward)

Mike Sember appeared with the Chicago Cubs briefly.

S

Born: April 13, 1883, Hayden
Died: June 10, 1963, Los Angeles, Calif.
5'11", 188, Catcher
Pittsburgh, NL, 1909-13
St. Louis, FL, 1914
Brooklyn, FL, 1915
TR, BR, .225, 378 G, 1069 AB, 241 H

The back-up receiver at Pittsburgh jumped to the Federal League when it began. After the Federal League folded he never return to the majors.

Syl Simon (Sylvester Adam)
Born: Dec. 14, 1897, Chandler
Died: Feb. 28, 1973, Chandler
5'10", 170, Infielder
St. Louis, AL, 1923-24
BR, TR, .242, 24 G, 33 AB

Simon cracked into the majors in 1924, but couldn't stay as a regular. In 1926 he lost four fingers in an industrial accident. When he returned to baseball the following year, a specially built glove and bat were made for him. He played in the minors until 1932. His bat and glove were enshrined in the National Baseball Hall of Fame.

Hosea Siner (Hosea John)
Born: March 20, 1885, Shelburn
Died: June 11, 1948, Sullivan
5'10", 185
Boston, NL, 1909
BR, TR, .130, 10 G, 23 AB

John Slagle (John A.)
Born: Lawrence
Pitcher

Cincinnati, NL, 1891
0-0, 0.00 ERA, 1G

Joe Slusarski (Joseph Andrew)
Born: Dec. 19, 1966, Indianapolis
6'4", 195, Pitcher
Oakland, AL, 1991-93
TR, BR, 10-12, 5.34 ERA, 37 G

A member of the 1987 Pan American Team and 1988 Team USA, Slusarski spent only two years in the minors before advancing to the major leagues. However, shoulder problems and his propensity to give up the long ball landed him back in the minors in 1993.

Although Slusarski was born in Indianapolis, he was raised in Illinois. He played Little League baseball as a youth in Springfield, the state capital, and was graduated from Griffin High School. After two years at Lincoln Land Community College, he attended the University of New Orleans, where he compiled a 13-6 record with 160 strikeouts over 146 innings.

The Seattle Mariners selected him in the sixth round of the draft, but Slusarski decided to return to his birthplace in the summer of 1987 and play for the Pan American Team, which played its games at Bush Stadium. The following year he was selected in the second round of the free agent draft by the Oakland A's. This time he signed a major league contract. Instead of pitching in the minors, though, he joined Team USA to earn a gold medal in the Summer Olympics at Seoul, South Korea.

In 1989 he pitched the entire season for Class A Modesto, Calif., compiling a 13-10 record with a 3.18 ERA. Baseball American rated him as the tenth best prospect in the California League.

Slusarski began 1990 at Class AA Huntsville, Ala., but ended the year at Triple A Tacoma, Wash. He spent a week on the disabled list in May with bicep tendinitis and was promoted to Tacoma on July 17. He actually pitched better at Tacoma then at Huntsville, lowering his ERA from 4.47 at Huntsville to 3.40 at Tacoma.

After spring training in 1991, Slusarski was sent to Tacoma, but before he could start a game he was summoned by the A's to replace Eric Show, who was put on the DL. The A's put him on a morning flight to Oakland on April 11 so that he could start a game that afternoon! He shutout the Twins for seven innings to earn his first major league win.

The A's put Slusarski on the frequent-flyer program in 1991, as they shuttled the pitcher between Tacoma and Oakland all year whenever injuries beset the pitching staff. His best performance in the majors came on July 27, when he tossed his only complete game. He went 5-7 in Oakland with a 5.27 ERA in twenty appearances.

1992 began with Slusarski on the A's starting rotation. He began the year by winning four of his first five decisions. His best outing came May 10 against the New York Yankees when he allowed just two hits and two runs over eight innings in a 5-2 victory. However, he came on hard times in late May and June, as American League batters started taking him out of the yard with the long ball. After giving up fifteen homers on the young season and an ERA over 5.00, the A's sent him back to Tacoma on June 24.

In August tendinitis problems surfaced again, so Slusarski was put on the DL for a week to give his shoulder a rest. At the end of the season the A's called him up again. He made one start against Baltimore and the tendinitis problem reared its ugly head again, putting him on the shelf for the rest of the season. On Oct. 19 the A's team orthopedist, Dr. Rick Bost, performed the surgery to alleviate the recurring problem.

While Slusarski pitched well in spring training, the A's sent him to Tacoma to start the 1993 season. He was called up in May, but spent less than a month there before being optioned back to Tacoma. He was called up again in June. He appeared in only two games for the A's in 1993. His ERA was 5.19.

The transplanted Hoosier now makes his home in Kenner, La., with his wife Kristine and daughter, Meagan.

Ed Smith (Rhesa Edward)
Born: Feb. 21, 1879, Mentone
Died: March 20, 1955, Tarpon Springs, Fla.
5'11", 170, Pitcher
St. Louis, AL, 1906
TR, 7-10, 1 SV, 3.72 ERA, 19 G
BR, .204, 54 AB, 11 H

S

Harry Smith (Harry W.)
Born: Feb. 5, 1856, North Vernon
Died: June 4, 1898, North Vernon
6', 175, Second baseman, catcher, outfielder
Chicago, NL, 1877
Cinncinnati, NL, 1877
Louisville, AA, 1889
BR, TR, .220, 35 G, 132 AB

Red Smith (Willard Jehu)
Born: April 11, 1892, Logansport
Died: July 17, 1972, Noblesville
5'8", 165, Catcher
Pittsburgh, NL, 1917-18
BR, TR, .156, 26 G, 45 AB

Jock Somerlott (John Wesley)
Born: Oct. 26, 1882, Flint
Died: April, 21, 1965, Butler
6', 170, First baseman
Washington, AL, 1910-11
BR, TR, .204, 29 G, 103 AB

By Speece (Byron Franklin)
Born: Jan. 6, 1897, West Baden
Died: Sept. 29, 1974, Elgin, Ore.
5'11", 170, Relief Pitcher
Washington, AL, 1924
Cleveland, AL, 1925-26
Philadelphia, NL, 1930
TR, 5-6, 4.73 ERA, 62 G
BR, .167, 54 AB

Speece spent two full seasons in the majors during his twenty-three years in professional baseball.

Born in Indiana, his family moved to Nebraska, where he spent his boyhood. His career nearly ended soon after it began in 1920 when he suffered an elbow injury and was out for a year. His pro career began at Norfolk and he spent some years with the Indianapolis Indians in the 1920s.

Speece was an underhanded pitcher and threw until he was forty-eight.

Paul Splittorff (Paul William)
Born: Oct. 8, 1946, Evansville
6'3", 205, Pitcher
Kansas City, AL, 1970-84
TL, 166-143, 3.81 ERA, 429 G
BL, .182, 121 AB
4 LCS, 37 IP, 2-0, 2.68 ERA
1 WS, 2 IP, 0-0, 5.40 ERA

Splittorff attained a number of firsts for the Kansas City Royals during his fifteen-year career with the team. He was the club's all-time leader in games, innings pitched, starts, wins, and losses when he retired. The crafty left-hander threw three one hitters in the majors.

Splittorff lived in the state for less than a year, because his steel working father was reassigned to Chicago. His family moved again to Minneapolis when he was in kindergarten. At eight years of age he began to play organized baseball. He played outfield and first base in the Edina Little League. It wasn't until he was twelve that he started pitching. His family moved back to Chicago when he was in sixth grade. He didn't pitch his first year in the Babe Ruth League.

"I pitched a lot in high school," he said. Besides playing varsity baseball for three years, he lettered in basketball as well

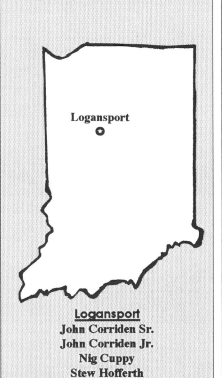

Logansport

Logansport
John Corriden Sr.
John Corriden Jr.
Nig Cuppy
Stew Hofferth
Red Smith

at Arlington Heights High School. Splittorff also played for American Legion Post 208. He helped his Legion team get to the World Series in Aberdeen, N.D., in 1964, the same year he graduated from high school.

Splittorff wasn't drafted by any team after he finished high school. He attended Morningside College in Sioux City, Iowa, and majored in business administration, while playing for the school baseball team. In his junior year he was drafted in the twenty-second round by the Royals, which had just become an expansion team. He signed in June 1968 and pitched in his first game on June 21 in the Rookie League at Corning, N.Y. "It was a strange feeling not having a major league team yet," he explained. "We didn't have a lot of veteran leadership and I missed that."

In the off-season he went back to finish his degree before going to the Royals first spring training camp. After a good spring, he was assigned to Class AAA Omaha, Neb. He was predominantly a starter and went 12-12 on the year in aiding Omaha to the American Association championship. "Jack McKeon was the manager and he really liked younger players," he said.

The next year he returned to Omaha, which again won the league championship. After the season was over, he was called up to the Royals. On a cold, wet Sept. 20 he started his first game in the majors against the Chicago White Sox. "Rick McKinney hit a homer in the seventh.

The scoreboard I liked so much as a kid went off," he explained as if the game were yesterday. He lost the game and had one relief appearance before the end of the season.

In May 1970 the Royals brought him up for good. The pitcher with the riding fastball, sinker, slider, and straight change started in twenty-two games. In August he limited the Washington Senators to one hit in a game called because of rain after five innings. Splittorff finished with a 8-9 mark, as the Royals surprised everyone by finishing second in the league after just three seasons in the majors.

Splittorff became the Number One starter for the club in 1973 and pitched the first game for the Royals in its new stadium. He also became the first Royal to win twenty games in a season. His 20-11 mark helped KC to a second-place finish with McKeon at the helm.

After an off year with a 13-19 record, Splittorff had the best game of his career in 1975. The crafty lefty one-hit the first-place Oakland A's on Aug. 3. He gave up a hit and a walk in the first inning before retiring twenty-six in a row. He ended the season with a 9-10 mark.

The only time he was put on the disabled list during his career came in 1976. He tore a tendon on the second finger of his pitching hand and was out all of August. The Royals won the Western Division and faced the New York Yankees in the League Championship Series. In Game Two after Dennis Leonard

S got off to a rocky start, Splittorff relieved in the third inning. He shut down the Yankees and the Royals won 7-3, giving him the Royal's first-ever post-season victory. Leonard again was shelled in Game 5 and Splittorff was called on in the first inning. He threw two more innings before being relieved. The Royals lost the game 7-6 and dropped the series.

Splittorff had the best winning percentage in the American League in 1977 in helping lead the Royals to their second pennant in a row. In thirty-seven starts he ended with a 16-6 record and 3.69 ERA. The lefty got the call in the first LCS game against the Yankees. He went eight innings and allowed only two runs in the Royals win. He started again in Game Five and held his own in another eight-inning performance. However, the relievers were hit hard in the ninth and the Royals lost 5-3. It was a disappointment for both the team and Splittorff.

The Royals made it a three-peat in 1978 with the help of the Hoosier hurler, who went 19-13 in the regular season. Splittorff got the call in Game Three and gave up four runs in seven innings. The Royals bounced back in the eighth inning, but the Yankees won the game in the ninth. The Royals were eliminated from the playoffs.

After a losing record in 1979, Splittorff suffered lower back problems the next year and was put in traction for a week. It wasn't serious enough to put him on the DL though. In the playoffs he started in Game Three and gave up just one run in five innings. The Royals finally scored late in the game to pick up the victory and sweep the Yankees in the LCS. Manager Jim Frey decided lefties wouldn't fare well against the Philadelphia Phillies in the World Series, so Splittorff didn't get any starts. "That was probably the biggest disappointment of my career," he commented. His only relief appearance came in the last game of the series, a loss to the Phillies.

In the strike season of 1981, the Royals finished first in the second half of the split season. Splittorff was 5-5 on the year and was bypassed in the three-game playoffs, which Oakland swept. It was a .500 season as well for Splittorff in 1982, as he finished with a 10-10 mark.

The lefty got back on the winning trail in 1983, as he had the most victories (13) for the Royals and the best ERA (3.63) among starters. The following year Kansas City decided it was time for a change and brought up rookie pitchers. After Splittorff had two poor starts in April, Manager Dick Howser relegated him to the bullpen. By the end of June, he had only worked twenty-eight innings.

"My goal was to have a good year and that wasn't happening. A trade was out of the question. I didn't want to stay in uniform anymore," he explained. Although he thought he had something left, Splittorff retired on July 1 and went to the radio booth on a trial basis. The trial worked and he's been behind the microphone ever since.

"My goal was to have a good year and that wasn't happening. A trade was out of the question and I didn't want to stay in uniform anymore." Paul Splittorff

He now lives in Kansas City with his wife, Lynn, and two children, Jennifer and Jamie. Jamie has followed in his father's footsteps and was drafted by the Royals in the twenty-fifth round.

Freddie Spurgeon (Fred)
Born: Oct. 9, 1901, Wabash
Died: Nov. 5, 1970, Kalamazoo, Mich.
5'11", 160, Infielder
Cleveland, AL, 1924-27
BR, TR, .285, 316 G, 1177 AB

An elbow injury ended the promising career of Spurgeon, an infielder for the Cleveland Indians for four years.

Spurgeon's family moved to Michigan when he was growing up, and he played baseball and football at Kalamazoo High School. After high school he went to Valparaiso College and continued playing football and baseball. When he came up short with tuition money for the next year, he decided on professional baseball and played under the name of Jackson with the Dubuque team in the Mississippi Valley League, probably to keep his college eligibility intact.

An elbow injury as a result of an automobile accident ended his baseball career. After baseball he became a liquor salesman.

Chick Stahl (Charles Sylvester)
Born: Jan. 10, 1873, Avila
Died: March 28, 1907, West Baden
5'10", 160
Boston, NL, 1897-00
Boston, AL, 1901-06

BL, TL, .307, 1303 G, 5062 AB, 37 HR
1 WS, .303, 8 G

Stahl was a good hitter and base-stealer who hit .358 as a rookie with the Boston Braves. He contributed three triples in the first World Series to help Boston to victory. The following season he led the league in steals with nineteen. He may be the only brother who played and managed against his brother, Jake, player-manager for the Washington Senators. However, it cannot be documented that the two were actually brothers.

Ace Stewart (Asa)
Born: Feb. 14, 1869, Terre Haute
Died: April 17, 1912, Terre Haute
5'10", 176, Second base
Chicago, NL, 1895
BR, TR, 97 G, .241, 365 AB

Stewart spent only a year in the majors, but he was a team leader and spent twenty years in professional baseball.

His first professional team was Terre Haute of the Indiana-Illinois League. In one game he was loaned to the other team, the St. Louis Peach Pies, to fill out the other team's roster, a common practice in those days.

His career hop-scotched through the minor leagues: 1890, Anderson; 1891-92, Wisconsin State League; 1893, Pennsylvania State League; 1894, Sioux City, Iowa.

In 1895 he went to the Chicago Colts of the National League. Cap Anson was the player-manager of the team and was high on Stewart right away,

Ace Stewart

S as Ace hit a home run in each of the first two games of the season. The team captain didn't hit another dinger until a month later when he had probably the best game of his career. He knocked in eight RBI with a homer, triple, and a single against Philadelphia.

In June, Ace began slumping. In August, the team signed a new second baseman and Stewart became disgruntled. His great-great-grandson, Patrick Stewart, thinks Anson expected too much from the rookie, which led to Ace's release.

Stewart went to Indianapolis in 1896 where he got some revenge against the Colts in an exhibition game, as Indianapolis won 8-4. He was named team captain and helped Indianapolis finish in second place in the Western League. The next year Stewart helped his team finish first again in 1899.

In 1900 Indianapolis joined the American League and Stewart left from Kansas City of the Western League before ending the season back home with Terre Haute. The next year he convinced fellow Hoosier Mordecai "Three Finger" Brown to go with him to Omaha of the Western League. Stewart became team captain.

Stewart again returned to Terre Haute in 1904 before going to New Orleans of the Cotton State League that same

CHICAGO BASEBALL TEAM OF 1895.

Ace Stewart, back row far right, played for only one season with the Chicago Colts. The coach of the team was Cap Anson, sitting in the middle.

year. He spent part of 1905 with Terre Haute before ending his baseball career in the Cotton State League, 1906-09.

Nick "Jumbo" Strincevich
(Nicholas Mihailovich)
Born: March 1, 1915, Gary
6'1", 180, Pitcher
Boston, NL, 1940-41
Pittsburgh, NL, 1941-42, 44-48
Philadelphia, NL, 1948
TR, 46-49, 4.05 ERA, 203 G
BR, .158, 272 AB, 43 H

Strincevich played in the majors during the war years and two good seasons with the Pittsburgh Pirates. His biggest payday in the majors came when he was presented with an automobile.

Strincevich began playing baseball while he was in elementary school. His high school, Lew Wallace in Gary, didn't have a baseball team, so he played American Legion ball.

In 1933 he began playing semipro ball for the Barnes Ice Company. A year later a Yankees scout was impressed with him when he struck out eighteen batters in a game. He tried out for the Yankees at Comiskey Park and was signed for $65 a month.

"Jumbo," as he was called, began minor league ball at Akron, Ohio, a Class C team. The following year he pitched for Butler, Penn. Then in 1937 he was promoted to Class B Norfolk, Va. Strincevich was released by the New York team in 1938 and he played for Newark of the International League. Then he was drafted by the

Boston Bees of the National League in 1939 and was sent to Sacramento. He was 6-2 the last two months of the season with Sacramento.

1940 became Strincevich's rookie year with the Bees. The twenty-five-year-old Hoosier struggled to a 4-8 record and 5.51 ERA the first season in the big leagues. He started fourteen games and relieved in eighteen others.

The following year the Bees changed their name to the Braves. Strincevich had relieved in three games when the Braves decided to trade him on May 7 to Pittsburgh for Lloyd Waner. Jumbo spent some time in the minors and appeared in just seven games for the Pirates.

In 1943 Jumbo pitched at Toronto of the International League and helped them to a pennant. He also was the starting pitcher in the Minor League All-Star Game.

His excellent performance at Toronto earned him a promotion back to the Pirates staff in 1944 where he became a starter. He responded by going 14-7 with a 3.08 ERA for the second-place Pirates. He was an mentioned for the All-Star Team, but there was no game that year because of the war.

Strincevich continued his winning ways in 1945. The right-handed sidearm curveballer had the most wins (16) on the Pittsburgh staff and a career high for himself.

Jumbo couldn't get on track in 1947 nor did his team. His ERA ballooned to 5.26 and his record dived to 1-6. The next

Nick Strincevich got his start with the Pittsburgh Pirates during the war years.

Tim Stoddard

⊘ East Chicago

East Chicago
Bob Anderson
Larry Fritz
Jim Hicks
Danny Lazar
Kenny Lofton
Stan Perzanowski
Tim Stoddard

year Pittsburgh used him only in relief before they traded him to Philadephia for cash on May 15. He appeared in just six games for the Phillies that year, his last in the majors.

His biggest thrill in the majors was having his folks come to Wrigley Field to see him play. The Cubs held a Gary Day and Major Joe Firnerty gave him the keys to an automobile.

Strincevich now lives in Portage with his wife, Mary. They have two children, Nick Jr. and Carol. He had a stroke in 1991 and it affected his speech.

Tim "Big Foot" Stoddard (Timothy Paul)
Born: Jan. 24, 1953, East Chicago
6'7", 250, Relief Pitcher
Chicago, AL, 1975
Baltimore, AL, 1978-83
Chicago, NL, 1984
San Diego, NL, 1985-86
New York, AL, 1986-88
Cleveland, AL, 1989
TR, 41-35, 76 SV, 3.95 ERA, 485 G
BR, .100, 20 AB, 2 H, 1 HR
1 LCS, 0-0, 4.50 ERA
1 WS, 1-0, 5.40 ERA

Stoddard was the starting forward for the North Carolina State 1974 NCAA basketball championship team, but chose a career in baseball instead.

He signed with the Chicago White Sox in 1975 and made his debut on Sept. 7. The White Sox sent him back to the minors the next two years before releasing him.

Stoddard signed with Baltimore in 1978. The following year he set a World Series record

when he singled in an RBI in his first ever Major League at-bat. He saved a career-high twenty-six games in 1980 for the Orioles.

In 1984 he was dealt to Oakland before going to the Chicago Cubs. He helped the Cubs to a pennant with his career high ten wins. He also had seven saves during the season. He went to the Yankees and Indians before his career ended.

Bobby "Sturge" Sturgeon (Robert Harwood)
Born: Aug. 6, 1919, Clinton
6', 175, Shortstop
Chicago, NL, 1940-42, 46-47
Boston, NL, 1948
BR, TR, 420 G, .257, 1,220 AB, 313 H

Sturgeon admittedly wasn't the best of shortstops, but his love for the game and his desire to do the best job led him to play six years in the majors during the 1940s. He also managed for five years in the minors.

The Hoosier-born player's family moved to California when he was four. He didn't play any organized baseball until high school. "The first year I went out for the baseball team at Long Beach Polytechnic High I got cut the first day because I was a 'Baseball Joe.' I had baseball shoes that I'd gotten with brown coupons for selling *Liberty* magazines and I wore Levis and I walked in with my glove strapped on my belt," he explained. The coach took one look at him and cut him the first day. Sturgeon joined an American Legion team and his manager,

St. Louis scout Bob Hughes, convinced the high school coach to keep him the next year. He played on the reserve squad.

In his senior year he played with Chuck Stevens, another player who would eventually make it to the majors with the St. Louis Browns. The team won the Southern California championship that year with Sturgeon's help.

After Sturgeon graduated from high school in 1937, Hughes signed him to a professional contract and he was assigned to Class D Albuquerque, N.M. He wasn't given a bonus. "I was one of those guys that thought baseball was one of the greatest things in the world. There were many who didn't get bonuses in those days," he said.

Sturgeon said another reason he didn't get a bonus was because Branch Rickey was the owner and was notorious for being a tightwad.

The infielder began 1938 at Sacramento, Calif., but he hit only .122 and didn't play much. When the club asked him if he wanted to go back to Albuquerque, he jumped at the opportunity because he knew he'd get a chance to play every day. His batting average leaped back to .335.

After a good spring in 1939, he was assigned to Columbus, a Class AA team in Ohio. He hit .297 on the year.

The Cubs bought him in January 1939, reportedly for $75,000. The Cubs thought he would be another Billy Herman, another Hoosier who later became a Hall of Famer. Stur-

geon went to Jersey City and played in the International League in 1940 until being called up in September by the Cubs. His first hit in the majors was a wind-blown double over the head of St. Louis' Pepper Martin in Wrigley Field.

1941 became Sturge's rookie year in the majors with the Cubs. He was the starting shortstop. On July Fourth in a doubleheader against the Cardinals he had the best baseball day of his life. In the eighth inning of the first game, Sturge knocked in the winning run with a single. In the second game the bases were full when he singled to knock in the winning run again. He hit .245 on the season with fifteen doubles and three triples.

Sturge suffered a leg injury in 1942 and lost his shortstop job to Lennie Merullo. He filled in at short and second and played in sixty-three games, hitting .247.

With the United States embroiled in a world war, he decided to enlist in the U.S. Navy Reserve. He was assigned to the Small Craft Training Center in San Pedro. He spent the next three years in the service.

He returned to baseball in 1946 and had his best year at the plate, hitting .296. "Also, oddly enough, the best year I had hitting is the same year I didn't field quite as well. Naturally, the media, who knew everything, said I was a good fielder and no hit and that I became a good hitter and no fielder," he said. He smacked his only major league home run during year. He shared shortstop duties with Merullo and Billy Jurges, a

"Naturally, the media, who knew everything, said I was a good fielder and no hit and that I became a good hitter and no fielder." Bobby Sturgeon

163

S

Bobby Sturgeon played before and after World War II.

former starting shortshop with the Cubs before the war. In 1947 Sturgeon filled in at shortstop and second base for seventy-five games.

In 1948 he was traded to the Boston Braves. He didn't play very much because he was traded by Stanky. "That was the year Alvin Dark broke in and hit something like three and a quarter," he said. The Braves won the pennant and went on to lose the World Series to the Cleveland Indians. He watched the series from the bench. Although he was with a championship team, he didn't play much and didn't feel he contributed.

The following year he went to play for Seattle of the Pacific Coast League for a couple of years. He later managed minor league ball for the Los Angeles Angels, Sacramento, Edmonton, and Salt Lake City. He retired from baseball in 1955.

Now he belongs to a baseball club that meets monthly in Long Beach, Calif. Club members include former players Chet Lemon, Herman Rich, and Cliff Dapper.

Ed "Kickapoo" "Chief" Summers (Oron Edgar)
Born: Dec. 5, 1884, Lodoga
Died: May 12, 1953, Indian-
apolis
6'2", 180, Pitcher
Detroit, AL, 1908-12
TR, 68-45, 5 SV, 2.42 ERA, 138 G
BB, .162, 352 AB, 57 H, 2 HR
2 WS, 0-4, 21 IP

Park Swartzel
Born: Nov. 21, 1865,

Knightstown
Died: Jan. 3, 1940, Los Angeles, Calif.
Pitcher
Kansas City, AA, 1889
TR, 19-21, 1 SV, 4.32 ERA, 48 G
BR, .144, 174 AB, 25 H

**Arlas "Lefty" "Foxy" Taylor
(Arias Walter)**
Born: March 16, 1896, War-
rick County
Died: Sept. 10, 1956, Dade
City, Fla.
5'11", 175, Pitcher
Philadelphia, AL, 1921
TL, BR, 0-1, 22.50 ERA, 1 G

**Ben Taylor (Benjamin Harri-
son)**
Born: April 2, 1889, Paoli
Died: Nov. 3, 1946, Martin
County
5'11", 163, Pitcher
Cincinnati, NL, 1912
TR, 0-0, 3.00 ERA, 2 G
BR, .000, 2 AB, 0 H

Harry Taylor (James Harry)
Born: May 20, 1919, East
Glenn
6'1", 190, Pitcher
Brooklyn, NL, 1946-48
Boston, AL, 1950-52
TR, 19-21, 4.10 ERA, 90 G
BR, 124 AB, 20 H, .161

Taylor's best year in the majors was his rookie year with the Brooklyn Dodgers in 1947, when the right-handed hurler went 10-5 and helped lead the team to the World Series. Arm troubles near the end of his rookie season dimmed his career.

The coal miner's son grew up in Shirkieville playing youth baseball. He played infield and pitched. As an eighth grader, he whipped a high school team with his fastball and curve. His high school didn't have a team.

At eighteen he joined the Fisher Auto Sales team, a semi-pro team in nearby Terre Haute. At the end of the season a scout from Nashville saw Taylor pitch in the post-season state tournament and offered him a contract. He declined, but the scout persisted and finally signed Taylor to his first professional contract for $100 a month. In 1938 he was assigned to the Class D Georgia League. He compiled a 3-4 record before breaking his middle finger playing the outfield. He was released on July 1.

Taylor returned to his home and hooked up with a semipro team in nearby Brazil. After pitching a good game, he was offered a contract by Class AA St. Paul, a farm club of the Chicago White Sox. His contract was for $250 a month. In 1939, after a good spring, he couldn't get in the win column with St. Paul, so he was sent down to Richmond, Va., in the Piedmont League. Taylor didn't have much luck there either; he was a slow starter and gave up runs early in the game. In 1939 and 1940, he continued his minor league career in St. Paul.

World War II broke out and Taylor was drafted right during spring training in 1941. The Army sent him south for training. At Camp Shelby, Miss., he hurled three no hitters in an intramural league. "They couldn't hit my overhand or sidearm curveball," Taylor explained. He was nearly unbeatable at Camp Livingstone, La., in 1943, losing only one game on an error. In 1944 he was shipped to Hawaii where he played ball for a local brewery semipro team. In one game he was playing shortstop and hit a runner upside the head acciden-

T

Harry Taylor

Harry Taylor still has all his mementos from his days with the Dodgers.

T

tally with the ball still in his hand. Taylor broke his right thumb on the play and thought his playing days were over. He managed while his thumb healed.

After the war he rejoined St. Paul, now a farm club of the Brooklyn Dodgers. In 1946 he compiled a 15-9 record and was called up to the Dodgers in September. His first appearance in the majors was in relief against the Boston Braves with Dodgers ahead by a run. "Two men were on and one out. The third and fourth batters were coming up. I was a little wild and took the count to 3-2. Then I struck him out. I did the same to the next guy. Got him out on a 3-2 count," remembers Taylor, the memory still fresh in his mind. The Dodgers won the game and Taylor was credited with a save. He was an instant hit with manager Leo Durocher, who used his heroics as a example to others the rest of the season. The first major leaguer to get a hit off of Taylor was fellow Hoosier Hall of Famer Billy Herman.

1947 was Taylor's rookie year. The right-hander won his first four games before giving up his first loss in the majors. In a game against the Cubs, Taylor was surprised that manager Burt Shotton, Durocher's replacement after his suspension from baseball, put Hoosier rookie Gil Hodges behind the plate to catch him. Taylor threw his best game of the year. "He [Hodges] was a helluva ball player! We took Chicago by storm that night!"

Taylor considers a shutout against St. Louis in July as his best major league game. He shut down the Cardinals, tripled in two runs and scored himself to win the game single handedly.

In mid-August he was in the middle of another game against St. Louis when the temperature dropped and his arm locked up, pinching something in his elbow. After that he couldn't straighten his arm and lost the snap in his curve ball. His sinker wouldn't dip as well. He went to Johns Hopkins Hospital, but doctors couldn't do anything for the growths in his elbow. "When I hurt my arm, I came back too soon," he said. As it was, he ended the season holding opposing batters to a .225 average and 7.2 hits per game, best in the NL.

The Dodgers won the pennant and Taylor was called upon to start the fourth game of the World Series against the Yankees. The notoriously slow starter wasn't helped in the first inning when a booted double play loaded the bases. He was too careful pitching to Joe DiMaggio and walked him. Taylor was lifted, but the Dodgers came back to win the game. Taylor looks back at the game wishing things had turned out differently, but he's glad he didn't give up a grand slam to DiMaggio.

In 1948 he won his first game against the Giants. Then he had surgery to remove his appendix. He was out nearly a month, but when he returned he felt it was much too soon. His performance tailed off and he was 2-7 before being sent down to St. Paul. Taylor spent all of 1949 and most of 1950 in the minors even though he felt he pitched well enough to be called up again.

In the fall of 1950 the Boston Red Sox purchased his contract, and he joined the club immediately. He pitched in three games and won two of them for his new team. He shutout the Philadelpia Athletics in one game. In 1951 the Red Sox went on a movement toward youth, resulting in the thirty-two year old getting a start only once in two weeks. "I needed to pitch every four or five days to be effective," Taylor said. He got only eight starts that season and ended with a 4-9 mark in thirty-one appearances. "In '51 they [Boston] couldn't buy a base hit."

After winning one game in 1952, Taylor was shipped to Louisville. "I got home that fall and took over the farm from my father-in-law. I had been living out of a suitcase since 1938."

But after a year away from baseball, Taylor was itching to get back and went to North Dakota to play semipro ball with Williston. The league included teams from Canada. In 1955 he played for Paris, Ill., in a Class D league — the same class he had begun with seventeen years earlier. His career had come full circle and it was time for him to retire. He reluctantly called it quits, rather than manage.

In 1992 Taylor suffered a stroke and has to watch his health more closely now. He lives near New Goshen and likes to golf. Every year he plays in a tournament put on by the the pitcher who replaced him at Brooklyn — Carl Erskine.

Walt Tauscher (Walter Edward)
Born: Nov. 22, 1911, LaSalle
6'1", 186, Relief Pitcher
Pittsburgh, NL, 1941
Brooklyn, NL, 1941
TR, 1-0, 1 SV, 5.71 ERA, 23 G
BR, .167, 6 AB, 1 H

Walt Terrell (Charles Walter)
Born: May 11, 1958, Jeffersonville
6'2", 205, Pitcher
New York, NL, 1982-84
Detroit, AL, 1985-88
San Diego, NL, 1989
New York, AL, 1989
Pittsburgh, NL, 1990
Detroit, AL, 1990-92
TR, 111-124, 4.22 ERA, 321 G
BL, 192 AB, .120, 23 H, 3 HR
1LCS, 1 G, 0-0, 9.00 ERA

Terrell was a workhorse on the mound, logging more than 200 innings pitched in seven of his eleven seasons in the majors. He tossed fourteen shutouts and a one-hitter during his career.

His professional career began when he was the thirty-third selection in the 1980 amateur draft by the Texas Rangers. Because of his pitching experience in college at Morehead State University, Ky., Terrell bypassed the Rookie League and went to Sarasota, where he was 3-2 with a 1.42 ERA. That earned him a promotion to Asheville where he was 1-1 with a 6.75 ERA the remainder of 1980.

During spring training the following year, he was traded to the New York Mets with pitcher Ron Darling for outfielder Lee Mazzilli. The Mets assigned him

T

"I needed to pitch every four or five days to be effective." Harry Taylor

Walt Terrell

To Class AA Tulsa. He went 15-7 during the year and chalked up a 3.10 ERA.

In 1982 he was elevated to Class AAA and played the whole season at Tidewater, Va. In September the Mets called him up and he made his Major League debut against St. Louis on Sept. 18. He lost that game as well as the next two starts, and finished with a 3.43 ERA.

The Mets again put him at Tidewater to start the 1983 season. Terrel went 10-1 with a 3.12 ERA, which earned him a call from the Mets on June 16. Four days later he won his first Major League game against the Cardinals. On Aug. 6 he homered twice off Hall of Fame pitcher Ferguson Jenkins in a game at Wrigley Field. He spent the rest of the season with the Mets and finished with a 8-8 mark and 3.57 ERA. The International League named him Pitcher of the Year.

But when the Jeffersonville pitcher went 11-12 in 1984, the Mets decided to deal him to Detroit for infielder Howard Johnson. He won his first four games with the Tigers. Terrell combined with Willie Hernanadez for a one-hitter against Minnesota on July 14. He recorded his first winning season with a 15-10 mark.

In 1986 Terrell no-hit California for eight innings before Wally Joyner doubled with two outs in the ninth inning.

The sinkerballer recorded a career high seventeen wins in 1987 for the Tigers, who won the Eastern Division of the American League. He started the third game of the League Championship Series and gave up six runs in six innings, but the Tigers went on to score two runs in the bottom of the ninth to beat Minnesota. It was the only win in the LCS for Detroit.

After a dismal 7-16 record in 1988 — mainly due to lack of hitting support — the Tigers dealt him to San Diego for infielders Chris Brown and Keith Moreland.

Terrell's performance continued to slide with the Padres. He won three of his first five decisions before losing ten of his next eleven. So, the Padres traded him on July 22 to the New York Yankees with a player to be named later for infielder Mike Pagliarulo and pitcher Don Schulze. His record improved to 6-5 with the Yankees the rest of the season. He hurled over 200 innings for his sixth year in a row.

The Hoosier became a free agent at the end of the season and signed with Pittsburgh. But his 2-7 record led the Pirates to release him in July. Terrell found his way back to the Tigers, who signed him as a free agent on July 28. He responded with a 6-4 record the rest of the year.

1991 saw Terrell start off slowly, but he caught fire after the All-Star break. First he reached his 100th career victory in a shutout of the Yankees on Aug. 10. Then he was named American League Player of the Week, Aug. 19-25, going 2-0 with a 1.50 ERA in two complete games. He tossed another shutout against the Chicago White Sox on Aug. 20. He finished the year with a 12-14 record.

In 1992, his last year in the majors, Terrell dropped below 200 innings as he was used more in relief than as a starter. In all he appeared in thirty-six games and finished with a 7-10 mark and 5.20 ERA.

Terrell is married to the former Karen Forge and they have three children: Ryan, Erin, and Michael.

Yank Terry (Lancelot Yank)
Born: Feb. 11, 1911, Bedford
Died: Nov. 4, 1979, Bloom-
ington
6'1", 180, Pitcher
Boston, AL, 1940, 42-45
TR, 20-28, 2 SV, 4.09 ERA, 93
G
BR, .145, 145 AB, 21 H

Tommy Thevenow (Thomas Joseph)
Born: Sept. 6, 1903, Madison
Died: July 29, 1957, Madison
5'10", 170, Shortstop
St. Louis, NL, 1924-28
Philadelphia, NL, 1929-30
Pittsburgh, NL, 1931-35
Cincinnati, NL, 1936
Boston, NL, 1937
New York, NL, 1938
BR, TR, .247, 1229 G, 4164 AB, 1030 H

Injuries on and off the field hampered Thevenow's career.

He broke in with St. Louis in 1924. Then he led the league in putouts and assists to help his team to the World Series. In the series, he scored a home run when Babe Ruth dropped his fly in Game 2. Thevenow's ten hits

helped lead his team to the World Championship.

His injury woes began the following season when he suffered a fractured ankle, which left him with a permanent limp.

Then in 1931 he was involved in a car accident and broke his jaw, a finger, and a leg. He was a protege of Cardinal manager Rogers Hornsby.

Sam "Big Sam" Thompson (Samuel Luther)
Born: March 5, 1860, Danville
Died: Nov. 7, 1922, Detroit
6'2", 207, Outfielder
Detroit, NL, 1885-88
Philadelphia, NL, 1889-98
Detroit, AL, 1906
BL, TL, .331, 6005 AB, 1986 H

Thompson hit more home runs in the dead-ball era than anyone else. He set several hitting records during his days. He was named to the National Baseball Hall of Fame in 1974 and the Indiana Baseball Hall of Fame in 1979.

The sandlot player began his professional career in 1884 at Evansville of the Northwest League. He hooked on with Indianapolis of the Western League the following year and played for manager Bill Watkins. When Watkins went to Detroit the next year, he convinced the team to sign "Big Sam." The only problem was that Detroit couldn't find a uniform big enough to fit him. In his first at-bat with the Wolverines, Thompson hit a triple and split the seat of his ill-fitting pants rounding second. He hit .303 in his rookie season with

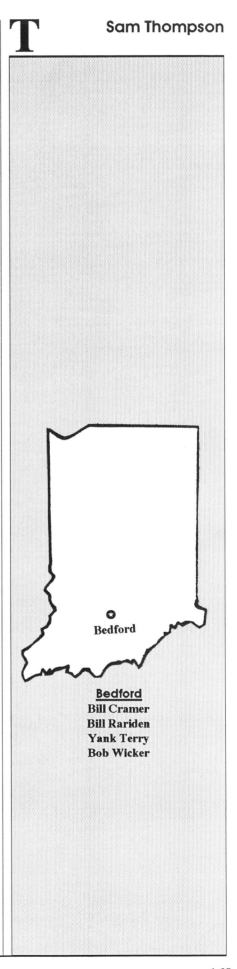

Bedford

Bedford
Bill Cramer
Bill Rariden
Yank Terry
Bob Wicker

T seven homers.

Thompson became a fixture in the outfield for Detroit in 1886 by hitting .310 and driving in eighty-nine runs. Defensively, he became the first player who could reach home with his throw. He led Detroit to a championship in 1887 when he drove in 166 RBI with his twenty-three triples, ten homers, and a .406 batting average.

When Detroit dissolved in 1888, he was sold to Philadelphia. He led the league in more runs (20) in his first year for the Phillies. He led the league again in 1895 with eighteen dingers.

He retired from baseball after the 1898 season, but the injury-riddled Detroit Tigers persuaded him to play the last eight games of the season when he was forty-six. He had trouble hitting the spitter, but still managed a .226 average.

Three times during his career he led the league in hits, and twice in RBI and slugging average. His career home run total lasted until Babe Ruth exceeded the record in 1921.

Dickie Thon (Richard William)
Born: June 20, 1958, South Bend
5'11", 175, Shortstop, second and third baseman, designated hitter
California, AL, 1979-80
Houston, NL, 1981-87
San Diego, NL, 1988
Philadelphia, NL, 1989-91
Texas, AL, 1992
Milwaukee, AL, 1993
BR, TR, .264, 1387 G, 4449 AB, 71 HR

Thon was one of the best shortstops in the game before being beaned in 1984. The third-generation player received the Tony Conigilaro Award, presented annually by the Boston Red Sox for overcoming his injury problems to continue in the major leagues. He's also notorious for breaking up no-hitters.

While Thon was born in South Bend, he grew up in Puerto Rico. He played baseball, basketball, and volleyball at San Antonio High School in Rio Piedras. During the summers he played American Legion baseball. After he was graduated in 1975, the California Angels signed the seventeen year old as an undrafted free agent on Dec. 23.

Thon spent his first year in the minors at Class A Quad Cities, Minn., in the Midwest League, where he hit .276 and stole nineteen bases. The following year he was promoted to Double A Salinas in the Texas League. His .316 average earned him a promotion to Class AAA Salt Lake City midway through the season. The following year he spent the whole season at the Triple A Utah team, hitting .257, including seventeen doubles.

After spring training in 1979 he again went to Salt Lake City, but the Angels called him up on May 27. In his first major league at bat, he singled against the Chicago White Sox. In all he played in thirty-five games for the Angels during the year and hit .339.

California again assigned him to Salt Lake City after

spring training in 1980. After he hit a league-leading .394 in forty games, the Angels called him up on May 27, exactly a year after they had first called upon him. The night after being called up Thon had one of his best games of his career — a 5-for-5 performance against Texas. He played second, third and designated hitter until he became the regular shortstop for the team in September. He played winter ball in Puerto Rico and led the league in hitting with .331.

During spring training in 1981, California dealt Thon to the Houston Astros for pitcher Ken Forsch. During the strike-shortened season, he played in forty-nine games at second, shortstop, and third base. He hit .274 on the season.

1982 found him as the starting second baseman on the team; he went out and proved his worth. Just after the All-Star break, he went on a hitting rampage and had a twenty-one-game streak. Ten of his hits that year went for triples to lead the National League. He also hit a career high thirty-one doubles and stole thirty-seven bases.

While 1982 was good, he topped his performance the following year, earning him a spot on the All-Star team. Thon showed he could hit the long ball as well and stroked twenty homers into the seats on the year. And he did a lot of clutch hitting as well to lead the league in game-winning RBI (18).

Then tragedy.

In the fifth game of the 1984 season, a pitch from New York Mets Mike Torrez glanced off the left flap of Thon's batting helmet and struck him in the temple area. He suffered a fracture of the interior orbital rim of the left eye and underwent surgery three days later. Surgeons wired a small piece of bone back into position. His vision began to improve late in the season, but headaches prohibited him from returning to action.

Thon's sight was still impaired the following season and he suffered from blurred vision. Houston put him on the DL May 19-June 8. He played in eighty-four games on the season and hit .251, but his power numbers were way down. Houston granted him free agency on Nov. 12, but he resigned from the club on Jan. 7.

Vision problems again haunted Thon in 1986. He was placed on the DL again June 9-23. He helped the Astros to a Western Division crown and started three of the six games League Championship Series games against the Mets and hit .250. Houston lost the series.

During spring training in 1987 Thon had vision problems again and left the team. However, he returned on April 19 and was assigned to Tucson on a rehabilitation assignment. He was activiated on May 11 by Houston, but after hitting just .212 in thirty-two games, he left the team on July 4 and was put on the disqualified list the rest of the season. Thon signed a contract with San Diego on Feb. 19 and played the 1988 season with the Padres.

The Philadephia Phillies

T

purchased his contract on Jan. 17, 1989. The Phillies made him their regular shortstop and he responded with his best year since his injury. Breaking up Tom Browning's perfect game in the ninth inning on July 4 seemed to be the turning point on Thon's season. After the All-Star break he hit .311 and bested that during the last month of the season with a .363 average. He topped NL shortstops with seventeen homers on the year. The Philadelphia Sportswriters Association voted him the Most Courageous Athlete for over-coming his injury.

Thon continued playing well in 1991 for the Phillies. He may have played in more games during the year, but he was suspended for three games for bumping umpire Terry Tata on June. 26. His eight homers on the season included two in one game against Houston and a grand slam off Mets hurler Frank Viola to spoil that pitcher's bid at a no-hitter.

Thon repeated his two-homers-in-one-game perform-ance the following year against Montreal — the second homer was the game winner. Thon broke up another no-hit bid in 1991. This one came off of St. Louis' Ken Hill with a one-out single in the eighth inning. At the end of the season, the Boston Red Sox presented him with the Tony Conigliaro Award for overcoming his adversity through spirit, determination, and courage.

During the off-season Thon became a free agent and signed a contract with Texas. He got off to a hot start with a .300 average in his first twelve games, but his average dropped off to .246 by the time he was put on the DL with a bone bruise on his right shoulder on Aug. 7. Texas put him on waivers on Oct. 6 to give him his release.

He became a free agent again and signed with Milwau-kee on Jan. 29. Getting off to an excellent start in April, the Hoosier shortstop and had a twelve-game hitting steak for the Brewers. He finished the year hitting .276 in eighty-five games.

Thon now resides in Sugar-land, Texas, in the off-season, with his wife, Maria, and four children: Soleil, Vanessa, Mari-ana, and Richard.

Gary Thurman (Gary Montez)
Born: Nov. 12, 1964, Indian-apolis
5'10", 180, Outfielder
Kansas City, AL, 1987-92
Detroit Tigers, AL, 1993
TR, BR, .241, 400 G, 767 AB, 185 H

Thurman hasn't been able to crack the everyday lineup during his time in the majors. His excellent speed has made him a good defensive outfielder and base stealer, but he hasn't been able to hit righthanded pitchers. He was a member of the gold-medalist U.S. baseball team at the National Sports Festival in 1982.

As a youth Thurman was good at many sports and started playing baseball in Little League. He moved up to a Connie Mack League, but he didn't play baseball in high school until his junior year at North Central in Indianapolis. Excellent speed and throwing ability allowed him to play centerfield and pitch. "Because of his speed, he'd get a lot of doubles and triples. He'd make a triple out of a routine double," said Glen Schmucker, Thurman's former coach.

"Probably the thing that turned his baseball career around was the National Sports Festival in the summer of 1982," Schmucker said. The festival was played in Indianapolis, and Thurman helped the North team to a gold medal in the games.

In his senior year, he was an all-state quarterback for North Central and was offered a football scholarship at Purdue. However, he gained even more attention on the baseball diamond. Former North Central baseball manager Tom Bradley remembered about twenty-five major league scouts coming to a game in Lafayette to see Thurman play. Thurman pitched that particular game, which led one scout to tell Bradley, "We didn't come to see him pitch." In his senior year he set home run and stolen base records at North Central, as well as leading his team to a 24-2 finish.

Miami University offered him a baseball scholarship, but Kansas City drafted him in the first round of the 1983 June draft. He was the twenty-first player taken overall. The Royals offered him a contract in the ballpark of $100,000, so Thurman asked Bradley what he thought he should do. Bradley didn't like his boys going to

professional baseball right after high school, but he advised him to sign it because he knew his family could use the money. Thuman had a twin sister and triplet brothers and sisters at home in a single-parent environment. Bradley kiddingly told Thurman, "Don't you think you ought to share it?"

Thurman signed and went to Sarasota, Fla., of the Rookie League for the short season. The following year he went to Charleston, S.C., where he hit .228 on the season and stole forty-four bases. His professional career began to take off in 1985 at Fort Myers in the Florida State League. He hit .302 and set a team record of seventy stolen bases, while finishing second in the league in swipes and triples. *Baseball America* named him as one of the top ten major league prospects in the league.

He began 1986 at Class AA Memphis, Tenn., where he continued to bat well with a .312 average and fifty-three stolen bases before he moved up to Triple A Omaha, Neb., by the end of the season. After spring training in 1987, he was again assigned to Omaha and batted .293 on the season. He also led the American Association in stolen bases with fifty-three and earned a promotion to the Royals at the end of the season.

Thurman's major league debut came Aug. 30 in Chicago. His first major league hit, stolen base and run scored came that night off Richard Dotson of the White Sox. In the same series at Chicago he recorded his first extra-base hit and first RBI. His

Gary Thurman was waived by Kansas City during spring training in 1993. He was picked up by the Detroit Tigers.

Tbest game during his first season in the majors was a 3-for-4 performance off Oakland on Sept. 13. He hit .296 in twenty-seven games for the Royals.

1988 found Thurman at Omaha to start the year. When Bo Jackson was injured, Thurman was recalled to the Royals on June 3. He played for nearly a month and hit a dismal .129 before going back to Omaha. At the end of the season he was again brought up to the majors.

Late in spring training in 1989, Thurman pulled a groin muscle, yet the Royals kept him on the Opening Day roster. He was activitated from the disabled list on April 13 and again found himself on the DL on June 10 from a sprained left wrist. Rehabilitating the injury, he remained at Omaha for seventeen games before going back to the Royals. During the season he was successful on all sixteen stolen base attempts, tying the American League record for stolen bases without being thrown out.

Thurman started the season with the Royals in 1990, but was optioned to Omaha on May 1 when the rosters were reduced to twenty-five players. He was re-called to the Royals on Sept. 11 following the Triple-A playoffs.

1991 became Thurman's first full year in the majors. He picked up his first major league home run on May 15 off Denis Boucher in Toronto and put together a nine-game hitting streak from Aug. 3 to Sept. 22. However, the streak was interrupted by an injury — a partial tear of the medial collateral ligament in the right knee from a home-plate collision. He ended up appearing in eighty games for the Royals and batted .277.

Thurman was again used as a reserve outfielder for the Royals in 1992. His numbers were down, including an average that dropped off to .245. He did have a six-game hitting streak from May 22-30.

Because he was not protected by the Royals in the expansion draft after the season was over, the Colorado Rockies and Florida Marlins passed on him. Before spring training, the former Indianapolis Northside star signed a one-year contract with the Royals for $425,000, a $137,500 raise. However, he wanted to be traded so that he could play everyday. "He was unhappy and asked to be traded," said Bradley. The Royals couldn't trade him, so they did the next best thing and put him on waivers. Detroit picked him up.

Early in the 1993 season, Thurman's play with the Tigers was limited, but he contributed significantly to helping the Tigers to first place with a game-winning RBI in one game. He showed he still has good speed, scoring from second on a passed ball. In all, he played in seventy-five games and hit .213 on the season.

"Gary's a fine player. He needs to play all the time to be good," explained Bradley.

Thurman now calls Kansas City his home in the off-season. He is married to Paula and they have two children: Andrew and Brytoney.

Gary Timberlake (Gary Dale)
Born: Aug. 8, 1948, Laconia
6'2", 205, Pitcher
Seattle, AL, 1969
TL, 0-0, 7.50 ERA, 2 G
BR, .000, 1 AB, 0 H

Walt Tragesser (Walter Joseph)
Born: June 15, 1887, Lafayette
Died: Dec. 14, 1970, Lafayette
6', 175, Catcher
Boston, NL, 1913, 15-18
Philadelphia, NL, 1919-20
BR, TR, .215, 272 G, 689 AB, 148 H

Tragesser attended Purdue University before he signed a professional contract in 1910. He was an excellent defensive catcher, but a weak hitter at .215 lifetime in eight years in the majors. He hit six home runs during his career, which was during the dead-ball era.

Ken Trinkle (Kenneth Wayne)
Born: Dec. 15, 1919, Paoli
Died: May 10, 1976, Paoli
6'1", 175, Pitcher
New York, NL, 1943, 46-48
Philadelphia, NL, 1949
TR, 21-29, 21 SV, 3.74 ERA, 216 G
BR, .138, 80 AB, 11 H

Dizzy Trout (Paul Howard)
Born: June 29, 1915, Sandcut
Died: Feb, 18, 1972, Harvey, Ill.
6'2", 205, Pitcher
Detroit, AL, 1939-52

Boston, AL, 1952
Baltimore, AL, 1957
TR, 170-161, 35 SV, 3.23 ERA
521 G
BR, .212, 961 AB, 205 H, 20 HR
2 WS, 1-2, 1.71 ERA

Dizzy was a solid pitcher, broadcaster, and director during his more than thirty years in professional baseball. After he died, his son, Steve, carried on the family tradition as a pitcher in the majors.

Trout broke in with Terre Haute in 1935. Then he played at Indianapolis for a couple of seasons before going to Toledo and Beaumont, finally cracking into the majors in 1939 with Detroit.

The Hoosier had four sub-par seasons until he led the American League in 1943 with twenty wins and five complete games.

The following season he had twenty-seven victories and led the league in complete games (33), shutouts (7), and ERA (2.12). His performance earned him a spot on the All-Star team.

1945 was probably more satisfying for the hurler, because he helped the Tigers to a pennant when he hurled six games in nine days and won four during the pennant drive.

Trout retired in 1952 after being traded to Boston, but five years later he signed with Baltimore when he impressed the Orioles in an Old-Timers Game. However, he was unimpressive in two games and ended with an 81.00 ERA!

After baseball, he was a Tiger broadcaster and the director of the Chicago White Sox

Dizzy Trout

T speaker's bureau until 1972.

His son Steve pitched for the Chicago Cubs and the Seattle Mariners.

Pat Underwood (Patrick John)
Born: Feb. 9, 1957, Kokomo
6', 195, Pitcher
Detroit, 1979-80, 82-83
TL, BL, 13-18, 8 SV, 4.42 ERA,
113 G

A Number One draft pick in 1976 by the Detroit Tigers, Pat was a promising All-State, left-handed hurler like his brother, Tom, who was already in the majors. However, elbow problems doomed his career.

He played baseball before he was old enough to go to school. His father — a former minor league player with the Philadelphia Phillies — was the president of the local Little League. "He was always at the park in the summer. We were exposed to it early," Pat explained.

Yet his father didn't push them into baseball. Instead, he let the boys fall into it naturally. Pat began playing Little League when he was seven. He was a pitcher from the beginning. "I had the talent to throw hard," he said. In the minors he was forced to pitch from Little League distance because he threw so hard. When he wasn't on the mound, he was behind the plate or roaming the outfield. He was named to the Little League All-Star Teams when he was eleven and twelve.

Pat advanced to Babe Ruth League and became an All-Star pitcher there, too. After his team finished as runner-up in the state when he was fifteen, the American Legion Post in Kokomo picked him up to play in the state tournament alongside his brother, who was eighteen and in

his last year with the Legion team. It was the only time the brothers played on the same team. Pat pitched in a couple of games, and the team went on to win the state championship.

At Kokomo High School, Pat shone as a pitcher. As a sophomore he was named as an alternate to the All-State Team, and in his junior year he was nearly unhittable. At one stretch he threw three consecutive no-hitters! The rare feat earned him a spot in *Sports Illustrated.* Pat became nationally known overnight. He also received a trophy from the magazine, which he still cherishes.

Kokomo High went to the state championships behind Pat's arm during his senior year. At the semi-finals he threw seven innings and was pulled because he had reached the maximum innings allowed. His team lost to Sullivan. But the day wasn't a total loss, as the Detroit Tigers followed their top pick home to sign him to a contract. He had asked for and received a $70,000 signing bonus with $7,500 in incentives at his brother's advice. Pat went to Class A Lakland, where he posted a 7-2 record and his team won the league.

The next year Pat was promoted to Montgomery, Alabama, a Class AA team. He started the year with a 9-2 mark, so he was elevated to Triple A with Evansville in June 1977. "I got a rude awakening. It was big jump for me," he said. He got his first taste at a losing record, finishing the rest of the season with a 3-5 mark. The following year he was again assigned to

U-V

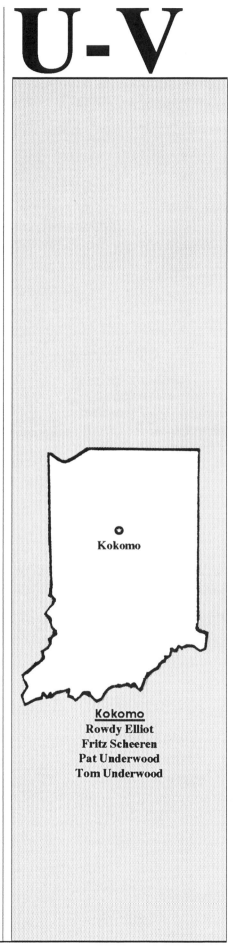

Kokomo

Kokomo
Rowdy Elliot
Fritz Scheeren
Pat Underwood
Tom Underwood

Pat Underwood

Pat Underwood followed in the footsteps of his brother as a pitcher in the majors.

U Evansville for more seasoning. After posting a 5-5 record, his season ended prematurely when he collided at first base with Champ Summers in Indianapolis and his shoulder separated.

In 1979 Pat got off to a good start and was called up in May and put in the bullpen. On his first road trip, Manager Les Moss called Pat into his office to tell him he would get his first start of his career. Against his brother! He was taken back about it at first, but the decision didn't bother him, because he respected his brother. "He showed me it was possible to make it to the majors," he explained.

The two were staying in the same hotel room. The night before the game they played a friendly game of backgammon. While they were keeping the brotherly battle ahead low key, the team was playing up the event in the press. Toronto even flew their families and friends up to the park to see the game. To this day Pat doesn't know whether or not the two teams decided to match the brothers up on purpose for a publicity stunt or by accident, but it doesn't really matter to him. Just before the game, Tom said to him, "Let's give 'em a good show."

Both had good stuff that night, May 31, 1979. Going into the eighth inning there was no score. Then Jerry Morales hit a home run off Tom to give the Tigers a 1-0 lead. In the bottom of the ninth, Pat gave up a double, so Moss put in a reliever to save the game for Pat's first major league win. After the game the brothers shook hands

at home plate. It was the first and last time they ever faced each other. The loss gave Tom a 0-7 record on the year at the time. "It's the basis for a lot of trivia questions, now," Pat said.

By the following week Moss was fired and replaced with Sparky Anderson, who made Pat a regular starter. The first win gave Pat increased confidence and was the impetus for a winning streak of five games.

Another game during that streak was even more memorable for baseball. Just before the All-Star Game, Detroit was in Chicago for a weekend series. On Friday night, White Sox owner Bill Veeck decided to hold a "Disco Sucks Night" and admit anyone with a 45 rpm record for fifty cents. The publicity stunt worked, and people jammed into Comiskey Park for the doubleheader, which featured Pat on the mound in the first game. The crowd of long-haired hippies became rowdy, flinging records like frisbees and shooting off firecrackers. Constant interruptions resulted in the game's going over four hours. Pat didn't let the distractions bother him and beat the White Sox.

Between games the records were gathered up in centerfield where they were dynamited! The explosion caused a riot. "All of these people came out on the field and tore up chunks of turf. We all got scared and went to the clubhouse and locked the door," he explained. Order was never restored and the White Sox forfeited the game. "Needless to say we partied that night."

Pat finished the season with a 6-4 record and 4.57 ERA and decided to go home after the season was over and give his arm a rest. He was confident the Tigers would need him again. Pat had a good spring in 1980 and made the team as a reliever. He was used mainly in middle relief or as a set-up man.

"They brought me in some save situations and I didn't do well," he said. However, Pat did have five saves on the year and ended up with some good numbers, although he had a losing record of 3-6. He did improve his ERA to 3.58 and was second on the team in appearances.

At spring training the next year, Sparky told Pat that he didn't have a spot on the roster. He would have to earn it. "Sparky jacked me over!" he said angrily. As it turned out, Pat had a poor spring and was sent to Evansville. "It shocked me!"

Detroit kept him on the forty-man roster, so he was still paid a major-league salary. In fact, they had doubled his salary to $50,000 because of his 1980 numbers. His shoulder was giving him some troubles as it kept tightening up. Pat attributed it to all the warming up he had to do the year before as a reliever. At Evansville he was made a starter again and went 9-7 on the year.

In 1982 Pat had lackluster 4-8 season, and began the following season at Evansville with a sore elbow. Detroit soon called him up again, but he proved ineffectual on the mound in four relief appearances.

Detroit decided to trade the younger Underwood to Cincinnati on July 1 for Wayne Krenchicki. The Reds assigned Pat to Class AAA ball at Indianapolis. He went 6-3 as a starter for the Indians the rest of the season. The trade was nullified and Pat was sent back to the Tigers and assigned to Evansville again. "I'm assuming they (Cincinnati) weren't aware of the elbow problems. They probably didn't want the liability of surgery," Pat surmised.

Soon after the trade was turned around, Pat was considered a free agent and the Texas Rangers drafted him off the Evansville roster. At spring training the Rangers cut him. The Hoosier hurler landed a job with the Rochester Red Wings in New York, a Baltimore AAA team. Within a month he couldn't continue and asked to be released.

Pat enrolled at Indiana University at Kokomo to get a degree in business. During the summer of 1985 he played for the Kokomo Highlanders, a semipro team.

Pat went on to receive a bachelor's degree from IU and a master's degree from Indiana Wesleyan in Marion. He's now a supervisor with Delco Electronics in Kokomo, developing electronic components for the air bag. He has a wife, Debbie, and two boys, Ryan, 8, and Evan, 6. Both boys are involved in baseball already. Maybe some day there will be another set of Underwood brothers playing in Major League Baseball.

Indiana High School Record Book

COMPLETE GAMES IN A CAREER
1. 54 — Robbie Clark
2. 43 — Guy Finch
3. 40 — *Pat Underwood*

CONSECUTIVE SCORELESS INNINGS
1. 57 — Don Leslie
2. 48 — Casey Whitten
3. 46 — John Clements
4. 38 — *Pat Underwood*

INNINGS PITCHED IN A CAREER
1. 364 — Robby Clark
2. 343 — Scott Fritz
3. 343 — Tom Browning
4. 338 — *Pat Underwood*

STRIKEOUTS IN A CAREER
1. 637 — *Pat Underwood*
2. 553 — *Tom Underwood*

NO HITTERS IN A CAREER
1. 8 — Marvin Julien
2. 7 — Dave Highmark
3. 6 — *Pat Underwood*

SHUTOUTS IN A SEASON
1. 10 — Tom King
2. 9 — Don Leslie
3. 8 — *Pat Underwood*

ERA IN A CAREER
1. 0.39 — David Gandolph
2. 0.43 — Jim Wiskotoni
3. 0.43 — Tim Lebo
4. 0.44 — Rick Ponto
5. 0.58 — *Pat Underwood*

U

Tom Underwood (Thomas Gerald)
Born: Dec. 22, 1953, Kokomo
5'11", 185, Pitcher
Philadephia, NL, 1974-77
St. Louis, NL, 1977
Toronto, AL, 1978-79
New York, AL, 1980-81
Oakland, AL, 1980-83
Baltimore, AL, 1984
TL, 379 G, 86-87, 3.89 ERA
3 LCS, 5 IP, 0-0, 3.86 ERA
BR, .117, 154 AB, 18 H

Tom became the first Underwood brother to make it to the majors. He had a career high fourteen wins in his rookie year and was named on the Topps All-Rookie Team.

Tom began building his pitching arm when he was three. His father, a former minor leaguer, didn't push him into baseball. Nor did he try to change Tom when he began throwing the ball left handed. By the time he was seven he was well ahead of the other boys in the Pee Wee League. And by the time he got into Little League at age nine, he was a strong pitcher. "I was pretty talented. I could throw it harder," he recalled.

At thirteen he went into the Babe Ruth League. At Kokomo High School he lettered in football, basketball, and baseball. He was not that impressive on the mound the first two years in high school, but he made up for that his last two years. In his senior year he went 10-1. Toward the end of his senior year, the scouts started to hover like vultures over the team. In one game Tom struck out nineteen batters. Then just before the draft, he gunned down twenty-five batters in a ten-inning game. "I was hounded relentlessly," he said.

The draft came and Philadelphia selected him in the second round. Tom waited until after the American Legion season was over before signing.

In his last Legion season, he had the opportunity to play on the same team with his brother, Pat. The left-handed duo led the team to a state championship. The day before the regionals, Pat was at a light football scrimmage for the high school team when he was tackled and broke a collar bone. "It cost us a pitcher, which probably cost us the World Series," Tom explained. The Legion team lost at the regionals without Pat. After the season was over, Tom signed with the Phillies for $50,000.

Philadelphia sent him to Class A Spartanburg, S.C. He went 14-6 on the year, leading the league in many categories and was selected as Pitcher of the Year. The following year he was promoted to Double A Reading, Pa. His excellent performance there coupled with injuries on the Phillies staff resulted in his being called up in August. The day he reported, the Phillies were playing in a nationally televised game in Cincinnati. He was called in to relieve. He struck out his first batter before the Reds shelled him for six runs. After two weeks, he was sent back to the Toledo Mudhens, a Class AAA team. "I should have really gone to Triple A all year," he admitted.

In spring training the next

Tom Underwood had a longer career than his brother did in the majors.

year, a couple of pitchers were hobbled with injuries, so Tom began the 1975 season with the Phillies and never looked back at the minors. The rookie pitcher tossed one of the best games of his career in his first start, a complete game shutout. He's very proud of another shutout he had that year on May 13 against the Big Red Machine in Cincinnati. Tom started thirty-five games that season and finished with a 14-13 record.

The following season the Hoosier improved his ERA to 3.52 and recorded a 10-5 mark on the season to help the Phillies win the division.

1977. "That was a season to forget," Tom summed up the year. The Phillies decided to use Tom as a reliever because they had a wealth of starting left handers. By June the Phillies decided he was expendable and traded him to St. Louis. "When the trade came, mentally it killed me," he explained. "I had just bought a home in Philly!"

The Cardinals reinstated him to a starting role, but Tom was devastated by the mid-season trade and didn't pitch well the rest of the season. He ended up with his first losing season in the majors, going 6-9 at St. Louis and 9-11 for the year. The Cardinals weren't impressed and traded him to Toronto.

Although Tom pitched well for the Blue Jays, the club didn't have much power and lots of times he lost close ones. He was 6-14 in 1977 with a 4.09 ERA. It got him used to losing.

The following year he improved his ERA, but the losses continued to mount. His best game with Toronto came against his own brother. Pat had been elevated to the majors by the Detroit Tigers in May. In Pat's first road trip, the Tigers were up against Toronto, so the clubs scheduled a "family feud". Tom lost to his brother. It was the only time the two faced each other.

Tom ended the 1977 season with a 9-16 record and led the Jays in strikeouts for both years.

In November, Toronto traded Tom to the Yankees. Tom went from a last-place team to a first-place team, as the Yankees won the American League East in 1980. Tom's losing record did a turnabout and he finished with a 13-9 record. In the playoffs he made two brief relief appearances.

In the strike-plagued 1981 season, Tom started poorly, so the Yankees traded him on May 20 to Oakland. Tom pitched well in the strike interrupted season and ended with a 3-2 record for the A's. Ironically, the A's ended up facing the Yankees in the LCS. Tom made two brief relief appearances that meant nothing, as the A's were swept.

The A's continued to use Tom mainly in relief in 1982. He was pitching the best baseball of his career. With a month to go he was leading the league in ERA when a home-plate collision put him out of action for ten days with a separated rib cage, which ruined the rest of his season.

The following year he had a bad start and by All-Star break was 5-5 with a 5.55 ERA. He remembered those numbers all

U

too vividly.

During the winter he declared himself a free agent and signed a one-year deal with a two-year option with the Baltimore Orioles. He got a $100,000 bonus with a salary of $500,000 for the year. The Orioles decided not to pick up Tom's option the next year and bought out his contract for $50,000. After he was released, no other teams made him an offer. Tom retired.

Today he lives in Fort Lauderdale. He's married to Chrissy Morra of New Jersey, whom he met after his baseball career. He has two children, Danielle and John Dominick.

Dick "Foghorn Dick" Van Zant (Richard)
Born: Nov. 1864, Indiana
Died: Aug. 6, 1912, Wayne County
Third baseman
Cleveland, AA, 1888
.258, 10 G, 31 AB, 8 H

Willie "Peek-a-Boo" Veach (William Walter)
Born: June 16, 1862, Indianapolis
Died: Nov. 12, 1937, Indianapolis
Pitcher, First baseman
Kanas City, UA, 1884
Louisiana, AA, 1887
Cleveland, NL, 1890
Pittsburgh, NL, 1890
3-10, 2.55 ERA, 13 G
.215, 100 G, 353 AB, 76 H

Veach acquired an unusual nickname during his fourteen years in professional baseball.

The penniless orphan boy took up playing amateur baseball around Indianapolis before he broke into pro ball with the Fort Wayne Golden Eagles for $25 a month and board. He later played in Terre Haute on his way to Kansas City of the Union Association.

At Kansas City Veach acquired his nickname. He was bothered by men on base, so his manager told him to look at the bench for a signal to indicate when Veach should throw to first. After he picked off two men, the opposition got wise to the signal. So the manager moved the signal to a person in the grandstand, but the other team figured out what was going on. Everyone began calling him "Peek-a-boo."

After baseball, Veach joined Teddy Roosevelt's Rough Riders in the Spanish-American War.

Beverly Volkert
Born: Redkey
AAGPBL, 1949-51

Kate Vonderau (Kathryn E.)
Born: Fort Wayne
Catcher
Fort Wayne, AAGPBL, 1946
Muskegeon, AAGPBL, 1947
Chicago, AAGPBL, 1948
Fort Wayne, 1949-53
.187, 400G, 1272 AB, 238 H
(1946-48, 50-53 stats)

Vonderau completed a college degree while playing in the league for eight season.

Before she joined the pro league, Vonderau played on a championship softball team in her hometown. She bounced around the girl's league the first three years before landing back with her hometown Daisies in 1949.

W-Z

Richmond ⊙

<u>Richmond</u>
Claude Berry
Eli Cates
Glenn Chapman
Bill Prough
Huck Wallace

Huck "Lefty" Wallace (Harry Clinton)
Born: July 27, 1882, Richmond
Died: July 6, 1951, Cleveland, Ohio
5'6", 160, Pitcher
Philadelphia, NL, 1912
TL, BL, 0-0, 0.00 ERA, 4 G

Lefty Wallace (James Harold)
Born: Aug. 12, 1921, Evansville
Died: July 28, 1982, Evansville
5'11", 160, Pitcher
Boston, NL, 1942
Boston, NL, 1945-46
TL, 5-6, 4.13 ERA, 51 G
BL, .079, 38 AB, 3 H

Frank Warfield (Frank)
Born: 1895, Indianapolis
Died: July 24, 1932
Second and third baseman
Detroit, NNL, 1920-22
Philadelphia, NNL, 1923-30
Baltimore, NNL, 1929-31
Washington, NNL, 1931-32
.262, 685 G, 2548 AB, 667 H

Warfield played and managed in the Negro National League for eleven seasons.

Jack Warner (John Ralph)
Born: Aug. 29, 1903, Evansville
Died: March 13, 1986, Mount Vernon, Ill.
5'9", 165, Third baseman, shortstop
Detroit, AL, 1925-28
Brooklyn, NL, 1929-31
Philadelphia, NL, 1933
BR, TR, .250, 478 G, 1546 AB, 1 HR

Warner played, coached, and scouted in professional baseball for some sixty years. The best he could do in the majors was hit a career high .267 in 1927 with one home run, his only homer in eight seasons. He was a regular for just two seasons with Detroit.

Art "Watty" Watson (Arthur Stanhope)
Born: Nov. 11, 1884, Jefferson
Died: May 9, 1950, Buffalo, N.Y.
5'11", 170, Catcher, Outfielder
Brooklyn, FL, 1914-15
Buffalo, FL, 1915
BL, TR, .337, 53 G, 95 AB, 32

Eric Wedge (Eric)
Born: Jan. 27, 1968, Fort Wayne
6'3", 215, Catcher
Boston, AL, 1991-92
Colorado, NL, 1993
BR, TR, .250, 37 G, 80 AB, 5 HR

Injuries have limited Wedge's ability to perform behind the plate during his brief professional career. He showed he can hit the long ball with five homers in only sixty-eight at bats in 1992 with Boston.

Born and raised in Fort Wayne, Wedge was graduated from Northrop High School in 1987. He then attended Wichita State University. In his senior year he hit .380 in helping his team win the College World Series. The Missouri Valley Conference Player of the Year led the NCAA in walks (88) and total bases (106), second in RBI (99), runs scored (98) and tied for second in homers (23).

His college performance earned him a third-round draft pick by the Boston Red Sox in 1989. Wedge started the short season at Class A Elmira. He played for the Red Sox in the Hall of Fame Game in Cooperstown on July 24 and hit a home run. He was promoted to New Britain where he caught in fourteen games. He was a finalist for the 1989 Golden Spikes Award, given to the top amateur player in the country.

Wedge played all of 1990 at New Britain and caught 103 games. He hit five home runs on the year, including a grand slam on August 9 at Williamsport.

1991 was an injury-riddled season for the Hoosier. He started the season at Pawtucket, but hit just .138, because he was bothered by a strained muscle in his right forearm. He was moved to Class AA New Britain and was there only two games before injuring his right knee. Wedge had surgery on the knee and was put on the disabled list. Afterwards, he was sent to Winter Haven on a rehabilitation assignment, appearing in eight games. The Red Sox purchased his contract on Sept. 17 and he made his first major league appearance as a pinch hitter on Oct. 5, singling off Milwaukee's Chris George.

In 1992 Wedge started at Class AAA Pawtucket where he hit .299 in 65 games with eleven homers and 40 RBI. Boston called him up Aug. 19. The Red Sox used him mainly as a designated hitter because he was suffering from a sore right elbow. Wedge responded by yanking five balls out of the park during his brief major league appearance in twenty-seven games. His first homer was a two-run shot off Seattle's Shawn Barton on Aug. 21 in Fenway Park. The next day he started at catcher and went 2-for-2 with two runs scored. After the season was over, he had surgery on the elbow.

The Red Sox decided to leave Wedge off the protected list, so the Colorado Rockies selected him in the eleventh round of the major league baseball expansion draft. During spring training in 1993 he hurt the elbow again and went through surgery. The Rockies put him on the disabled list on March 28. He spent most of the season injured and played in only nine games for the Rockies.

Wedge is single and now resides in Malden, Mass.

Violet Weitzman
Born: Fort Wayne
AAGPBL, 1946

Dutch Wetzel (Franklin Burton)
Born: July 7, 1893, Columbus
Died: March 5, 1942, Burbank, Calif.
5'9", 177, Outfielder
St. Louis, AL, 1920-21
TR, BR, .246, 67 G, 138 AB

Bill Whaley (William Carl)
Born: Feb. 10, 1899, Indianapolis
Died: March 3, 1943, Indianapolis
5'11", 178, Outfielder
St. Louis, AL, 1923

BR, TR, .240, 23 G, 50 AB

George "Heavy" Wheeler (George Harrison)
Born: Nov. 11, 1881, Shelburn
Died: June 14, 1918
5'9, 180, Pinch hitter
Cincinnati, NL, 1910
BR, TR, .000, 3 G, 3 AB, 0 H

Harry Wheeler (Harry Eugene)
Born: March 3, 1858, Versailles
Died: Oct. 9, 1900, Clinton
5'11", 165, Pitcher, outfielder
Providence, NL, 1878
Cincinnati, NL, 1979
Cleveland, NL, 1880
Cincinnati, AA, 1882
Columbus, AA, 1883
St. Louis, AA, 1884
Kansas City, UA, 1884
Chicago, UA, 1884
Pittsburgh, UA, 1884
Baltimore, UA, 1884
TR, 7-6, 4.70 ERA, 14 G
BR, .228, 257 G, 1122 AB

Jack White (John Wallace)
Born: Jan. 19, 1878, Indianapolis
Died: Sept. 30, 1963, Indianapolis
5'6", Outfielder
Boston, NL, 1905
BR, TR, .000, 7 AB, 0 H

Frank "Hooker" Whitman (Walter Franklin)
Born: Aug. 14, 1924, Marengo
6'2", 175, Infielder
Chicago, AL, 1946, 48
BR, TR, .045, 20 G, 22 AB, 1 H

Bob Wicker (Robert Kitridge)
Born: May 25, 1878, Bedford
Died: Jan. 22, 1955, Evanston, Ill.
6'1", 195, Pitcher
St. Louis, NL, 1901-03
Chicago, NL, 1903-06
Cincinnati, NL, 1906
TR, 64-55, 1 SV, 2.73 ERA, 138 G

Wicker's best season in the majors came in 1903 when he was 20-9 with Chicago. His best game was a near no-hitter in 1904.

Janet Wiley
Born: South Bend
First baseman
South Bend, AAGPBL, 1950-53
Rockford, AAGPBL, 1953
.206, 33 G, 102 AB, 22 H
(1953 stats)

Wiley was a batgirl for the girls league before coming to play in 1950. "There are many kinds of love, and playing baseball for South Bend was one of the loves in my life," she was quoted as saying in 1953.

Cy Williams (Fred)
Born: Dec. 21, 1887, Wadena
Died: April 23, 1974, Eagle River, Wisc.
6'2", 180, Outfielder
Chicago, NL, 1912-17
Philadelphia, NL, 1918-30
BL, TL, .292, 2002 G, 6780 AB, 1981 H

Williams was the first National League player to hit 200 home runs in a career. He led the league four times in home runs

Casey Wise was a second generation major leaguer.

and set records that lasted decades.

The Hoosier attended Notre Dame and played football with Knute Rockne. He broke into the majors in 1912 with the Cubs. Early in his career he didn't pound out home runs, but it was the dead-ball era of baseball. Still, he led the league in dingers in 1916 with a dozen. The Cubs dealt him to Philadelphia for thirty-six-year-old Dade Paskert, one of the worst trades ever.

Williams liked the short right field in the Baker Bowl and again led the league in homers in 1920 (15), 1923 (41), and 1927 (30). He also hit .300 or better six times, including a career high .345 in 1926.

He had a dozen inside-the-park homers, seven grand slams, and eleven pinch homers during his career — all records until 1960.

After baseball, he became a well known architect in Wisconsin.

Casey Wise (Kendall Cole)
Born: Sept. 8, 1932, Lafayette
6', 170, Utility infielder
Chicago, NL, 1958
Milwaukee, 1957-58
Detroit, AL, 1960
BB, TR, .174, 321 AB, 126 G

A second-generation major leaguer, Wise spent parts of four seasons in the big leagues as a switch-hitting utility infielder. In that short time he did play once in the World Series. He never hit over .200 in the majors.

Wise became interested in baseball at age five because of his father, Hugh Wise, who was

managing a minor league team at the time. His dad, a Purdue graduate, had a cup of coffee with Detroit in 1930, but spent fifty years in baseball. One of his accomplishments was getting a stadium built in Owensboro, Ky. Casey became the bat boy.

When Wise wasn't handing out bats, he played sandlot baseball. His father went to war, and the family moved to Hollywood, Fla. He attended South Broward High School and lettered in football, baseball, basketball and track. All-state in basketball, he also set the school's pole vault record. During the summers he played American Legion ball.

After he was graduated, Wise went on to play semipro. He was playing in Spencer, Iowa, in 1953 when his father arranged him to tryout for the majors. However, the tryout was washed out and he went to Milwaukee to try out for the Braves. Then Gene Mauch drove him to Chicago to tryout for the Cubs. The Northsiders liked what they saw and signed him to a contract for $26,000, which allowed him to attend the University of Florida to earn an engineering degree.

Wise began at Sioux Falls, a Class C team in 1953. The shortstop moved up to Class A Des Moines the following year. Then he went to Beaumont, a Class AA team. In 1956 he played for Los Angeles of the Pacific Coast League.

In 1958 Wise was on the opening-day roster as the second baseman for the Chicago Cubs. In his first game in the majors he faced Warren Spahn. He hit the ball hard off of Spahn but for an out. A few games later Wise got a single up the middle for his first hit.

"We got into June and they started to bring in the veterans," he explained. He got sent back to the minors.

In the off-season he was traded in a six-player deal to the Milwaukee Braves, so Spahn was now a teammate. Wise did some time in the minors that season, but he did play in thirty-one games for the Braves at second and short. The Braves went to the World Series and Wise appeared in two games as a pinch hitter. He didn't get a hit, but the experience was one he will never forget. The Braves lost the series in seven games to the New York Yankees.

In 1959 Wise continued his utility role with the Braves, who finished in second place. During the winter he continued his trade in Winter Ball in Cuba. One year his team won the Caribbean World Series. "It was good baseball, but not like the majors," he said. He was dealt to Detroit during the winter.

At Detroit in 1960 he hit .147 and played in 68 games. "After the 1960 season, I decided to bag it," he said. "I couldn't get in there enough to establish myself."

Wise worked in engineering for Dow Chemicals for a couple of years before he decided he wanted a new career in dentistry. However, he couldn't afford the tuition, so he went back to baseball to help pay for his education. He landed a three-year contract that would pay for schooling while he played and coached at the minor leagues.

In the second year of the contract at Jacksonville, the manager quit and Wise was thrown into managing the team. One of his players was another Hoosier — Tommy John. "That was quite an experience," he commented. Cleveland decided he wasn't right for the part and fired him after the season.

Wise went on to finish his degree and completed a career in dentistry. Now retired, he lives in Naples, Fla., with his wife, Joan Palda of Cleveland. They have two children, Kendall and Kendra.

Andy Woehr (Andrew Emil)
Born: Feb. 4, 1896, Fort Wayne
Died: July 24, 1990, Fort Wayne
5'11", 165, Second and third baseman
Philadelphia, NL, 1923-24
BR, TR, .244, 63 G, 193 AB

Clarence Woods (Clarence Cofield)
Born: June 11, 1892, Woods Ridge
Died: July 2, 1969, Rising Sun
6'5", 230, Pitcher
Indianapolis, FL, 1914
TR, BR, 0-0, 4.50 ERA, 2 G

Bob Wright (Robert Cassius)
Born: Dec. 13, 1891, Greensburg
6'1", 175, Pitcher
Chicago, NL, 1915
TR, BR, 0-0, 2.25 ERA, 2 G

Z

Joe Wyatt (Loral John)
Born: April 6, 1900, Petersburg
Died: Dec. 5, 1970, Oblong, Ill.
6' 1", 175, Outfielder
Cleveland, AL, 1924
BR, TR, .182, 4 G, 11 AB, 2 H

Harlan "Cy the Third" Young (Harlan Edward)
Born: Sept. 28, 1883, Portland
Died: March 26, 1975
6'2", 190, Pitcher
Pittsburgh, NL, 1908
Boston, NL, 1908
TR, 0-3, 2.61 ERA, 14 G

Rollie "Bunions" Zeider (Rollie Hubert)
Born: Nov. 16, 1883, Auburn
Died: Sept. 12, 1967, Auburn
5'10", 160, Utility fielder
Chicago, AL, 1910-13
New York, AL, 1913
Chicago, FL, 1914-15
Chicago, NL, 1916-18
BR, TR, .239, 938 G, 3213 AB

Zeider set the American League record for steals by a rookie in 1910 with forty-nine — a record that stood until 1986. The following season, he scored five runs on Oct. 8. Then on June 21, 1912, he swiped four bases in one game. The versatile player earned his nickname when Ty Cobb spiked him in his bunion.

The National Baseball Hall of Fame in Cooperstown has inducted the following Indiana players (year of induction in parentheses):

Mordecai Brown (1949)
Max Carey (1961)
Oscar Charleston (1976)
Billy Herman (1975)
Chuck Klein (1980)
Sam Rice (1963)
Edd Roush (1962)
Amos Rusie (1977)
Sam Thompson (1974)

The Indiana High School Baseball Coaches Association Hall of Fame in Jasper has inducted the following players, coaches, and contributors to the game of baseball in Indiana (year of induction in parentheses):

Players

Mordecai Brown (1979)
Donie Bush (1979)
Max Carey (1979)
Oscar Charleston (1981)
Bob Coleman (1980)
Clyde Crouse (1981)
Carl Erskine (1979)
Fred Fitzsimmons (1993)
Pete Fox (1980)
Bob Friend (1979)
Billy Herman (1979)
Gil Hodges (1979)
Wayne LeMasters (1988)
Chuck Klein (1981)
Art Nehf (1989)
Al Pilarcik (1987)
Roman Pfeffer (1979)
Ron Reed (1990)
Sam Rice (1979)
Glen Rosenbaum (1991)
Edd Roush (1979)
Amos Rusie (1979)
Everett Scott (1986)
Sam Thompson (1979)

Paul Trout (1981)

Coaches

Dave Alexander (1985)
Frank Baird (1981)
Don Barnett (1983)
Emory Bauer (1980)
Gene Bottorff (1988)
Tom Bradley (1980)
Len Buczkowski (1991)
Ken Cox (1988)
Charles Dagwell (1981)
Don Dunker (1984)
Paul Fields (1979)
Walt Floyd (1983)
Marvin Groh (1979)
Orval Huffman (1987)
Ray Howard (1990)
Don Jennings (1988)
Bill Jones (1982)
Jack Massucci (1993)
Quentin Merkel (1990)
Bill Nixon (1993)
Don Noblitt (1982)
Don Poole (1990)
Jim Reinebold (1979)
Ken Schreiber (1979)
Howard Sharpe (1989)
Don Sherman (1992)
Dick Siler (1992)
Keith Slaughter (1986)
Chris Stavreti (1991)
Jim Turner (1980)
Paul Wolfe (1987)

Contributors

Lowell Barnett (1989)
William Bolton (1982)
Paul Eksew (1983)
Charles O. Finley (1980)
Ford Frick (1983)
Paul Frisz (1982)
Harry Geisel (1993)
Don Jellison (1992)
Judge Kenesaw Landis (1983)
Charles Maas (1984)
Alvin Ruxer (1983)
Stan Sajko (1984)
Larry Sigler (1993)
Barney Zoss (1991)

Hall of Fame

Photo Credits

Page 3 and 4: courtesy of Ernie Andres. **Page 5:** photo by author. **Page 8:** courtesy of Northern Indiana Historical Society. **Page 10:** courtesy of Andy Benes. **Page 13:** courtesy of Irma Bailey. **Page 18:** courtesy of Indiana State Museum. **Page 19:** photo by author. **Page 22 and 23:** courtesy of Darrel Chaney. **Page 28:** courtesy of John Corriden Jr. **Page 31:** courtesy of Delaware County Hall of Fame. **Page 35:** card courtesy of Nancy DeShone Rockwell. **Page 37 and 38:** photos by author. **Page 40:** courtesy of Dan Dumoulin. **Page 41:** photo by author. **Page 44:** courtesy of Scott Earl. **Page 48 and 51:** courtesy of Carl Erskine. **Page 57:** courtesy of Kerry Smith collection. **Page 66:** courtesy Chuck Harmon. **Page 69:** uncopyrighted photo, photographer unknown. **Page 71:** photo by author. **Page 73:** courtesy of Indiana State Museum. **Page 76:** courtesy of Stew Hofferth. **Page 81:** courtesy of Kerry Smith collection. **Page 86:** photo by author. **Page 88:** courtesy of Ron Kittle. **Page 95:** uncopyrighted photo, photographer unknown. **Page 98:** photo by author. **Page 99:** copyright TV Sports Mailbag Inc./Photo File, Elmsford, N.Y. **Page 101:** photo by Dave Swavel. **Page 102:** photo by author. **Page 104:** photo by author. **Page 106:** photo by author. **Page 109:** courtesy of Joe McCabe. **Page 112:** photo by author. **Page 114:** courtesy of Billy McCool. **Page 116:** courtesy of Dave McDonald. **Page 117:** photo by author. **Page 122:** photo by author. **Page 131:** photo by author. **Page 133:** photo by author. **Page 136:** courtesy of Chicago Cubs. **Page 143:** courtesy of Kerry Smith collection. **Page 149:** copyright TV Sports Mailbag Inc./Photo File, Elmsford, N.Y. **Page 153:** courtesy of Mike Sember. **Page 160:** courtesy of Patrick Stewart. **Page 161:** courtesy of Nick Strincevich. **Page 164:** Photo courtesy Bobby Sturgeon. **Page 166:** photo by author. **Page 173:** photo by author. **Page 178:** courtesy of Pat Underwood. **Page 180:** courtesy of Tom Underwood. **Page 186:** courtesy of Casey Wise.

Bibliography

While most research for this book was gathered through interviews, media guides, and from the files of the National Baseball Hall of Fame, the following publications also were used to gather facts for this book:

Amoruso, Marino, *Gil Hodges: The Quiet Man*, Paul S. Eriksson Publisher, 1991.

Baseball Weekly.

Chicago Cubs Vine Line.

Eidson, William G., *State Champs: The Final Four in Indiana Baseball*, Exponent Publishers, 1991.

James, Bill, *Stats 1994 Major League Handbook*, STATS, Inc., 1993.

John, Tommy, *T.J.: My 26 Years in Baseball*, Bantam, 1991.

Karst, Gene and Jones, Martin J. Jr., *Who's Who in Professional Baseball*, Arlington House, 1973

Kaufman, Alan S. and Jamec C., *The Worst Baseball Pitchers of All Time*, McFarland and Co., 1993.

Neft, David S. and Cohn, Richard M., *The Sports Encyclopedia: Baseball*, St. Martin's Press, 1992.

Porter, David L., *Biographical Dictionary of American Sports*, Greenwood Press, 1987.

Reddick, David B. and Rogers, Kim M., *The Magic of Indians Baseball: 1887-1987*.

Reichler, Joseph L., *The Great All-Time Baseball Record Book*, Macmillan Publishing Company, 1993.

Ritter, Lawrence S., *The 100 greatest Baseball Players*, Crown Publishing, 1986.

Shatzkin, Mike, *The Ballplayers*, Arbor House, 1990.

Smalling, R.J., *Baseball Address List, Number 7*, Edgewater Book Company, 1992.

Thorn, John and Palmer, Pete, *Total Baseball, Second Edition*, Warner Books, 1991.

Index

A

Henry Aaron, 54, 119
Ted Abernathy, 115
Charles Adams, 1- 2
Joe Adcock, 32
Tommie Agee, 80
Rick Aguilera, 86
Darrel Akerfelds
Jerry Akers, 2
Vic Aldridge, 2
Clifford Alexander, 41
Bernie Allen, 109
Richie Allen, 80
Walter Alston, 50, 52, 77
Bob Anderson, 2-3
Mike Anderson, 140
Sparky Anderson, 41, 44
Ernie Andres, 3-5
Luis Aparicio, 100
Harry Arndt, 5
Billy Arnold, 125
Lenna Arnold, 5
Cap Anson, 159-160
Martin Autry, 32
Jake Aydelott, 5-6

B

Dusty Baker, 119
Kirtley Baker, 7
Tom Baker, 55
Ernie Banks, 22, 23
Bruce Barmes, 7
Bill Barnes, 7
Tim Barrett, 7
Shawn Barton, 184
Earl Battey, 110
Emery Bauer, 112
Paddy Baumann, 7
Mary Baumgartner, 7-8
Buzzie Bavasi, 77
Johnny Beazeley, 48
George Beck, 8
Ollie Bejma, 8-9
Buddy Bell, 45
Andy Benes, 9-11
Joe Benz, 11
Yogi Berra, 81, 96
Moe Berg, 32
Al Bergman, 11
Tony Bernazard, 37
Claude Berry, 11-12
Monte Beville, 12
Charlie Biggs, 12
Emil Bildilli, 12-14
Harry Billiard, 14
Rae Blaemire, 14
Willie Blair, 100
Ray Blemker, 14

George Boehler, 14
Tim Bogar, 14-15
Wade Boggs, 98
Barry Bonds, 87
Luther Bonin, 15
Dr. Rick Bost, 155
Denis Boucher, 174
Larry Bowa, 60
Cy Bowen, 15-16
Ray Boyd, 16
George Bradley, 38
Phil Bradley, 16, 90
Tom Bradley, 173-174
Bill Brandt, 16
Sid Bream, 86
Bob Brenly, 106
Johnnie Briggs, 56
Mario Brito, 84
Pete Broberg, 150
Chris Brown, 168
Elmer Brown, 16
Kevin Brown, 15
Mordecai Brown, 16-18, 19, 160
Paul Brown, 66
Tom Browning, 172
Ron Bryant, 119
Steve Buechele, 87
Al Bumbry, 26
Sheldon Burnside, 18
Donie Bush, 18-19, 77
Mary Butcher, 19
Bill Butland, 19-20
Bill Byers, 20

C

Ivan Calderon, 84
Wes Callahan, 21
Johnny Callison, 115
Roy Campanella, 74, 76, 77, 96
Dave Campbell, 21
Mike Campbell, 100
Tom Candiotti, 44
John Cangelosie, 100
Chet Carmichael, 21
Max Carey, 1, 21-22
Camilo Carreon, 80
Jeff Carter, 84
Andy Carey, 95
Scott Cary, 22
Eli Cates, 22
Art Ceccarelli, 135
Rick Cerone, 38
Happy Chandler, 48, 55
Darrel Chaney, 22-25
Pete Chapman, 25
Oscar Charleston, 25-26
Hal Chase, 139
Dorothy Christ, 26
Fred Clarke, 22
Reggie Cleveland, 105
Ty Cobb, 1, 12, 28
Mickey Cochrane, 4
Rich Coggins, 26
Rocky Colavito, 3, 80
Bob Coleman, 26
Bill Collins, 27

Joe Collins, 51
Orth Collins, 27-28
Dave Concepcion, 23, 24
Chuck Connors, 50
Roy Corham, 27
Philip Corridan , 27
John Corriden, 27-28
John Corriden, 28-29
Kevin Costner, 120
Bill Cramer, 30
James Crandall, 30
Jim Crawford, 105
Ken Crawford, 31
Lou Criger, 31
Joe Cronin, 20
Frankie Crosetti, 13
Bucky Crouse, 31-32
George Crowe, 32-33
Nig Cuppy, 33
Chad Curtis, 33-34

D

John D'Acquisto, 120
Cliff Dapper, 162
Alvin Dark, 164
Ron Darling, 167
Cliff Daringer, 35
Rolla Daringer, 35
Hooks Dauss, 35
Bill Davidson, 35
Everett Dean, 107
Rob Deer, 90
Bill Denehy, 75
Nancy DeShone, 35-36
Bill DeWitt, 67
Dick Dietz, 36
Jo DiMaggio, 166
Dutch Distel, 39
Larry Doby, 66
Brian Dorsett, 36-39
Richard Dotson, 173
Red Downey, 39
Dorothea Downs, 39
Chuck Dressen, 51, 74
Elmer Duggan, 39
Dan Dumoulin, 39-42
Mike Dunne, 42, 124
Ryne Duren, 135
Leo Durocher, 74, 77, 166

E

Scott Earl, 43-45
Dennis Eckersley, 131
Bill Edgerton, 45-47
Stump Edington, 47
Hod Eller, 47
Rowdy Elliott, 47
Carl Erskine, 47-52, 74
Sammy Esposito, 5
John Eubank, 52
Bill Everett, 52
Darrell Evans, 10

F

Howard Farmer, 53
Stanley Feezle, 48, 73, 121
Bill Fehring, 53
Bob Feller, 4
Cecil Ferguson, 53
George Ferguson, 53
Joel Finch, 53
Rollie Fingers, 120
Joe Firnerty, 162
Chauncey Fisher, 53
Maury Fisher, 53-54
Tom Fisher, 54
Freddie Fitzsimmons, 54-55, 72
Darrin Fletcher, 84
Gene Fodge, 55-56
Ken Forsch, 171
George Foster, 41
Charlie Fox, 119
Pete Fox, 57
Herman Franks, 150
Charlie French, 57
Bob Friend, 57-59
Ford Frick, 12
Larry Fritz, 59-60
Jim Frye, 122, 158

G

Brent Gaff, 61-62
Joe Gates, 62
Lou Gehrig, 102, 149
George Gick, 62
Charley Gilbert, 70
Warren Gill, 62
Claral Gillewater, 62
Junior Gilliam, 95
Len Gilmore, 62
Tom Glavine, 10
Bob Glenalvin, 62
Harry Glenn, 62
Jot Goar, 63
George Goetz, 63
Doc Gooden, 15
Charles Gorman, 50
Burleigh Grimes, 1
Kevin Gross, 132
Harley Grossman, 63

H-I

Atlee Hammaker, 86
Don Hankins, 65
Donald Hanski, 65
Ed Hanyzewski, 65
Steve Hargan, 65
Bubbles Hargrave, 65-66
Pinky Hargrave, 66
Chuck Harmon, 66-68
Grover Hartley, 68
Bryan Harvey, 98
Ron Hassey, 90
John Heinzman, 68